D1420839

Royal Artists

Royal Artists

FROM MARY QUEEN OF SCOTS
TO THE PRESENT DAY

Jane Roberts

GRAFTON BOOKS
A Division of the Collins Publishing Group

LONDON GLASGOW
TORONTO SYDNEY AUCKLAND

Grafton Books
A Division of the Collins Publishing Group
8 Grafton Street, London WIX 3LA

Published by Grafton Books 1987

Copyright © Jane Roberts 1987

The illustrations of items in the Royal Collection,
and quotations from papers in the Royal Archives,
are here reproduced by Gracious Permission of
Her Majesty The Queen

British Library Cataloguing in Publication Data

Roberts, Jane, *1949–*
   Royal artists: from Mary Queen of Scots to the
present day.
   1. Kings and rulers as artists – Great
Britain 2. Great Britain – Kings and
rulers
   I. Title
   704'.0621   N8356.K5

ISBN 0-246-13015-6

Printed in Great Britain by
Butler & Tanner Ltd.,
Frome.

Photoset in Linotron Bembo by
Rowland Phototypesetting Ltd
Bury St Edmunds, Suffolk

All rights reserved. No part of this publication
may be reproduced, stored in a retrieval system,
or transmitted, in any form or by any means,
electronic, mechanical, photocopying, recording or
otherwise, without the prior permission of
the publisher.

CONTENTS

For my parents

FOREWORD

The most surprising people seem to enjoy drawing and painting.
I knew my eldest sister had studied at an art school in Paris, but
it certainly came as a great surprise to me to find out that my
father had been quite an accomplished water-colourist. I only
discovered this after I had caused some surprise to family and
friends by taking to oils myself. It has also come as a pleasant
surprise to find that at least one son has a real talent for watercolour.

I had always thought of "art" being for "artists", and that
only "experts" could appreciate good pictures. It was only
when I had been persuaded to try for myself that I discovered
how many "amateurs" there were among family and friends. I
also discovered that the mere attempt to paint suddenly gave
me an entirely new perception of pictures by "professionals"
and the great masters. I feel I can almost see the paintings from
the artists' points of view and share in their successes and
occasional failures.

I have never been altogether sure whether amateur efforts
should be seen in public, but I think Jane Roberts has put
together a very interesting account of the efforts of the painting
members of the "family". Some are obviously a great deal more
talented than others, but we have all done it for fun, and perhaps
it will encourage you to have a go. You never know, you may
be in for a surprise.

ACKNOWLEDGEMENTS

This book could not have been written without the generous help and encouragement of members of the Royal Family. I have been most fortunate to receive The Queen's permission to reproduce works in the Royal Collection, and to examine and quote from papers in the Royal Archives. HRH Prince Philip, Duke of Edinburgh, has kindly provided the Foreword and spared the time for discussions with me, as have other members of the Royal Family (in particular Queen Elizabeth The Queen Mother, the Prince of Wales, Princess Margaret and the Duke of Kent), who have also given me access to pictures and drawings in their possession.

The frequent marriage alliances between the princely families of Europe have meant that much relevant material is overseas. For permission to consult their family archives and for hospitality I am grateful to HRH Prince Ernst August of Hanover, Princess Margaret of Hesse and the Rhine, Prince Moritz and Prince Heinrich of Hesse, the Duke of Württemberg and Princess Charlotte of Hohenlohe-Langenburg.

Among the many descendants of Queen Victoria who have kindly allowed me to see material in their possession I would particularly like to thank Captain Alexander Ramsay of Mar and the Duke of Fife. The following are among those who have kindly answered my enquiries about past royal gifts, or have allowed me to reproduce works in their possession: the Duke of Argyll, the Duke of Buccleuch, the Duke of Northumberland, the Marquess of Bute, the Earl of Drogheda, Sir Marcus Worsley, The Hon. Mrs Gascoigne, Miss Eileen Hose and Miss Lynda Rae Resnick.

A very large number of curators of public and private collections throughout Europe and North America have become involved in this project. The completion of my text has been patiently supported and awaited by each of my colleagues in the

Royal Library and Archives at Windsor, and in the newly-formed Royal Collections Department. My debt to all of them, too numerous to name, is profound. Two honorary colleagues, Delia Millar and A. E. Sibbick, have been extraordinarily generous in allowing me access to their unpublished notes on nineteenth-century material. Without their assistance the voluminous and multifarious products of that period would have taken infinitely longer to identify and to explain. The Officers of the Order of St Michael and St George have kindly allowed me to reproduce an example of royal art in their care (Plate 58).

At the British Museum, Lindsay Stainton, Giulia Bartrum and Martin Royalton-Kisch have answered specific enquiries, as has Sarah Tyacke of the British Library. Material at the Victoria and Albert Museum has been made available to me by Clare Graham, John Murdoch and Gill Saunders, while Sir Roy Strong and Clive Wainwright kindly suggested possible lines of further enquiry. At the National Portrait Gallery I have corresponded with Kai Kin Yung. The Museum of London, now distanced from its original royal base at Kensington Palace, has a number of relevant items which I have discussed with Kay Staniland and Celina Fox. In the Ashmolean Museum and the Manchester City Art Gallery I have benefited from discussions with Christopher White and Nicholas Penny, and Julian Treuherz respectively. The curators of the Forbes Magazine Collection, New York, which contains a rich (and growing) collection of nineteenth-century royal art, have been unfailingly generous. Many works by Princess Louise and Lady Patricia Ramsay are now in the collections of the Public Archives and National Gallery of Canada. I am grateful for assistance from Jim Burant, Patricia Kennedy and Judith Roberts-Moore at the former and from Michael Gribbon, Catherine Johnston and Douglas Schoenherr at the latter. Dr Robert Hubbard of Rideau Hall, Dr Robert Brandeis of the Victoria University Library, Toronto, and Miss Catherine Hayes of the University of Rochester Library, New York, have all been most helpful. During two visits to Germany I was assisted by those charged with the care and well-being of many of the great historical collections. In other cases I have corresponded with the curators concerned. In this context I should particularly like to thank Göran Alm, Dr Blase, Baron Ludo van Caloen, Professor Dr E. G. Franz, Dr Giersberg, Elisabeth Handke, Sibylle Harksen, Willi Heberer, Nicolette Luthmer, R. Mattausch, Alheidis von Rohr and Willi Stubenvoll. In most of the above cases I have been supplied with photographs and reproduction permission, often at very short notice, and would like hereby to acknowledge my sincere thanks.

The following list of names of those other colleagues who have kindly assisted in various ways is inevitably far from complete, but any omission is unintentional: Herbert Appelts-hauser, Elaine Ashton, Veronika Birke, Charles Bone, Lorne Campbell, Rose Carter, Robert Common, Jane Cunningham, Victoria Cuthbert, Richard Dorment, Helen Dow, William Drummond, Terry Friedman, Charlotte Gere, Kate Gibson, Gay Hamilton, Eileen and John Harris, Graham Haslam, Paul Hulton, Jeremy Maas, James McGurk, Jennifer Montagu, Evelyn Newby, M. J. Peyton, Gordon and Simon Roberton, Mrs N. Round, Francis Russell, Reresby Sitwell, Nicola Smith, Lanto Synge, Veronica Tonge, Jehanne Wake, Richard Walker, Philip Ward-Jackson and Giles Worsley.

For the more immediate matters of publication, design and printing I should like to thank the following for their encouragement and help: Anne Charvet, Anne Engel, Kenneth Goddard, Andrew Hewson, Richard Johnson, Ronald Phillimore, Rosamund Saunders and Marianne Taylor.

As well as to my supremely long-suffering family, I owe an especial debt to two people: Olive Fortey, who has patiently typed, processed and duplicated my text from the earliest draft to the last footnote, and Elizabeth Johnston who first demonstrated that 'Royal Artists' was a subject worth pursuing, and has generously supported me through all stages of my work.

Windsor
July 1987

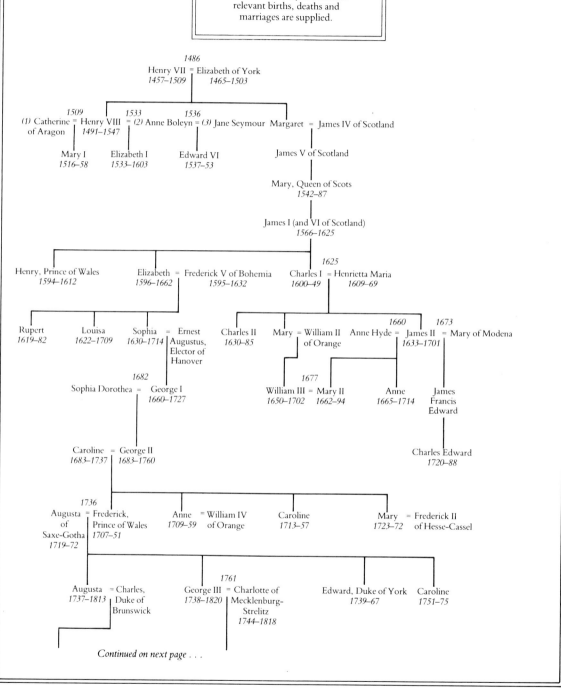

GENEALOGICAL TABLE

This table shows the relationship between those members of the Royal Family whose works are discussed in this book. Only the dates of relevant births, deaths and marriages are supplied.

1486
Henry VII = Elizabeth of York
1457–1509 | *1465–1503*

1509 | *1533* | *1536*
(1) Catherine = Henry VIII = (2) Anne Boleyn = (3) Jane Seymour   Margaret = James IV of Scotland
of Aragon | *1491–1547*

Mary I | Elizabeth I | Edward VI | James V of Scotland
1516–58 | *1533–1603* | *1537–53*

Mary, Queen of Scots
1542–87

James I (and VI of Scotland)
1566–1625

Henry, Prince of Wales | Elizabeth = Frederick V of Bohemia | *1625*
1594–1612 | *1596–1662* | *1595–1632* | Charles I = Henrietta Maria
| | | *1600–49* | *1609–69*

Rupert | Louisa | Sophia = Ernest | Charles II | Mary = William II | Anne Hyde = James II = Mary of Modena
1619–82 | *1622–1709* | *1630–1714* | Augustus, | *1630–85* | of Orange | | *1633–1701*
| | | Elector of | | | *1660* | *1673*
| | | Hanover

1682
Sophia Dorothea = George I | William III = Mary II | Anne | James
| *1660–1727* | *1650–1702* | *1662–94* | *1665–1714* | Francis
| | *1677* | | | Edward

Caroline = George II | Charles Edward
1683–1737 | *1683–1760* | *1720–88*

1736
Augusta = Frederick, | Anne = William IV | Caroline | Mary = Frederick II
of | Prince of Wales | *1709–59* of Orange | *1713–57* | *1723–72* of Hesse-Cassel
Saxe-Gotha | *1707–51*
1719–72

Augusta = Charles, | *1761* | Edward, Duke of York | Caroline
1737–1813 | Duke of | George III = Charlotte of | *1739–67* | *1751–75*
| Brunswick | *1738–1820* | Mecklenburg-
| | | Strelitz
| | | *1744–1818*

Continued on next page . . .

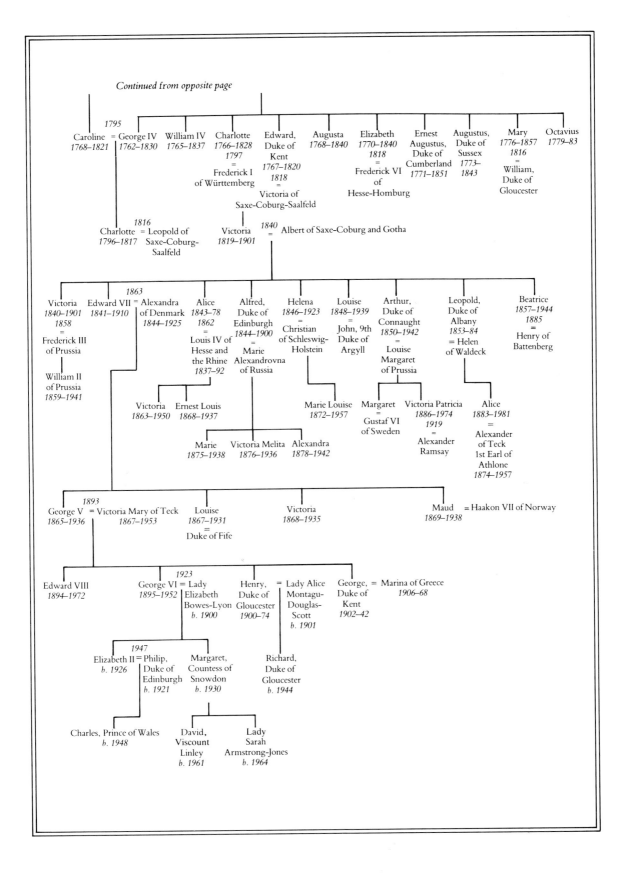

Continued from opposite page

INTRODUCTION

At the opening of an exhibition of works by former students of the Royal College of Art in 1923, one of the exhibitors was invited to give a formal address, which included the following statement:

> The artists of old believed in divine inspiration for their art, and many prayed for it before starting their daily work. I see no reason why that inspiration is not possible to-day. The hurry-scurry of modern life and the feeling that work must be rushed may retard our sense of creative beauty, but the joy of receiving and absorbing beauty and creating it afresh can be conveyed by painting, sculpture, design and architecture, so that it shows forth the inner inspiration as truly as ever.[1]

Although these words – and in particular the reference to divine inspiration – may strike an archaic note today, they have a certain relevance in the present context, for they were spoken by Princess Louise, the fourth daughter of Queen Victoria and Prince Albert, who was perhaps the most 'professional' of the royal artists whose careers will be charted in the following pages.

'The joy of receiving and absorbing beauty and creating it afresh' has been a feature of civilized life for many centuries. Today, with the assistance of the still and cinematographic camera, the 're-creation' of nature can be within everyone's grasp. The present study does not embrace the photographer's art, although a number of royal personages have taken an active interest in photography.[2] The discussion instead concentrates on the many other art forms which have been embraced by royal amateurs: painting with oils and watercolours, drawing, print-making (whether by mezzotint, etching or lithography),

Terra-cotta self-portrait bust
by Princess Louise.

sculpting, ivory-turning, enamelling, the cutting of silhouettes, japanning, embroidery, knotting, cut velvet work, painting on porcelain, penning on wood, the making of feather pictures, or architectural and decorative design. Activities such as needle-work and knotting are discussed only selectively. Queen Victoria gave the following advice on the inferiority of 'work' to draughtsmanship to her newly-married eldest daughter: 'I hope you will draw a little whenever you can. Papa & I used formerly always to draw of an Eveng. when we were read to – & you shd. do the same; it is much better than working.'[3]

Lord Melbourne, Queen Victoria's first Prime Minister, was evidently a willing subject for the Queen's pen. These sketches, almost scribbles, were made on a piece of blotting paper but are easily recognizable as portraits of 'Lord M'.

The reasons for this wide-ranging activity, spread over more than three centuries, are numerous. When the future Queen Victoria made the following note in her diary four months before her sixteenth birthday in 1835, she was voicing a basic (but unevenly distributed) human urge: 'I *love* to be *employed*: I *hate* to be *idle*.'[4] Her need to be constantly occupied was often satisfied by sketching. Literally thousands of drawings survive from her hand, ranging throughout her long life. At the other end of the spectrum, royal personages (like other artists) have painted or drawn to fulfil specific needs, such as (in Princess

Louise's case) a design for the badge of a newly-formed Canadian regiment, or (in Prince Philip's case) a certificate presented to his companions on an Antarctic cruise.

As early as the fourth century BC the teaching of drawing was justified for young men (that is, for free young men), 'not for the sake of avoiding mistakes in private purchases, and so that they may not be taken in when buying and selling utensils, but rather because it teaches one to be observant of physical beauty. But to be constantly asking "What is the use of it?" is unbecoming to those of broad vision and unworthy of free men.'[5] Over two thousand years later, Henry Peacham spelled out a number of particular benefits deriving from a knowledge of draughtsmanship, in the context of early seventeenth-century England:

> Should you, if necessity required, be employed, for your country's service in following the war, you can describe no plot, manner of fortification, form of *battalia*, situation of town, castle, fort, haven, island, course of river, passage through wood, marsh, over rock, mountain, etc. . . . without the help of the same. In all mathematical demonstrations nothing is more required in our travel in foreign regions. It bringeth home with us from the farthest part of the world in our bosoms whatsoever is rare and worthy of observance, as the general map of the country, the rivers, harbors, havens, promontories, etc.; the forms and colors of all fruits, several beauties of their flowers . . . the orient colors and lively pictures of their birds, the shape of their beasts, fishes, worms, flies, etc. It presents our eyes with the complexion, manner, and their attire . . . Besides, it preserveth the memory of a dearest friend or fairest mistress.[6]

After reading of the importance that Peacham attached to the military applications of draughtsmanship it should come as no surprise to discover that the first English prince from whose hand we have any number of works of art is Prince Rupert, the heroic Royalist Commander General in the Civil War and the nephew of Charles I. In the following century the sons of Frederick, Prince of Wales, received lessons in fortification and perspective for their practical (rather than their theoretical) application. The relevance of this instruction was stressed in John Gwynn's *Essay on Design*, published in 1749, following the Jacobite rebellion of 1745: 'In the Art of War, how requisite [the Art of Drawing] is, and how shamefully it has on our part been pretermitted, the recent experience of the four or five years last elapsed, does but too fully demonstrate.' During the nineteenth century, each of Queen Victoria's children was taught to paint and draw. But the coastal views and diagrams

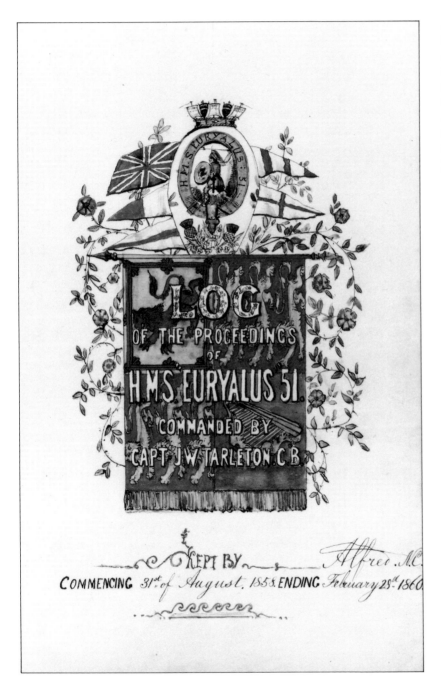

Basic draughtsmanship has long been part of a military or naval training. When Queen Victoria's second son, Prince Alfred, was sent to sea in HMS Euryalus in 1858, it was only natural that the resulting log-book should be decorated by the young naval cadet.

in the log-book kept by Prince Alfred, Duke of Edinburgh, when he was first at sea, and the instruction of his younger brother, Prince Arthur, Duke of Connaught, with the drawing

Three views of the coastline of Crete and the Southern Peloponnese by Prince Alfred, from his log of the voyage of HMS Euryalus, *1858–60.*

master of the Royal Military Academy, Woolwich, are instances of the continuation of the military application of draughtsmanship. The handicrafts taught to the future Edward VIII and George VI during their secondary schooling at Osborne College (the junior naval academy) bring this tradition into the context of our own times.

By the middle of the eighteenth century a practical knowledge of drawing was accepted as part of a gentleman's education. Two hundred years earlier few (if any) British children of whatever class received any artistic instruction. This change had come about as one of the by-products of the belated introduction of Renaissance ideas and styles to England. Foreign artists and works of art arrived on our shores as a result of the invitation and patronage of knowledgeable (native) men and women. The artist was a servant of these patrons. An outstanding example of the patron's skill and interest is provided by the early eighteenth-century aristocrat, Lord Burlington, who had both the theoretical knowledge and the executive skill to build houses, even palaces. The link between a practical interest in art and the patronage of art is crucial. Therefore it was only natural that the ten-year-old Prince George (later George III) was urged to consider the importance of drawing in the dedicatory address to *The Preceptor, containing a General Course of Education wherein the First Principles of Polite Learning are laid down* (London, 1748, printed for R. Dodsley): 'May you never suffer the false charms of Ease and Pleasure, to divert you from this glorious Pursuit, nor consider your exalted birth as exempting you from the Necessity of these Noble Attainments.' The Prince did indeed receive a very thorough artistic education, and continued to draw and design into his adulthood (see Chapter Two), but the majority of his time was inevitably occupied with affairs of state. For monarchs the other calls of office have ensured that any artistic activity has occupied a subsidiary place in their lives. Queen Victoria evidently thought that this was only right and proper, but the letters she received from her eldest daughter, the Princess Royal, following the latter's marriage in 1858 to the future Emperor Frederick III of Germany, reveal that the Princess (like her younger sister, Princess Louise) longed to spend more time engaged in her various artistic pursuits:

I make progress in my judgment and understanding of art (for I give myself much trouble with that) but I have long ceased to think that my own daubs are worth looking at. Could I sit and study – day after day – in a real, business-like

A page from a series of studies made by George III when Prince of Wales. Each sheet has a geometrical diagram occupying the upper part of the page, and an (unconnected) landscape composition below.

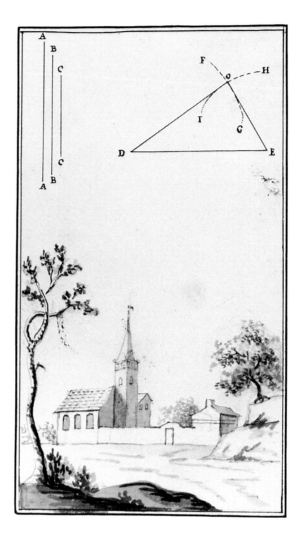

manner – having nature always before me – I feel that I could in time perhaps draw so as partially to please myself – but as it is, my drawing is a lamentable *hors d'oeuvre* and wretched dilettantism which only makes me sad to look at. Still it will ever remain a passion with me. I do love art more than I can say and no occupation has so great a charm as even my small way of practising it. I am often months without ever looking at a pencil. It is no satisfaction to me now to scribble over sheets of paper as I used formerly. I have learnt that all the work one does out of one's head without looking around at nature is only the utterest waste of time.[7]

Seven years later, in response to some firm advice from her

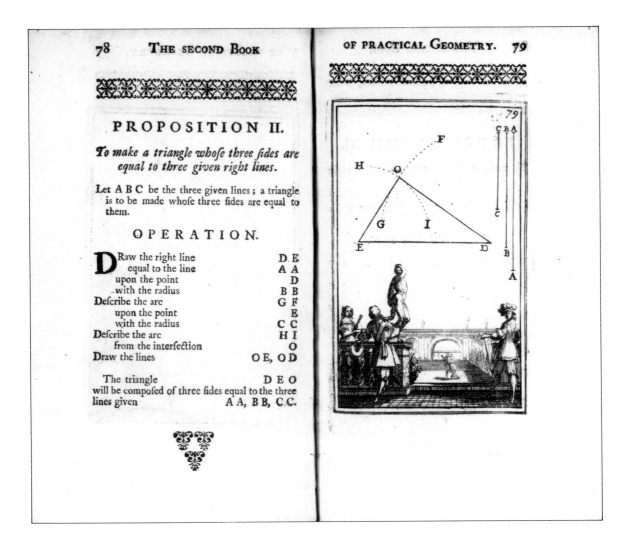

mother, the Princess regretfully concluded: 'As you say, so it is – Art cannot be our chief object in Life – in a position such as ours. But it may be – and I think it ought to be – its chief recreation.'[8]

Queen Victoria and Prince Albert, who were both proficient artists, realized the importance of a serious and informed interest in wider issues and ensured that the education of their children covered a broad range of subjects, including the natural sciences. During the previous hundred years, since the middle of the eighteenth century, circumstances had contrived to produce in England a situation in which the amateur artist thrived as never before, pursuing his or her art, often in the very real absence of other possible or potential activities.[9] Thus Horace Walpole

The source for George III's illustrations of geometrical propositions was Sebastien le Clerc's Pratique de la Géometrie. *In neither case were the accompanying designs (occupying the lower half of the sheet) related to the geometrical construction above.*

could look back from the eighteenth to the seventeenth century and describe the mezzotints by Prince Rupert in the following terms:

> Born with the taste of an uncle whom his sword was not fortunate in defending, Prince Rupert was fond of those sciences which soften and adorn a hero's private hours, and knew how to mix them with his minutes of amusement, without dedicating his life to their pursuit, like us, who wanting capacity for momentous views, make serious study of what is only the transitory occupation of a genius.[10]

Prince Rupert was one of a small group of distinguished amateur artists in the seventeenth century. In the eighteenth century practice of the arts became more widespread, and leisured hours more numerous. This activity was greatly assisted by the issue of detailed (and frequently illustrated) manuals, copies of which were to be found in the libraries of all the great houses of Britain by the end of the eighteenth century. With the help of a publication such as Robert Dossie's *Handmaid to the Arts* (first published in 1758), the reader could learn to draw, paint, sculpt, gild, japan, engrave, etch, mezzotint, paint china, and work with papier mâché. But in a noble or royal household tuition would also be provided by an instructor – or, in the case of George III's household, by quantities of instructors. In the eighteenth-century accounts of salaries paid to royal servants, the various teachers are listed each quarter and their wages noted. Although the masters of dancing, music, Italian and so on are specified in these lists, the drawing masters are almost invariably omitted. Their payments were apparently made at an irregular rate, and doubtless included varying amounts for the provision of materials. It is only in the nineteenth century, when individual lessons were charged and itemized, that we can be absolutely certain of the identity of the teacher, the length and frequency of his lessons, and the royal pupils who were in receipt of his instruction. In some cases artistic tuition was extended into adulthood. Both Queen Charlotte and Queen Victoria continued to practise painting and drawing alongside their own children, learning initially through copying the work of other artists, and later by depicting images from their imagination, or from nature.

While the position of Drawing Master first became established in the eighteenth century, by the mid-nineteenth century it had become so debased that Edward Corbould, the artist eventually

The highly competent work of Victorian amateur artists was largely the result of hours of practice, often under supervision of a professional master. William Leighton Leitch, the artist responsible for this sheet of drawings, taught Queen Victoria from 1846. He continued to teach both the Queen and her children until the 1870s, in spite of increasing infirmity. In the note (dated 9 August 1864) attached to this page, Leitch advised the sixteen-year-old Princess Louise to practise drawing compositions (such as these) 'a little now & then as Mr Leitch is quite sure The Princess would find the practice vy usefull as well as vy amusening'.

engaged to teach art to Queen Victoria's children, nearly refused the offer of the post. He explained his feelings on the matter in a letter dated 27 April 1852:

> Owing to the circumstance of a large class of persons who call themselves artists but whose only qualification to the title arises from, and consists in the reading of books on elementary art, and retailing the contents to listeners who place implicit faith in their artistic requirements – has caused 'the drawing master' to be looked *down* upon by the profession at large, as an individual incapable of earning an honest livelihood in painting . . . [Naturally there are exceptions and] it may in the particular case so graciously offered me be considered in the light of a very great distinction and a mark of honor . . . [therefore] I most cheerfully accept the office as Instructor in Drawing and Painting in Water Colors to the Royal Children.[11]

In spite of these forebodings Corbould appears to have enjoyed his lessons with the royal children, and he must receive considerable credit for their artistic proficiency.

In the twentieth century the ability to copy is little prized and imitations of other works are (sometimes with reason) dismissed with disdain. It is therefore not easy for us to appreciate the

value attached to copies in the past. Not only did furniture
makers, porcelain decorators, enamellers and textile manufac-
turers depend implicitly on the drawn and engraved work of
other artists, but more 'serious' masters such as miniature
painters often spent the greater part of their time producing
copies. It is in this context that the numerous copies produced
by George III's daughters should be viewed. The Old Master
drawings in the Royal Collection yielded many suitable subjects
for imitation. Studies by Leonardo were drawn and etched,
others by Raphael were traced by the princesses. The additions
to the Collection made by George III in 1762 included numerous
drawings by modern Venetian artists such as Marco and Sebasti-
ano Ricci, and Giovanni Battista Piazzetta, which were copied
in kind. Engravings by (or after) northern masters such as

Berchem, Barlow and Ridinger provided admirable models for the royal pen and brush, as did the works of contemporary British artists such as John Hamilton Mortimer, Thomas Gainsborough and Benjamin West. In 1838, between the time of her accession and her marriage to Prince Albert, Queen Victoria recorded how she and her Prime Minister, Lord Melbourne, had looked through a selection of volumes containing the drawings and prints which made up the Royal Collection at Windsor. 'Lord M.' told the Queen 'that there were every *sort* of print [and drawings], and most valuable, and that it was impossible to look at them all. We spoke of all this for some time, and of the use Lord M. said these original drawings would be to artists.'[12]

Although Queen Victoria does not appear to have copied

FAR LEFT: *This drawing of the Prophet Jonah, now attributed to Raphael's pupil G.F. Penni, is part of the unrivalled collection of Italian Old Master Drawings in the Royal Collection. It was copied by both Princess Elizabeth and Princess Alice.*

CENTRE: *Princess Elizabeth, the third daughter of George III, traced the drawing of Jonah on to a sheet of oiled paper, which was then pasted on to mounting card.*

LEFT: *Princess Alice, the second daughter of Queen Victoria, made this copy in 1866, four years after her marriage to the future Grand Duke Louis of Hesse.*

In this study dated 1860, Queen Victoria has copied a male nude from a drawing by Raphael. She was not working from the drawing itself (which was in the Malcolm Collection and is now in the British Museum), but from a photograph of the drawing which formed part of the Prince Consort's 'Raphael Collection'.

drawings by Old Masters, she used photographs of works of art as models and was adept at producing copies from the works of her contemporaries (who were sometimes also her masters), for example Westall, Hayter, Lear, Landseer, Leitch (Plate 3), Haag and Winterhalter. As we will see, she also copied the

Holbein's oil portrait of Georg Gisze was copied in watercolour by the Crown Princess as a gift for the Princess's art teacher, Heinrich von Angeli, in 1876. The inscribed note (printed on the wall above Gisze's head) contains the Princess's dedication to von Angeli.

work of other amateurs such as her cousin Ferdinand of Saxe-Coburg, the Prince de Joinville (one of Louis-Philippe's sons), or Charlotte Canning (a lady-in-waiting). Among the artistic products of Queen Victoria's daughters there are a few recorded instances of a return to copying Old Masters: in 1866 the second daughter, Princess Alice, copied the same Raphaelesque drawing (of Jonah) as her great-aunt Princess Elizabeth had traced around fifty years earlier.[13] A decade later Queen Victoria's eldest daughter, the Crown Princess of Prussia, gave the court portraitist, Heinrich von Angeli, her watercolour copy of an oil portrait by Holbein, which was hanging then (as now) in a Berlin museum.[14]

Once they had mastered the rudiments of art, these royal artists could then put their abilities to fine purpose by recording 'whatsoever is rare and worthy of observance', both at home and in the far corners of the world which they visited, either for pleasure or as part of their public duties. Although very few members of the Royal Family travelled (except to Hanover and within England) in the eighteenth century, the Grand Tour was so much an accepted part of civilized life that George III included it in his ideal educational programme. He suggested that the traveller visit Italy before moving on to the German princely courts. Sensibly he advised: 'I would recommend cultivating the acquaintance of all Men of Letters and not spending too much time with the English travellers.'[15] But we would search in vain for views of foreign scenery or costume by royal artists in the eighteenth century. With the new century the situation changed, and it is possible that two pencil views of the castle at Bad Homburg are by Princess (later Landgravine) Elizabeth, while several paintings by her sister-in-law, the Duchess of Kent, are specifically inscribed as views taken 'ad vivum' in Italy or Germany. When the Duchess's daughter, Queen Victoria, was on her travels she never ceased to observe, admire and record the curious scenery and inhabitants, and later took great delight in reviewing her sketches. Back home in July 1852 she: 'Finished some drawings from sketches I did in Scotland & of peasant women in Germany, & it gave me such a longing to go back to the latter again.'[16] The Princess Royal shared her mother's interest in unusual national costume, and derived great pleasure from sketching the local German variations that she encountered. She also sketched the scenery during her travels and wrote to the Queen with more than a hint of envy about her brother Prince Alfred's visit to India early in 1870: 'India must be *full* of sights wh. make one's mouth water when one is fond of colouring and of the picturesque and can draw. – I wonder whether Affie appreciates all that?'[17]

As the nineteenth century drew to its close, the opportunities for travel multiplied and the subject-matter of paintings by royal artists now extended from Venice and Florence through Menton and Cannes, Germany, Norway, Denmark, and on to Canada and even California. Princess Louise's travels through North America took place during the time that her husband, the Marquess of Lorne, was Governor-General of Canada. A few decades later, while Prince Arthur, Duke of Connaught, occupied the same position, the Prince's daughter (and companion) Patricia was very active artistically. A photograph in

A photograph from an album compiled by Princess Patricia of Connaught, relating to her father's time as Governor-General of Canada from 1911 to 1916. It is captioned: 'Expedition to Lake Louise from Banff. The arrival of my sketching things at Lake Louise. 4 Japs in single file carrying them.'

one of her albums has the following caption: 'Expedition to Lake Louise from Banff. The arrival of my sketching things at Lake Louise. 4 Japs in single file carrying them.' The considerable support on which any royal artist of the past could rely is thus very appositely indicated.

The difference between Princess Patricia's circumstances and those of other professional artists was immense. What is less easy to gauge is the extent of the difference (if any) between royal artists and other noble amateurs, some of whom occupied important positions at court. While Queen Charlotte sent her drawings and 'knotting' to members of the Harcourt family, in return she received from them examples of their etchings. The Duchess of Northumberland, whose family had received embroidery and drawings from (and by) members of George II's family, presented the young Princess Victoria on her fifteenth birthday with: 'a most beautiful album of crimson velvet embossed with gold, and filled with beautiful paintings by various ladies'.[18] The practice of art by the British Royal Family is very much a part of the activity of these 'various ladies' and gentlemen.

Equally (and perhaps even more) relevant to our present study is the artistic activity of other European Royal Families, especially those to which the British Royal Family is related through marriage. In such cases the lives and interests of the two families become almost inextricably combined, so that it is sometimes difficult to tell who is influencing whom. It can be said with some certainty, however, that the arrival of

George III's artistic daughters Charlotte and Elizabeth at the courts of Württemberg and Hesse-Homburg respectively, was at the time thought to be a source of inspiration to court life there, and that when Queen Victoria's eldest daughter, the Princess Royal, first moved to Germany in 1859, she was struck by the general atmosphere of inactivity and indolence that pervaded that court, and which merely persuaded her to draw, paint, sculpt and 'work' more than ever. To suggest that artistic talents and abilities were exclusive to English princes and princesses would be completely wrong, however. Less than ten years after her marriage the Princess Royal wrote to inform her mother of the portfolio of lithographs that the Queen Dowager of Prussia had had made from drawings by the late King Frederick William IV.[19] The palace at Charlottenburg, to the west of Berlin, still contains a firescreen made by the beautiful Queen Louise of Prussia. Yet earlier, Wilhelmina of Prussia (1751-1820), the wife of William V of Orange, was active as a miniaturist, copyist and decorative painter. A description of the royal palace of Het Loo in 1773 mentions white taffeta hangings painted by the Princess 'in the manner of Peking'.[20] Other artistic eighteenth-century German princesses include Maria Antonia of Bavaria, Queen of Poland and Electress of Saxony, and the Margravine Caroline Louise of Baden (1723-83, *née* Hesse-Darmstadt), who was taught to paint by Liotard.[21]

At a much earlier period the Habsburg line had produced a number of artists. Maximilian I (1459-1519) went to some pains to explain why he had learnt to paint. A panel on which his daughter, Margaret of Austria (1480-1530), had begun to paint is listed in an inventory of her possessions. Both Philip II (1527-98) and his son the Infante Pedro are known to have painted. Perhaps the most notable exponent was Philip II's third wife, Elizabeth of Valois, whom he married (following the death of his second wife, Mary Tudor) in 1559. Elizabeth was taught by Sofonisba Anguisciola (1527/8?-1626), an Italian artist of noble birth who had been invited to Spain by Philip II in the year of his marriage to Elizabeth. The young Philip IV (1605-65) received drawing lessons from the Dominican friar and artist Juan Bautista Maino (*c*.1569-1649), and there exists a signed picture of St Anthony and the Christ Child by Philip's brother Don Carlos.[22]

Of the two ruling houses of Germany with which the British Royal Family has been principally involved, that of Saxe-Coburg has produced considerably more artists than that of Hanover. Painted and drawn views by Queen Victoria's mother, Victoria of Saxe-Coburg, Duchess of Kent, have already been mentioned. The Duchess's brother, Leopold I, King of the Belgians, was also active artistically and during a stay at Buckingham Palace in February 1841 he produced an etching of two trees in a landscape.[23] He was doubtless inspired and encouraged on that particular occasion by the etching activities of the English royal couple, to both of whom he was uncle. Their own work is discussed in some detail in Chapter Three. Prince Albert and his elder brother, the future Duke Ernest II of Saxe-Coburg (1818-93), apparently learned to paint in oils during a stay with King Leopold in Brussels in the 1830s, on leave from their studies at Bonn University. Prince Ernest's 'Scene from Woodstock' (1836) is in the Royal Collection, while his painting of a Tyrolean mountain path, presented to Prince Albert in 1845, was formerly at Osborne House.[24] A mutual cousin of Queen Victoria and Prince Albert, Ferdinand of Saxe-Coburg (1816-85), who in 1836 married the Infanta (later Queen) of Portugal, was also active as an artist. His gifts of drawings and etchings were noted in the young Queen Victoria's Journal, and many have survived, with appropriate

Queen Victoria and Prince Albert's mutual first cousin, Prince Ferdinand of Saxe-Coburg, was also a skilled artist. His etching (dated 1848) shows Father Christmas distributing gifts to seven of the Prince's lively children at their home in Portugal.

inscriptions in pen or pencil, at Windsor. In addition to copies after other contemporary artists, he drew a favourite dog with her litter of puppies (1837), the various activities of his children Pedro and Louis (1839), the same children seated at table, propped up on cushions (1841), his father and brother Augustus (1843), and a hooded Father Christmas distributing gifts to seven delighted children (1848).

Prince Ferdinand's father (also Ferdinand, 1785-1851) had converted to Roman Catholicism in 1818, enabling this branch of the Saxe-Coburgs to marry into the French Royal Family, which they did on numerous occasions during the nineteenth century. The first such marriage took place in 1832, between the elder Ferdinand's brother Leopold (1790-1865, formerly married to Princess Charlotte of Wales) and Louise (1812-50), the eldest daughter of the 'citizen king' of France, Louis-Philippe (1773-1850). Two of Queen Louise of the Belgians' siblings married children of Duke Ferdinand. In 1840 Louis, Duke of Nemours (1814-96, Louis-Philippe's second son), married Victoire of Saxe-Coburg (1822-57), and in 1843 Clémentine (1817-1907, Louis-Philippe's youngest daughter) married Augustus of Saxe-Coburg (1818-81), King Ferdinand of Portugal's younger brother. With these marriages the Royal Family of France is (somewhat belatedly) introduced into our story.

During the 1730s the English writer George Vertue recalled the drawings and paintings of Francis I (1494-1547), and of 'the late Duke of Orléans', that is Philip d'Orléans (1674-1723), Regent of France from 1715 until his death, who was a child of the marriage between Louis XIII's second son and Charles I's youngest daughter, Minette.[25] He might also have mentioned Francis I's sister, Margaret of Navarre, or Réné of Anjou, whose daughter Margaret married Henry VI of England in 1445, and who was said to have been a gifted painter. Thereafter, it comes as no great surprise to discover that Louis XIV (1638-1715) was taught to draw. His youthful etching activity – resulting (for instance) in a print of houses and a watermill dated 1650[26] – could be paralleled with that of his contemporary Prince Rupert of the Rhine (see Chapter One). But in our context it is the French royal artists of the nineteenth century who are most relevant. Louis-Philippe's younger brother, the Duke of Montpensier, produced a number of chalk lithographs dated 1805-6 during a stay in Twickenham.[27] The English watercolour painter William Callow taught at least three of the children of Louis-Philippe in Paris during the 1830s: Louis,

Duke of Nemours, Clémentine d'Orléans, and François, Prince of Joinville (1818-1900).[28] During this period Princess Victoria often records her receipt of drawings from the French princes and princesses.[29] Following the popular uprising in February 1848, Louis-Philippe's abdication and the election of Napoleon III as ruler of France, Queen Victoria welcomed the exiled Royal Family in England, and encouraged them to settle at Claremont House, Surrey. In 1850 she described in her Journal Joinville's sketches made on a recent visit to his cousin Ferdinand in Portugal and Spain.[30] During the next two years Joinville travelled around the British Isles, sketching in Scotland[31] and the West Country, as well as Switzerland.[32] In 1853 Callow was invited to Claremont to resume his drawing lessons with Joinville and Princess Clémentine, after a lapse of nearly twenty years. In his autobiography the artist records the pleasure with which he was greeted: 'Ah, ça me rappelle le bon vieux temps,' they said ('Ah, that reminds me of the good old days').[33] The painter recollected having met Joinville's children during his visits to Claremont. The eldest, Françoise (1844-1925), was mentioned by her father some years later in a letter to Queen Victoria during a visit to London in May 1888:

> I hope that the Queen still paints watercolours. It is one of the great joys of life. At the Watercolour Society I have seen a pretty child's head by your daughter Louise. I was not aware of her talent. My daughter also does pretty things. At present she is experimenting with pastels, which are very *à la mode*.[34]

The practical and therapeutic justifications for royal artistic activity have already been mentioned. Finished works were almost invariably produced specifically for presentation purposes. By the nineteenth century the anniversaries of birthdays and weddings, and of Christmas and the New Year, were invariably marked by the exchange of gifts which – in the case of children – would generally consist of something made by their own hands. The German custom of exchanging Christmas gifts had originally been introduced to England by Queen Charlotte. However, the following account, by the Queen's eldest daughter, of the Christmas celebrations at Schloss Homburg, the home of her younger sister Princess Elizabeth, suggests that Christmas back at home was still celebrated in rather a different way. The Princess Royal was writing to her friend Lady Harcourt in January 1821:

> You would have enjoyed the Christmas eve, when my sister gave all her presents . . . I was quite struck, thirteen tables filled, absolutely loaded, with gifts for us all . . . We saw an extraordinary sight in the Drawing Room, and being fearful of fire, I said, 'Lord, what is that?' My sister got up, and when she came to the room, there she found a Tree illuminated; which was prepared by her Grand Daughters for her, with a foot stool of Charlotte's work, who is the eldest; and a Cap of Pauline's work for Her.[35]

During the reign of Queen Victoria, however, such celebrations became very much a part of British life. Gifts were regularly exchanged throughout the year (e.g. Plates 12 and 13). Just as a large number of Queen Victoria's own early drawings and watercolours are inscribed with the date of her mother's birthday (17 August), so those of her children are frequently dated 10 February (her marriage), 24 May (her birthday), 26 August (Prince Albert's birthday) or – after 1861 – 14 December (Prince Albert's death). The well-ordered routine of Queen Victoria's family life was something about which she cared deeply. Two years after his death she was thinking of producing a biography of the Prince, which would include a description of – for instance – a typical New Year's Day. She asked the Princess Royal to assist her by providing an account

> beginning with you children standing in our room waiting for us with drawings and wishes; Grandmama at breakfast, then you children performing something or a tableau, and you playing and reciting and in the evening generally a concert or performance with orchestra – then our wedding day the same . . . and later my birthday perhaps . . . and put down any picture of darling Papa's manner.[36]

As well as gifts within the immediate family, presentations were also made to relations overseas. Queen Victoria's half-sister Feodora, who sent numerous drawings of her children to their English aunt, received examples of the Queen's art in return. After a parcel of etchings had arrived in Langenburg in early 1841, Feodora wrote: 'I think you are both greatly improved in your etchings, some of them I admire particularly and am so thankful you sent them me; I shall have such a nice collection of them, pray . . . continue to send me these precious drawings if you do more.'[37]

Like many members of George III's household, Lady

Watercolour by James Roberts showing Queen Victoria's birthday presents laid out at Osborne House in May 1856. In the centre (behind a Sèvres porcelain vase) is the fan painted by the Princess Royal illustrated as Plate 12. Above it is one of Prince Albert's gifts, Winterhalter's group portrait of Princess Louise with Princes Arthur and Leopold.

The royal children would often give drawings to their parents to celebrate anniversaries. Princess Alice's angel holds the flame of the New Year (1860), while that of the Old Year (1859) smoulders below.

Queen Victoria's half-sister, Feodora, moved from England to Langenburg (in West Germany) following her marriage in 1828. Thereafter she kept her family acquainted with the appearance and antics of her children through the charming drawings that often accompanied her letters. This sketch shows Princes Hermann and Victor and Princess Adelaide of Hohenlohe-Langenburg.

Harcourt and her husband received a number of drawings and pieces of work from the Royal Family. This tradition has continued through the centuries, for an autograph work by a member of the Royal Family was (and is) infinitely preferable (to the recipient) to a signed portrait, engraving or photograph. Princess Victoria evidently realized the potential value of a product of her hand early on. Shortly before her accession she obtained a number of American autographs (including that of Fenimore Cooper) through Mr A. Vail, the chargé d'affaires at the American Embassy in London, to whom she gave her drawing of a scene from *The Bravo*.[38] The numerous etchings made by Queen Victoria and Prince Albert during the 1840s were all privately printed, for distribution to family and friends. In Theodore Martin's biography of the Queen he quotes the letter, dated 3 May 1869, which had accompanied a complete series of these etchings: 'The Queen sends Mr Martin to-day a volume of the beloved Prince's and her own etchings, which she has had purposely bound for him, and which she hopes he will place in his library, as a trifling recollection of his kindness in carrying out so many of her wishes.'[39] Theodore Martin's professional role in preparing biographies of both the Queen and the Prince introduces a further possible use of royal art – to illustrate royal writings. Just as Queen Victoria illustrated her manuscript journal with pen sketches (occasionally ornamented with watercolour), so her first literary venture, *Leaves from the Journal of our life in the Highlands* (1868), in which parts of her journal were transcribed, included a small number of line illustrations based on these sketches. Drawings by the Queen's fourth daughter, Princess Louise, were reproduced in the

Occasionally royal artistic talents have been applied to charitable causes. Princess Elizabeth's designs of the Power and Progress of Genius (first published in 1806) were reissued in lithography in 1833 specifically to raise funds for a crèche in Hanover. One might have wished that the subject-matter had been as down-to-earth as the purpose. In this plate Fancy tickles Genius with a feather from her wing, but fails to arouse him from the trance into which he has fallen, 'quite exhausted and overpowered by the perfume of the flowers of Fancy'.

context of essays by herself and her husband, the Marquess of Lorne, and as illustrations to the ballad of *Auld Robin* by her husband's cousin, Walter Douglas Campbell (1894).

In a surprisingly large number of instances royal works of art have been used to raise funds for charitable concerns. In 1833, Princess Elizabeth published a volume of lithographs after her designs to raise money for a crèche for the daughters of working mothers in the city of Hanover, the home of her brother Adolphus, Duke of Cambridge. A few years later we find the young Princess Victoria copying a successful drawing several times, once 'for Foreign Bazaar', and once 'for Dss. Beaufort's Bazaar' (see p.95). In 1900, the year before her death, Queen Victoria (and other members of her family) contributed works

In 1855 five of Queen Victoria's children contributed works of art to the London exhibition in aid of the victims of the Crimean War. Contemporary critics decided that the star of the show was the Princess Royal's painting of The Field of Battle. *It sold for 250 guineas, and was later reproduced in chromolithography, to raise yet more income for the 'Patriotic Fund'.*

to the Artists' War Fund exhibition and auction.[40] There are a number of other instances of Queen Victoria's children contributing their work to charitable causes, most notably the 'Patriotic Fund' to help dependants of Soldiers fighting in the Crimea in 1855. The exhibition of amateur work (in Bond Street, then at Burlington House) which was arranged specifically for the Patriotic Fund, included works by each of the five eldest princes and princesses. The Princess Royal's watercolour of *The Field of Battle* fetched 250 guineas at auction during the fund-raising effort, and was later reproduced in chromolithography, the income resulting from the sale of the prints being put to the same purpose. The Princess also contributed to the exhibition at the New British Institution in aid of the German war wounded in 1870 (as did Princess Louise) and to a number of charitable causes in Prussia, her married home. *Queen Alexandra's Christmas Gift Book*, consisting of reproductions of her own photographs, was published by the *Daily Telegraph* in aid of charity in 1908. The exhibition tour of 'Queen Mary's Carpet' through America in 1950, and its subsequent sale (for $100,000), all in aid of the British dollar crisis, is one of the most remarkable of such ventures. A more recent example is Prince Philip's donation of one of his paintings to his very successful Award Scheme.

It must by now be clear that the practice of art among the British Royal Family has at times been widespread, and that surviving examples date from the middle of the seventeenth century to the present day. Because of the formidable size of the families of George III (seven sons, six daughters) and of

Queen Victoria (four sons, five daughters), even by limiting our discussion to the immediate Royal Family the careers of an extraordinarily large number of people become involved. The main sources for the illustrations (and information) contained in this book are the Royal Library and Archives at Windsor Castle, in which the majority of the surviving art, journals and correspondence relating to the later British monarchs is to be found. The pictures are sometimes individually mounted, occasionally still framed up, but more often part of sketchbooks, or pasted on to the pages of an album, with appropriate inscriptions (including title and date) below. The meticulous way in which these apparently insignificant items were thus recorded has enabled the present study to be written.

Queen Victoria's drawing of her eldest daughter, the Princess Royal, was made within weeks of her marriage to the future Emperor Frederick III of Germany on 25 January 1858.

Drawings by King George III, Queen Charlotte and their children are mentioned in Inventory A, the manuscript list of all the drawings and watercolours in the Royal Collection compiled at the start of the nineteenth century. Other early works by the King re-entered the Collection with the majority of George III's papers in 1912, during the librarianship of Sir John Fortescue.[41] The collection of Victorian royal art has remained at Windsor in (or not far from) the Print Room, organized and equipped by Prince Albert during his last years. In a detailed note of her wishes for the drawings and watercolours most personal to her, the Queen itemized a number of albums which 'I desire should be placed in the Royal Library at Windsor, there to remain and to be considered heirlooms of the Crown.'[42] These included:

> The fine Album in red morocco containing all the sketches I and my beloved Husband made of our children –
> All my own sketchbooks from nature – (these to be kept separate from all the others) . . .
> My beloved Husband's own Drawing book – His Drawings, and the books with His valuable musical compositions written in His own precious hand . . .
> Two large Volumes containing Drawings by our Children –
> The large Volume containing Drawings by the Princess Royal.

These wishes were presumably drawn up soon after the Prince's death, for in addition to the above volumes there are two albums of drawings by Princess Louise in the Print Room. Other more recent additions to the Collection include sketchbooks by Queen Alexandra and Queen Mary.

However, there is very little relevant material at Windsor from before the accession of George III in 1760. Items relating to the family of Charles I's sister, the Queen of Bohemia, are now in the Historisches Museum am Hohen Ufer, Hanover, while the Hesse-Cassel archives at Fulda contain a volume of drawings by Princess Mary, daughter of George II, who married the Landgrave Frederick II of Hesse-Cassel in 1740. These references to Hanover and Fulda remind us that it has been more normal for a British prince or princess to marry a member of a foreign (Protestant) Royal Family than a fellow country-man. The careers of our royal artists must therefore be traced both at home and overseas. In the time and space allotted for the present study this could only be done selectively, and there are doubtless many collections containing relevant material which have not been consulted. The family archives of the ruling houses of Belgium, Denmark, Greece, Norway, Portugal, Spain and Sweden, for instance – each of which is related to the British Royal Family – have not been visited. But several princely collections in Germany have yielded unexpected (and plentiful) examples of royal art. The later drawings and artefacts by George III's eldest daughter, Charlotte Augusta Matilda, are now scattered between the Württemberg family collection, Schloss Ludwigsburg and the Staatsgalerie in Stuttgart, the capital of the Principality (then Kingdom) of Württemberg, whose heir Princess Charlotte married in 1797.[43] Most of the library and remaining archive of the second daughter, Princess Elizabeth, also survives in Germany, the Princess's home following her marriage in 1818. Like her sister Charlotte, Princess Elizabeth, the Landgravine of Hesse-Homburg, was childless and her heir was her husband's niece, Caroline, Princess Reuss (1819-72). The collection is now divided, part remaining at Bad Homburg (in the Schloss and the nearby Gothic House), with the greater part at Princess Caroline's home at Greiz, now in the German Democratic Republic.[44]

A large group of drawings and watercolours by Queen Victoria's eldest daughter, the Empress Frederick, has survived at Fulda. These are either loose-leaf, in their original sketch-books, or pasted into albums – following the example set by her parents. The Princess Royal spent the majority of her later years (after the death of her husband in 1888) at Kronberg in the Taunus mountains, to the north-west of Frankfurt. There she was within easy reach of her youngest daughter Margaret (1872-1954), who married Frederick Charles, Landgrave of Hesse, in 1893. Following the death of the Empress in 1901 her

property was bequeathed to this daughter, hence the presence of so many items of Prussian (and British) interest in the Hesse family archives. The papers and drawings of Queen Victoria's second daughter, Alice, are also in Germany, in the private family collection of another branch of the Hesse family, the Grand Dukes of Hesse and the Rhine, at Wolfsgarten and Darmstadt. Princess Alice married Prince (later Grand Duke) Louis of Hesse in 1862. Their grandson, Grand Duke Louis V, died in 1968, having named as his ultimate heir his adopted son Prince Moritz of Hesse (born 1926), the head of the Hesse-Cassel line (and the grandson of Princess Margaret of Prussia). The papers and collections of two of Queen Victoria's gifted daughters, Princesses Victoria and Alice, will thus eventually be united. Most of the family collections of Queen Victoria's half-sister Feodora, and of her second son Prince Alfred, Duke of Edinburgh, are at Schloss Langenburg, also in Germany.[45] The majority of the drawings and papers of Princess Patricia of

George III's third daughter, Elizabeth, worked in a wide variety of different media. This lithograph is in the collection of her work at her married home, Bad Homburg.

Connaught and of both Princess Louise, Duchess of Argyll, and her niece Princess Louise, Duchess of Fife, have remained with the families into which they married.

As a result of the various gifts, presentations, and sales of royal art for charitable purposes, other pieces are now scattered among the public and private collections of the world. In return for their services royal teachers (and particularly art teachers) must often have received gifts of paintings and drawings as tokens of affection from their pupils. Edward Corbould, the drawing master to the children of Queen Victoria and Prince Albert, was evidently showered with presents from his pupils, which he then carefully (and considerately) inscribed with the date and circumstance of presentation. Items formerly in Corbould's collection are to be found in both the British Museum and the Forbes Magazine Collection. In 1862 William Corden, who painted for the Queen (but never taught the Royal Family), was given her cylindrical watercolour box with folding palette, which is still in the possession of the artist's descendants.[46] Albums of juvenile royal art were formed by the children's governesses Fräulein Bauer and Madame Rollande, and doubtless by others besides.[47] In spite of Queen Victoria's wish that her own drawings should become 'heirlooms of the Crown', at least three of her sketchbooks have been removed from the Royal Collection.[48]

Although all this artistic activity was very much the private occupation of the Royal Family in its leisure hours, from time to time (particularly in the nineteenth century) works by royal artists were exhibited for public inspection. Horace Walpole and others claimed that some of the paintings exhibited by George III's master Joshua Kirby were actually by his royal pupil. Queen Victoria contributed two napkins made from yarn spun by her own hand, and a number of her etchings, to the Philadelphia Exhibition in 1876.[49] In the 1890s four drawings (or maybe etchings) by the Queen were lent to the Victorian exhibition at the New Gallery,[50] and a further seven were included in the 'Royal Room' exhibition at Earl's Court.[51] As we will see, the Prince Consort instituted legal proceedings against the organizers of an exhibition of royal etchings in the 1850s, specifically because royal permission had been neither sought nor granted. In 1925 the Brook Street Art Gallery, London, staged a whole exhibition of *Etchings by Her Majesty the late Queen Victoria and the Prince Consort*, and Osbert Sitwell wrote a preface to the catalogue, which also included a watercolour portrait by the Queen of Violet Granby (later Duchess

On the eve of her departure for Germany (and three days after her mother had portrayed her: see p.27), the Princess Royal inscribed this drawing to her master Edward Corbould.

of Rutland), and a piece of sculpture thought to be by Princess Louise (from Sitwell's collection).

Three of Queen Victoria's daughters exhibited their work in the context of professional artists. The fact that the first such instance occurred in Germany, where the Princess Royal lived following her marriage in 1858, may be relevant. In 1859 she informed the Queen that: 'we frequently have painters to dinner, they are much more received here than in England.'[52] The Princess was elected a member of the Berlin Academy the following year and exhibited there with regularity during the next decades. In the German Exhibition at Earl's Court,

Princess Louise's portrait of Major de Winton was exhibited at the Royal Society of Painters in Watercolour in 1880–1 and is now in the National Gallery of Canada. Major (later Sir Francis) de Winton (1835–1901) was Secretary to the Marquess of Lorne from 1878 to 1883. His portrait was painted in cool tones: the brown coat and black hat are silhouetted against a grey ground.

London, in 1891, her watercolour of a girl's head (painted in San Remo) was item 1 in the Drawing and Watercolour section. The Princess was an Honorary Member of the Institute of Painters in Watercolour from 1880, and her works were exhibited on various occasions in London galleries. The Queen's fourth daughter, Princess Louise, was probably the first member of the Royal Family to show her work at the Royal Academy of Arts. Her exhibits there (in 1868, 1869 and 1874) were pieces of sculpture, and specifically portrait busts of members of the Royal Family and Household. She was an Honorary Member of the Society of Painters in Watercolour from 1877, and her pictures were included in the Society's exhibitions from 1880.

In the following year the Society was formally redesignated the Royal Society of Painters in Watercolour, and the Princess of Wales (later Queen Alexandra) joined Princess Louise, Sir Richard Wallace, John Ruskin and others, as an Honorary Member. Although the Princess of Wales does not appear to have shown her work in public, Princess Louise's exhibits at the RSPW continued into the present century. During her time in Canada she contributed regularly to exhibitions and was partly instrumental in founding the Royal Canadian Academy. Her works were shown at the Grosvenor Gallery on a number of occasions and some also went north for exhibitions in Glasgow and Edinburgh. Princess Beatrice was an Honorary Member (with the Princess Royal) of the Royal Institute of Painters in Watercolour, and was thus a co-signatory of their Jubilee Address to the Queen in 1887. She exhibited at three of the Institute's exhibitions.[53] Other public displays of royal art include the contributions by the Princess of Wales and the Duchess of York (later Queen Alexandra and Queen Mary) to the exhibitions sponsored by the Home Arts and Industries Association in the Albert Hall during the 1890s.

In the next generation Princess Patricia, daughter of Prince Arthur, Duke of Connaught, was a member of the New English Art Club (from 1931) and an Associate of the RSPW (from 1940). She exhibited regularly in both Canada (where she resided with her father from 1911 to 1916) and London, where she had three one-man shows between 1928 and 1959. The wives of two of her cousins were also exhibiting their work in London in these years. Princess Marina, Duchess of Kent, as a Patroness of the Society of Women Artists (along with Queen Mary and the Princess Royal), exhibited portraits at the Society's exhibitions in 1936 and 1937. Another portrait by the Duchess was included in the Jubilee exhibition of the Women's International Art Club in 1950. Princess Alice, Duchess of Gloucester, had two one-man exhibitions at Walker's Galleries, New Bond Street, in 1933 and 1935, but after her marriage she exhibited only occasionally.

These works were exhibited to be judged alongside pieces by other, professional artists, with which they could well hold their own. In the later nineteenth and earlier twentieth centuries there were many highly accomplished amateur artists, of which the members of the Royal Family were only a small group. A number of the factors contributing to their activity have already been mentioned. In an oft-quoted remark by Prince Albert in 1860, some others are added:

I consider that persons in our position of life can never be distinguished artists . . . Our business is not so much to create, as to learn to appreciate and understand the works of others, and we never do this till we have realised the difficulties to be overcome. Acting on this principle myself, I have always tried to learn the rudiments of art as much as possible. For instance, I learnt oil-painting, watercolours, etching, lithography, etc. etc., and in music I learnt thorough bass, the pianoforte, organ, and singing, – not of course, with a view of doing anything worth looking at or hearing, but simply to enable me to judge and appreciate the works of others.[54]

Indeed, the Royal Family are and always have been considerably more important as patrons and collectors than as artists. The following study should be read less as a part of the history of art and more as an element in the social history of Britain, and particularly of the Royal Family of Britain. It also has a certain relevance for the history of British art, for princes and princesses have drawn and painted when there were artists to teach them to do so. They have continued to draw and paint into the present reign, and thus experience the time-honoured 'joy of receiving and absorbing beauty and creating it afresh', so appositely described by Princess Louise.

1

THEORISTS AND EARLY PRACTITIONERS

'Before we launch into this subject,' the Count replied, 'I should like us to discuss something else again which, since I consider it highly important, I think our courtier should certainly not neglect: and this is the question of drawing and of the art of painting itself. And do not be surprised that I demand this ability, even if nowadays it may appear mechanical and hardly suited to a gentleman. For I recall having read that in the ancient world, and in Greece especially, children of gentle birth were required to learn painting at school, as a worthy and necessary accomplishment, and it was ranked among the foremost of the liberal arts . . . From painting, which is in itself a most worthy and noble art, many useful skills can be derived, and not least for military purposes: thus a knowledge of the art gives one the facility to sketch towns, rivers, bridges, citadels, fortresses and similar things, which otherwise cannot be shown to others even if, with a great deal of effort, the details are memorized. To be sure, anyone who does not esteem the art of painting seems to me to be quite wrong-headed.'

Thus did the great Italian writer Baldassare Castiglione (1478-1529) pronounce on the importance of artistic education as part of the upbringing of the perfect courtier. Although his book *Il Cortegiano* (The Courtier) was written in the context of an Italian princely court (specifically Urbino), at the start of the sixteenth century, Castiglione's theories were gradually introduced throughout Europe, providing a useful justification and handbook for rulers and nobles alike concerning the proper behaviour and upbringing of the courtier successor to the medieval knight. His ideas lie at the heart of post-Renaissance educational theory.

Castiglione's book was first published, in its original Italian, in 1528. The first educational treatise or 'courtesy book' in the

English language appeared only three years later. *The Boke Named the Governour* by the English writer Sir Thomas Elyot (*c.*1490-1546) depended to a very large extent on Castiglione's example, but made subtle adjustments for the English character. Elyot introduced his discussion by noting that excessive activity in the military and other arts could lead to overstrain unless punctuated by periods of relaxation, through music, painting or carving. The following passage is taken from Chapter VIII, headed 'That it is commendable in a gentilman to paynt and kerve exactly, if nature therto doeth induce hym':

> If the chylde be of nature inclyned (as many have been) to peynte with a penne, or to fourme ymages in stone or tree: he shuld not be therfrom withdrawen, or nature be rebuked, whiche is to him benevolent: but puttyng one to him, whiche is in that crafte, wherein he deliteth, most excellent, in vacant tymes from other more serious learnyng, he shulde be in the moste pure wise enstructed in painting or kerving.

Just as Castiglione had evoked the precedent of the Fabii, a Roman patrician family of the fourth century BC who had included a painter amongst their number, so Elyot noted 'Claudius Titus, the son of Vaspasian Hadrian, both Antonines, & divers other emperours and noble princis, whose warkes of long tyme remained in Rome and other citees'. If such men from our noble past had been active as painters, why could not modern princes follow? But

> I intend not by these examples, to make of a prince or noble mannes sonne a commune paynter or keruer, which shal present him selfe openly, stayned or embrued with sondry colours, or poudered with the duste of stones that he cutteth or perfumed with tedious sauors of the metalles by hym yoten. But veraily myne intente and meanynge is onely, that a noble chylde, by his owne naturall disposicion, and not by coercion, maye be induced, to receyve perfecte instruction in these sciences.

The earliest reference to a British monarch showing any practical interest in art occurs surprisingly early, in the writings of the chronicler Abbot Walter Bower concerning James I of Scotland (1394-1437), who delighted in 'protractioni et picturae' (drawings and pictures). Following Elyot's pronouncements one would have assumed that the Tudor monarchs were taught to paint and draw as part of their upbringing although few (if any) products have survived from such instruction.[1] Although the chief pastimes of Henry VIII (1491-1547) were 'hunt, sing and dance', he followed with great interest the progress of the numerous projects involving domestic and military architecture carried out during his reign. He composed music and poetry, but it is unlikely that he (or his son and heir Edward VI, 1537-53) drew or painted. Mary Tudor (1516-58) was probably too short-sighted to have embarked on close work. Elizabeth I (1533-1603) was a skilled performer on the keyboard, and wrote with an elegant hand, but is not known to have drawn.

Castiglione and Elyot were chiefly concerned with the education of gentlemen rather than gentlewomen. Until the seventeenth century there are comparatively few examples of female amateur artists. Upper-class women were expected to indulge in less cerebral and more practical arts such as embroidery and music-making. The tradition for such activity was well established by the sixteenth century. St Etheldreda (630-79), daughter of King Anna of the East Angles and abbess and patron saint of Ely, is said to have offered St Cuthbert a stole and maniple finely embroidered by herself and worked with gold and precious stones. Over three centuries later Queen Emma, wife of Ethelred the Unready (968-1016) and then of King Canute (994-1035), is stated to have embroidered vestments and altar cloths. Editha, the Norman wife of King Edward the Confessor (*c.*1003-66), embroidered her husband's coronation mantle (1042).

In the sixteenth century there are a number of documentary records of the handiwork of queens. Embroidery was evidently considered an essential part of a gentlewoman's education and the scarcity and high cost of the materials (especially silk and gold and silver thread) ensured that it was the preserve of the courtier class. In the accounts of King Henry VII's wife, Elizabeth of York, for the year 1502 there is a reference to 'an elne of linnyn cloth for a sampler for the Queene'. Apart from the fact that this is probably the first reference to a needlework sampler, it reminds us that in the sixteenth century (and for generations thereafter), embroidery did not require inventiveness so much as manual dexterity and industry.

The great English chronicler Raphael Holinshed described needlework as among the chief accomplishments of women at the court of Elizabeth I. Earlier in the century Henry VIII's first wife, Catherine of Aragon (1485-1536), whom Erasmus considered 'miraculously learned for a woman', had been described as having a skein of embroidery silk casually draped around her neck when she faced Cardinal Wolsey and the papal legate Cardinal Campeggio to answer Henry VIII's accusations. Queen Elizabeth was an active needlewoman. As a young girl she made a cushion for her governess in silk and wool, in tent- and cross-stitch, and she gave her young brother, the future King Edward VI, some shirts of her own making. Paul Hentzner, a German visitor to Windsor Castle in 1598, noted a cushion 'most curiously wrought by Elizabeth's own hand'.

But these few references pale into insignificance alongside the activity of Mary Queen of Scots (1542-87), who during her prolonged imprisonment (from 1568 until her execution) appears to have worked almost unceasingly with her needle.[2] Mary was brought up at the French court, during the period of her betrothal (1548-58) to the Dauphin, later Francis II. The Dauphin's mother, Catherine de' Medici, who was in charge of the education of the princesses (including Margaret of Navarre, noted above) and of Mary, was a notable early practitioner of lacis (darned net whitework), which she had apparently learnt at a convent in Florence. At her death in 1589, Catherine left over a thousand pieces of such work. When Mary returned to Scotland in 1561, following the death of her husband the previous year, she was accompanied by various French servants among whom were two embroiderers, Pierre Oudry and Servais de Condé. Their main function was to outline (in black silk) the designs to be followed by the needlewoman, but their actual duties went far beyond this, so that they came to occupy the role of the Queen's most intimate servants.

During her imprisonment there was evidently little else to do but sew, and there are numerous contemporary references to Mary's activity at this time. Her first period of imprisonment, following Darnley's murder and her remarriage to Bothwell, was at Lochleven (1567-8). There she was deprived of her faithful servants and had to petition the Scottish lords for 'an imbroiderer to draw forthe such work as she would be occupied about'. This work evidently included a piece featuring an embroidered thistle for Bothwell. After her unsuccessful plea for Elizabeth's mercy in May 1568, Mary spent much of the next sixteen years (1568-84) under the guardianship of the Earl of Shrewsbury. In March 1569 the Earl wrote to Sir William Cecil, Elizabeth's chief Secretary of State, describing how: 'This Queen [Mary] continueth daily to resort to my wife [Bess of Hardwick]'s chamber where with the Lady Lewington and Mrs Seton she useth to sit working with the needle in which she

Cross-stitch panel of a spider's web by Mary, Queen of Scots, and Bess of Hardwick (whose monogram it bears), the wife of her guardian, the Earl of Shrewsbury.

much delighteth and in devising works.' A month earlier Mary (at the time imprisoned at Tutbury) had been visited by another of Elizabeth's envoys, Nicholas White, who reported:

> I asked hir Grace, sense the wether did cut off all exercises abrode, howe she passed the thyme within. She sayd that all the day she wrought with her nydill, and that the diversitie of the colors made the work seme lesse tedious and contynued so long at it, till veray payn made hir to give over. Upon this occasion she entered upon a pretty disputable in comparison between carving, painting and work with the needle, affirming painting in her own opinion for the most commendable quality.

But we know of no painted works by Mary.

Apart from helping her to pass the time, Mary's needle was used to make and adorn gifts for her cousin, Queen Elizabeth. In May 1574 the French Ambassador, Le Motte, reported to Henri III:

> The Queen of Scots your sister-in-law is very well, and yesterday I presented on her behalf a skirt of crimson satin, worked with silver, very fine, and all worked with her hand,

to the Queen of England, to whom the present was very agreeable, for she found it very nice and has prized it much, and it seems to me I found her much softened towards her.

The following year Elizabeth received three nightdresses from Mary, also worked by herself. Sadly, these tokens did not have the desired effect (in achieving her release from prison), nor were they exchanged in kind.

For her son James (born 1566), the posthumous son of Darnley, Mary copied 'all with her own hand' a book of French verses, and 'wrought a cover for it with a needle, and [it] is now of his Majestie esteemed as a precious jewel'. It is evident from the inventory of Mary's belongings made in June 1585 that some at least of her needlework was intended for larger-scale pieces, and in particular bed hangings, which provided vital insulation against draughts in sixteenth-century houses and were traditionally the chief display area for the embroiderer's art. The inventory lists a number of unfinished bed hangings 'wrought with needlework of silk, silver and gold, with divers devices and arms, not thoroughly finished'. In addition there were numerous small pieces, presumably to be applied to the hangings, which included 51 flowers in petit point, 124 birds, 116 others, 16 four-footed beasts and 52 fish.

For surviving examples of Mary Queen of Scots' work we must turn to the so-called Oxburgh hangings, one of which is dated 1570. The hangings are large curtains employing a ground of green velvet, to which are applied a number of canvas panels worked chiefly in cross-stitch, with silk thread. One of the original set of four hangings has been cut up, and parts are in the Victoria and Albert Museum, London, and the Palace of Holyroodhouse, Edinburgh. Of the remaining three (at Oxburgh Hall, Norfolk, on loan from the Victoria and Albert Museum), two were worked by Bess of Hardwick, the formidable wife of Mary's guardian Shrewsbury, and one is attributable to Mary herself. Thirty of the appliqued petit point panels on Mary's hanging are 'signed' with her royal or personal monogram. These include the central one, which shows a hand reaching from the sky while a sickle prunes a vine, between two fruit trees. Above is the motto VIRESCIT VULNERE VIRTUS (virtue flourishes by a wound). The same design had appeared on a cushion sent by Mary to the Duke of Norfolk and the cushion was cited as evidence of her complicity in Norfolk's plot to kill Elizabeth. The design, it was claimed, showed Queen Elizabeth in the guise of the unfruitful vine that was to be cut

The central panel from one of the Oxburgh hangings, incorporating (at left and right) Mary's cipher and arms. It was claimed that the panel symbolized the removal of the unfruitful vine (Queen Elizabeth) so that the fruitful one (Mary, Queen of Scots) could replace it.

down so that the fruitful branch, Mary, could rule in her stead. It is disappointing, but hardly surprising, to find that little or no inventiveness was involved in the designs used on the Oxburgh hangings. They are derived from the books of emblems or *imprese* which were published from *c.*1560 and were evidently quite readily available in England for use in the applied arts.

Following Queen Elizabeth's death in 1603 there was a new King and a new dynasty, for Mary Queen of Scots' son, James VI of Scotland, succeeded to the English throne as King James I. At the same time there was a renewed interest in art. During the previous reign the portrait had dominated artistic life. Artists had painted little else, and collectors purchased few pictures that were not portraits. In consequence, the social status of the artist remained debased, in spite of Elyot's pleas at the beginning of the century. The first signs of change appear *c.*1600, with the *Treatise concerning the Arte of Limning* by the miniaturist Nicholas Hilliard (1547-1619). Far from having to present arguments for the practice of miniature painting (or limning) by gentlemen as well as more menial artists, Hilliard wrote: 'Now therefore I wish it were so that none should meddle with limning but gentlemen alone, for that it is a kind of gentle painting of less subjection than any other.' Hilliard's work, although intended for publication, was not issued until early in the present century. However, a similar theoretical line was followed in the writings of Henry Peacham, who was tutor to James I's eldest son, Prince Henry (1594-1612), from 1606. Peacham's *The Art of Drawing with a Pen*, first published in 1606, was reissued (with revisions) as *Graphice*, or *The Gentleman's Exercise*, six years later. As the title would suggest, this was not a painter's handbook but 'the first art manual written specifically for an audience of non-professionals'. Peacham rightly believed that in their lack of artistic attainment the English (and Scottish) monarchs were falling behind their continental equivalents. Painting was 'favoured in times past of the greatest Monarches, and of late daies practised even by Princes, and the greatest personages themselves, as *Francis* the first [1494-1547] King of France, *Charles Emanuel*, Duke of Savoy [1562-1630], with many others who are reported to have been excellent with the pencill.'[3] In Chapter XV of *Graphice* Peacham discussed in some detail the artistic ability of the Dutch nation:

> Since the greatest persons among them as Dukes, Earles, and in a manner all the Gentlemen doe beare an inbred love of drawing, and of themselves by their owne practise grow more times wonderfull expert herein: yet none at this day, who favoureth a good picture, or an excellency in that kinde, more than Rudolph the Emperor [1552-1612] now living.

The ability to draw or paint was thought to be inextricably linked to informed patronage of the arts, and thus to the encouragement of the work of professional artists. Peacham's better-known work, the *Compleat Gentleman* (1622), which was to some extent an updated version of Elyot's *Governour*, naturally repeated the earlier writer's advocacy of the teaching of drawing as an essential part of the education of a gentleman.

The first decades of the seventeenth century were a period of peace and prosperity in strong contrast to the troubles of Elizabeth's reign. The atmosphere was thus well suited to the flowering of the arts. Peacham's call for the teaching of painting to the leisured classes found a willing audience, and when writing the history of English art of the seventeenth and early eighteenth centuries George Vertue, and later Horace Walpole,

were able to cite the names of numerous noble amateur prac-
titioners, in both painting and architecture.[4] King James I,
characterized by the nineteenth-century Whig historian
Macaulay as 'the wisest fool in Christendom', is not known to
have drawn or painted, but he published a number of books
and was a noted poet and patron of the arts. His wife, Anne of
Denmark, was said to prefer pictures to the company of living
people. Their three children Henry (1594-1612), Elizabeth
(1596-1662) and Charles (1600-49) each inherited these artistic
interests. The start of the Stuart dynasty thus heralded a fertile
period both of royal patronage and collecting, and of royal
artefacts.

In spite of the comparative peace of these years, Prince Henry
considered the martial arts as of prime importance. In his
miniature portrait by Isaac Oliver the Prince is depicted in a
rich suit of armour, before a military encampment. But his
Treasurer, Sir Charles Cornwallis, noted that 'He greatly delighted in . . . Building and Gardening; in Music, Sculpture and
Painting, in which last art he brought over several valuable
works of great Masters from all countries.' Among those who
worked for and advised the Prince in artistic matters was Salo-
mon de Caus (1576-1626), the French engineer and architect.
According to the preface of his book on perspective, dated
October 1611, de Caus had instructed the Prince on this subject
for two or three years, that is since 1608.[5] We are reminded of
the importance of the application of art to military use, for a
knowledge of perspective would assist the correct making of
plans and views of fortifications.

Henry's younger brother Charles, who succeeded as Prince
of Wales following Henry's early death in 1612, was described
by Bainbrigg Buckeridge as having 'delighted more in Painting
than in all the other sciences, as much a master was he of all'.[6]
Contemporary opinion, when it mentioned Charles I's artistic
output, was likely to be particularly biased. In another early
biography, Perrinchief claimed that: 'In painting he has so
excellent a fancy that he would supply the defect of art in the
workman, and suddenly draw those lines, give those airs and
lights, which experience and practice had not taught the
painter.'[7] Conversely, the early eighteenth-century antiquary
George Vertue recorded a statement by Hugh Howard that
'K. Charles first drew very handsomly several drawings of his
with his own handwriting, corrected by Rubens', while himself
observing that this was 'not likely'.[8] Perrinchief goes on to say
that the King

could judge of fortifications, and censure whether the cannon were mounted to execution or no. He had an excellent skill in guns, knew all that belonged to their making. The exactest arts of building ships for the most necessary uses of strength or good sailing, together with all their furniture, were not unknown to him. He understood and was pleased with the making of clocks and watches. He comprehended the art of printing.

No tangible evidence has survived of this remarkable activity, and no works by the King (or by Prince Henry) were specified in the very full Inventories and Valuations of Charles's possessions made between 1649 and 1651. However, the lists include references to limnings of a Faulconer and of Tobias and the Angel 'by the King's Neece', that is Louisa Hollandina (1622-1709), the second daughter and sixth child of the 'Winter Queen' (James I's daughter, Elizabeth Stuart) and Frederick V of Bohemia.[9] Both Louisa and her younger sister Sophia (1630-1714) were said by the contemporary French art critic, Roger de Piles, 'to distinguish themselves by their skill with the paint brush', while Buckeridge stated that 'all the children of the queen of Bohemia, daughter of King James I, were taught to paint by Honthorst.'[10] The lessons with Gerard van Honthorst, who was much patronized by the Winter Queen and her family, presumably took place in The Hague where the family was resident in exile (from 1620), and where Honthorst was employed as painter to the Stadtholder and had a sizeable studio. When the English diarist John Evelyn visited The Hague in 1641 he met members of the Queen of Bohemia's family. He described Princess Louisa as:

> so rarely accomplisht in the art of Painting, that by a peculiar talent she would draw the Pourtraicture of any she saw by memory onely: I have of this Princesses hand the Picture of the Vicountesse Mourdaunt, which she sent my Wife in Oyle, and a long ingenious & facetious letter, all in *Rebus's*, & *Hieroglypics*, drawn with a pen very Curiously, expressing (without words) what pass'd at the Hague, directed to the old Earle of Norwich from whom it came to my hands.[11]

In 1669 Princess Louisa is specified as the artist responsible for 'A Nostre Dame in litle', noted as hanging over the chimney of Queen Henrietta Maria's bedchamber at Colombes. By now the Princess had entered the convent at Maubuisson, of which she later became Abbess, and where she ended her days in 1709. When questioned by her niece, the notorious Liselotte, Duchess of Orleans (1652-1721), about the possibility of tedium in this cloistered life, her response was characteristic: 'She answered

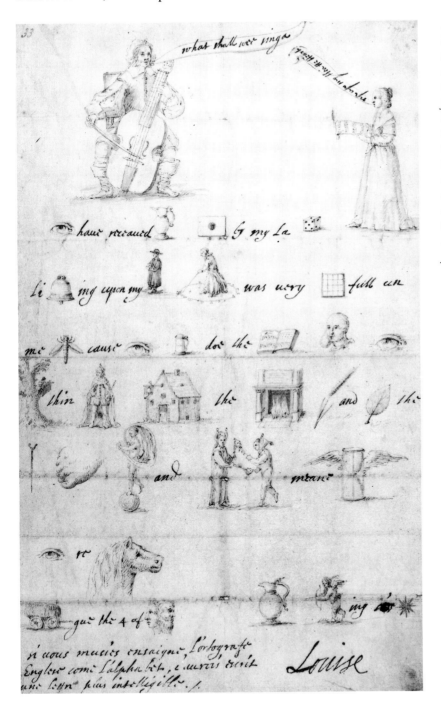

A picture letter sent by Princess Louisa to Lord Goring (later Earl of Norwich). It may be tentatively construed as follows: 'I have received your letter by my Lady libelling upon my Father which was very painful un[to] me because I can do the part many are thinking in the great . . . and leave the rest to Fortune and [fools], meantime I remain Your loving sister Louise. Hague the 4 of January.'

laughing that I well knew what painters were; they liked to see dark places, and the shadows that the light caused, and this gave her every day fresh taste for painting. She could turn everything this way that it should not seem dull.'[12]

When Elizabeth of Bohemia died in 1662, the greater part of her collection passed to her close friend and supporter William, 1st Earl of Craven (1606-97), in whose London house she expired. The Craven collection, which remained intact until comparatively recently, included a number of paintings by (or attributed to) Elizabeth's children. The obvious dependence of these pictures on the style of Honthorst makes secure attributions extremely difficult. However, a portrait of a lady wearing a disc-shaped hat and holding a rod is inscribed as a self-portrait by Princess Louisa, and a picture of her sister, Princess Sophia, is inscribed 'Foace par Madame La Pr. Lowisa'.[13] A picture once thought to represent Prince George of Hanover, later King George I of England, but actually of the young William III (1650-1702), by the Electress Sophia, another of Elizabeth's daughters, was also once in the Craven collection.[14] Although few paintings or drawings by Princess Sophia, the mother of the future King George I, are known, a number of

A number of the children of Charles I's sister the 'Winter Queen', Elizabeth of Bohemia, painted and drew. The second daughter, Princess Louisa, painted this self-portrait before entering a nunnery. Like other members of her family she was taught by Gerard van Honthorst, the court painter at The Hague.

her pieces of needlework have been identified. Among the most remarkable of these is the altar frontal presented by her to the convent at Loccum (near Hanover) in 1691, representing a display of blue and white china ranged on shelves, all worked in cross-stitch.[15] While Princess Louisa had become a convert to the Catholic faith, Princess Sophia adhered to her Protestant religion and was thus in 1701 declared eligible to succeed to the throne of England.

Prince Rupert (1619-82), Louisa and Sophia's elder brother, is the first royal artist by whom a substantial body of work has survived. Apparently Rupert's talent for drawing only became evident during his time at the University of Leyden, where he matriculated in 1628. As was the case with his great-grandmother, Mary Queen of Scots, a period of imprisonment (from 1638 to 1641, in the castle of Linz on the Danube) provided him with an enforced period of leisure during which he 'diverted himself sometimes with drawing and limning'. His military training taught him the importance of the art of perspective, and he perfected an instrument to assist artists in perspective drawing, which many years later he presented to the Royal Society in London. A few of his sketches, and some of his etchings, have survived. In the sale of the painter Charles Jervas, Vertue noted 'some small figures drawn loosely with the pen. on white paper a clean free pen writing . . . under writ. – dessinati per il principe Ruberto a Londra 23 Septembro'.[16] One of the Prince's sketches in the British Museum represents a

Princess Sophia, a younger sister of Prince Rupert and Princess Louisa, worked this altar hanging in cross-stitch for presentation to the convent at Loccum (Bad Rehburg, near Hanover) in 1691. Her eldest son succeeded to the throne of England in 1714 as King George I.

This view and section of a boat-mounted mortar reminds us of Prince Rupert's ingenuity as an inventor. He was a founder member of the Royal Society.

mortar mounted on a boat. This may be related to the new method of boring cannon invented by Prince Rupert. Other experiments included an improvement in the manufacture of gunpowder, a new type of powder flask, a water machine, and a method of painting colours on marble which when polished would be permanent. Vertue noted 'a piece of marble in a frame' of the *Woman taken in Adultery*, 'curiously painted and stained by Pr. Rupert'.[17]

At least two of Prince Rupert's etchings are definitely datable to his years at Linz. The etched portrait of Queen Christina of Sweden (which is almost certainly by him), probably dates from 1655 when he and his cousins Charles, Henry and Mary Stuart met Christina at Königstein, after her abdication and before her journey to Rome. Soon after this date Rupert seems to have begun working in mezzotint. According to John Evelyn, to whom he imparted the technique in 1661, both the invention and the introduction of the mezzotint to England were due to the Prince. However, others have concluded that the invention of the technique should be ascribed to the German soldier and amateur artist Ludwig von Siegen. Whatever the case, Prince

Prince Rupert is often credited with the invention of the technique of mezzotint engraving. This print of the 'Great Executioner', copied from a painting by a follower of Ribera, is the largest and most impressive of his mezzotints. It is signed and dated 1658 along the lower edge of the plate.

Rupert corresponded in detail on the subject of the new printing method with his cousin, Landgrave William VI of Hesse-Cassel (whose groom of the bedchamber von Siegen was), during the years 1657-8. Thus, on 28 December 1657 Rupert wrote: 'You can rest assured that bone-black is best of all for the varnish [ink], but it must first of all be well rubbed and crushed with something and it will then mix very well.' On 5 February 1658: 'I am sending with this several instruments that have already been completed. You should simply whet them on an oilstone until they draw evenly upon the copper. The proofs which you promise will be a heartfelt delight to me.' Finally, on 26 March: 'I must inform you that I have invented an instrument that works over the whole of the copper with little effort and time. I also have other things in hand which will soon be completed.'[18]

It appears from the above that if Rupert did not invent the art of mezzotint, he was principally responsible for devising the mezzotint rocker, the tool used to work up the burr on the surface of the plate. Of the seventeen mezzotints by or attributed to Rupert, one (*Titian's self portrait*) is dated Vienna 1657, and

two others (*The Great Executioner* and *The Standard Bearer*) are
dated 1658. In the latter year Prince Rupert met the Dutch artist
Wallerant Vaillant, to whom he revealed the new process. The
secrets of the new art were later propounded in full to John
Evelyn in London, where both Vaillant and Rupert had transferred at the time of the Restoration of the monarchy in 1660.
On 24 February 1661, Evelyn noted in his diary: '*Prince Rupert*
first shewed me how to Grave in M[e]zzo Tinto.' A further
session took place on 13 March, when 'This after noone his
hig[h]nesse *Prince Rupert* shewed me with his owne hands the
new way of Graving call'd *Mezzo Tinto*', enabling Evelyn to
publish in the following year his book entitled *Sculptura: or the
History, and Art of Calcography and Engraving on Copper . . . To
which is annexed A new manner of Engraving*, or Mezzo Tinto,
communicated by His Highness Prince Rupert *to the Author of this
Treatise*. Thereafter the art of mezzotint developed apace as an
almost exclusively English medium, hence its description as *la
manière anglaise*.

Through his membership of the Royal Society from its foundation in 1660, and through his ready accessibility in London
and Windsor (where he was resident as Governor and Constable
of the Castle from 1668), Prince Rupert was associated with
many of the scholars and artists of his time. Although aesthet-
ically his surviving works are not of the first rank, his ingenuity
and industry cannot be doubted. In his last years at Windsor,
where he had a laboratory, forge, workshop, studio and library,
he doubtless enjoyed the leisure to pursue his many interests to
the full. His apartments in the Round Tower are now occupied
by the Royal Archives, which retain so many of the references
to royal artists that are quoted on these pages.

Prince Rupert's cousin, King Charles II, is known to have
received lessons from a number of artists, although a hundred
years later the indefatigable Horace Walpole stated that Charles
'had a turn to mechanics, none to the politer sciences'.[19] Walpole
also noted that Van Dyck's pupil David Beck (1621-56) 'was in
favour with Charles I and taught the Prince, and the Dukes of
York and Gloucester, to draw'.[20] A drawing by Charles II of
the Isle of Jersey, noted by Vertue at Leipzig and by Walpole
in the Imperial Library at Vienna,[21] was presumably made
while Prince Charles was on the island, between April and June
1646 or between September 1649 and February 1650. It is
possible that the Prince's drawings provided the basis for
Hollar's etchings dated 1650 and 1651,[22] which are unlikely
for various reasons to have been based on designs by Hollar

himself. Hollar was doubtless introduced to the Royal Family by his patron, Thomas Howard, Earl of Arundel. In 1649, the year of Charles I's execution, three years after Arundel's death, Hollar stated that he had acted as domestic servant to the Duke of York (the future James II).[23] His association with the future Charles II is assumed by Vertue,[24] who noted:

> In a small pockett book [in the possession of the Earl of Oxford] several drawings of Hollar. as I suppose. tis said to be the book from which K. Charles the 2d learnt to draw, when he was *P. of Wales* on the cover is the impress of the feathers & Hollar taught him. there being eyes nose & mouth & several heads differently drawn. some after Holbein.[25]

Whether or not the drawings in the book were by Hollar, they appear to have been used by Charles II when Prince of Wales for the volume bore his impresa. It is perhaps worth noting briefly here that Anne, Countess of Buccleuch (1651-1732), who in 1663 married Charles's natural son James, Duke of Monmouth, was among the many pupils of Alexander Browne, author of various treatises on the art of drawing, published in the 1660s and 1670s. In the dedication to his *Ars Pictoria* (1675), Browne noted how 'Your Grace [i.e. Anne] was pleased from my poor instructions to draw a nobler honour to this Art.'

Meanwhile, the two daughters of James II were similarly being taught, by the miniaturist Richard Gibson, nicknamed 'Dwarf' because of his diminutive stature.[26] Both Mary (1662-94) and Anne (1665-1714) were also noted as needlewomen. Queen Mary was said to have been more interested in embroidery than in state affairs, and was to be observed at work on her canvas even when travelling by carriage. In around 1712 Celia Fiennes (1662-1741), the indefatigable traveller and writer, noted that the Queen's Closet at Hampton Court was entirely furnished with hangings and seat furniture 'all of satten stitch done in worsteads, beasts, birds, images and fruites all wrought very finely by Queen Mary and her Maids of Honour'.[27] Another tantalizing glimpse into the handiwork of the royal sisters is provided by a Shrewsbury sale catalogue of 1875: 'A fine piece of Old Silk tapestry – a garden scene, the offerings of Flora to Venus . . . etc. This screen, the work of Queen Anne, was presented by Her Majesty to the Rt. Hon. Richard Hill, Ambassador Extraordinary to the Court of Turin, 1703.'[28]

Before leaving the Stuarts we will pause to glance at the drawing of *St Jerome in Ecstasy* by Mary and Anne's nephew,

Charles Edward Stuart, the Young Pretender, is said to have drawn this figure of St Jerome in Penitence in 1733, at the age of twelve. It is based on a design by Guido Reni, known through a number of printed copies.

EX DONO EIUSDEM CAROLI PRINCIPIS WALLIÆ FILII JACOBI III. BRITANNIÆ REGIS AN. 1733.

the Young Pretender (1720-88), inscribed as having been drawn in 1733, when Prince Charles Edward had 'just turn'd of 12 years of age, without his Drawing Master Pompeo or any body else ever touching or putting an hand to it, as was known at the time to the whole Family. His Royal Highness made a present of it to Cardinal Imperiali, who put the Inscription below it, & esteeming it so much kept it with his jewels.'[29] The drawing is indeed remarkably proficient for a twelve-year-old, and well demonstrates the success of the more professional art teachers of the eighteenth century, in this case presumably the young Pompeo Batoni (1708-87).

2

THE EIGHTEENTH CENTURY

The Act of Settlement of 1701 established the succession of the English throne in the Protestant line represented by the Electress Sophia, sister of Prince Rupert of the Rhine and Princess Louisa. However, the Electress's death in 1714, two months before that of her cousin Queen Anne, meant that it was Sophia's eldest son, George (1660-1727), who actually succeeded to the throne. In spite of his Stuart ancestry, George I was a thoroughly German monarch and was furthermore not greatly interested in the visual arts. (However, his love of music was such that he was a patron of Handel in both Hanover and London: the *Water Music* was probably written for a royal progress on the Thames.) His estranged wife (and first cousin) Sophia Dorothea remained imprisoned at Ahlden (north of Hanover) throughout the reign, until her death in 1726. The King himself was frequently in Germany where, with the assistance of his eldest son Prince George, he pursued his military interests from the palace in Hanover.

Unlike his father, King George II (1683-1760), who succeeded in 1727, spoke good English (with a strong German accent), and with his intelligent and attractive wife Caroline of Ansbach (1683-1737) spent an increasing amount of time in England after his accession. Queen Caroline was a notable patron of the arts and is credited with the rediscovery of the volumes containing the unparalleled series of drawings by Leonardo and Holbein which are still in the Royal Collection. An embroidered quilt and two cushion covers, worked by Queen Caroline and her ladies, were given by the Queen to Lady Elizabeth Smithson (whose husband was later created 1st Duke of Northumberland) in 1742. The cultured atmosphere of royal family life at the time is charmingly suggested by Philip Mercier's conversation pieces showing Frederick, Prince of Wales, making music with his sisters Anne, Caroline and Amelia (*c*.1733). In addition to

*A painting by Princess
Caroline, the third daughter
of George II, based on a
picture by Philip Mercier. It
was presented by the Princess
to one of her ladies of the
bedchamber.*

his various appointments in the Prince of Wales's household,
Mercier was art teacher to Princess Anne (1709-59), and Vertue
quotes his indignant rebuttal of a story (published in a newspaper
in April 1734) according to which the Princess (married since
March 1734 to William IV, Prince of Orange) had painted the
likeness of the artist Herman van der Mijn.

Mr Merciere further says that at no time the Princess never
drew or painted any peece without his being witness – nor
ever drew from the life at any time. tho' she had drawn &
Coppyed many several copies in oyl painting done by her
that whilst she lately was in Holland at leisure she first begun

to draw. the picture (from the life) of one of her waiting mayds Mrs . . . in small.'[1]

With her husband Princess Anne formed notable collections of pictures, drawings and natural historical items. The artistic activities of her daughter-in-law, Wilhelmina of Prussia, were mentioned in the Introduction.

Although none of Princess Anne's work appears to have survived in England, we know of a number of pictures by her third sister, Princess Caroline (1713-57). Among them is an oil painting of a shepherd and shepherdess after Mercier, which she presented to her lady of the bedchamber from 1731 to 1736, Lady Susan Keck (née Douglas-Hamilton, d. 1755).[2] The handling of the paint is sufficiently competent to suggest that she painted other subjects. There is also a drawn copy by Princess Caroline of a mezzotint (by John Smith after Kneller, dated 1695) of the portrait of Lord Buckhurst and his sister Lady Mary Sackville with a hind. Princess Caroline's drawing is inscribed as having been presented by the Princess to Frances, Countess of Hertford, on 2 December 1732. Lady Hertford was lady of the bedchamber to Queen Caroline from 1726 (when she was Princess of Wales) until 1737. Like Queen Caroline's pieces of embroidery noted above, which were given to Lady Hertford's daughter Elizabeth Smithson, the drawing has remained in the collection of the Dukes of Northumberland. Another drawing by Princess Caroline, which is a copy of a picture by the French artist Pater, was reacquired for the Royal Collection earlier this century.[3] These charming copies appear to be the earliest surviving evidence of the serious artistic education of an English Royal Princess that has come down to us.

Following Mercier's fall from grace in the Royal Household, another drawing master was appointed: Bernard Lens III (1682-1740), who held the position of miniature painter to both George I and George II, is described specifically as having taught the latter's three younger children William Augustus (1721-65), Mary (1723-72) and Louisa (1724-51).[4] In 1735 Lens published a series of etchings of land- and seascapes that had been made expressly for his royal pupils. Five years later Princess Mary married Frederick II, Landgrave of Hesse-Cassel. Among the books from her library that have survived at Fulda is a leather-bound volume embossed with the initials 'P.M.' on the front cover and containing a number of landscape studies dated March and April 1733.[5] At the age of ten the young Princess was

George II's fourth daughter,
Princess Mary, was taught by
the miniaturist (and drawing
master) Bernard Lens III.
She was ten years old when
she made this drawing.

evidently receiving a thorough grounding in draughtsmanship.
Bernard Lens was the first of the fashionable drawing masters
who came to such prominence in the second half of the eighteenth century. His pupils included the young Horace Walpole.

Unlike his father and grandfather, but like his mother
Caroline of Ansbach, Frederick, Prince of Wales (1707-51),
was positively enthusiastic about the arts.[6] Vertue noted that
his 'affection and inclination to promote and Encourage Art and
Arts is daily more and more evident, by the imployments he
has given several artists'. Philip Mercier and then Joseph Goupy
were the Prince's favoured artists during the 1730s. Goupy
(c.1680-c.1780), the nephew and pupil of the French drawing
master Louis Goupy, worked for the Prince from 1733. Walpole
adds that Joseph Goupy 'had the honour of teaching her Royal
Highness the Princess of Wales',[7] and elsewhere we learn that
the future George III was among his pupils.[8] Before turning to
that prolific sovereign, it is interesting to compare a drawing
by his brother Edward, the future Duke of York (1739-67),
inscribed to the Princess Augusta on 21 November 1752,[9] with
the similar studies by his aunt, Princess Mary, carried out almost
twenty years before. Could they have been copying the same
models? There are four etchings ascribed to the Prince of Wales's
fourth son, Henry Frederick, Duke of Cumberland (1745-90),
in the British Museum.[10] From the style of dress they seem to

This Drawing is most humbly Dedicated to Her Royal Highnefs the PRINCESS
By Her most Dutyfull and most Obedient Son EDWARD. *Prince Edward Secit Nov. 21 1752*

The simple landscape style taught by Bernard Lens continued to inspire royal children long after his death in 1740. This drawing was presented to Princess Augusta of Wales by her second son, Edward, Duke of York, in 1752, when he was twelve years old.

date from the 1760s. Among the collection of pictures belonging to the family of the Earls of Harcourt there are two landscape drawings dated 1756, by Princes George and Edward, which are in the same style as the above-mentioned works, and were presumably given to the first Earl Harcourt, who was the Prince of Wales's Governor 1750-1 and remained a lifelong friend of the Royal Family.

Following the death of Frederick, Prince of Wales, in 1751, his eldest son George (1738-1820) became heir apparent. Nine years later he ascended the throne as George III, on the death of his grandfather, King George II. In 1764 the *London Chronicle* published an anonymous letter from Rome containing the following passage: 'The fine arts, hitherto too much neglected in England, seem now to rise from oblivion, under the reign of a Monarch, who has the taste to perceive their claims, and a propensity to grant his loyal protection to whatever can embellish human life'. In the heyday of the Grand Tourist, George III might well have travelled to Italy but he never even visited Scotland. However, his younger brothers Edward, William and Henry (respectively Dukes of York, Gloucester and Cumberland) had both the time and the opportunity to make the transalpine journey. The experience does not seem to have had any effect on their artistic production, which remained minimal.

Prince George had been carefully educated in most subjects,

and he appears to have drawn and designed throughout his long life. The record of the 'Establishment of His Present Majesty when Prince of Wales, and his Brother Prince Edward' from 1751 to 1756[11] notes annual payments of £100 to a Master of Fortification and Drawing throughout this period. In the latter year there is a single payment of the same sum to 'Joshua Kirby, Drawing Master'. Joshua Kirby (1716-74) was active as a topographical draughtsman in Suffolk before moving to London in 1755. It is very likely that most of the juvenile drawings by the young Prince that survive in the Print Room at Windsor Castle were carried out under Kirby's tutelage. A series of 38 such drawings, showing simple geometrical constructions in the 'sky' above crudely drawn landscape compositions, can be related to one of the standard geometrical textbooks, Sebastien le Clerc's *Pratique de la Géometrie*, first published in 1690 but later issued in English translation. This work, as well as the same writer's *Treatise on Architecture*, would certainly have been known to Kirby. George III's adaptations of le Clerc were noted in Queen Charlotte's Library at Frogmore House in 1819.[12] The Queen had found them in a desk four years earlier (illustrated pp. 8 and 9).

In the present context Kirby's mastery of the art of perspective, about which he lectured at the St Martin's Lane Academy, is crucial. When he published *The Perspective of Architecture* (at the King's expense) in 1761, it was dedicated to his royal pupil with the following words: 'May it please your Majesty, this

Joshua Kirby's book entitled The Perspective of Architecture *was published in 1761 at the expense of and with a dedication to George III. The illustrations included designs by the King, such as that shown here.*

work begun by your Majesty's Command, carried on under your Eye, and now published by your Royal Munificence, is most humbly dedicated to Your Majesty.' Elsewhere in the book Kirby notes that it was 'begun by command of His present Majesty when Prince of Wales by Joshua Kirby, designer in perspective to His Majesty'. In the captions to the plates Kirby avers that two (LXIV and LXXIII) were engraved from designs by others. The drawing on which plate LXIV is based has survived in the Print Room at Windsor, with the signature 'G.P.W. 1760' and the inscription: 'This Drawing was Designed & Executed for my Book on Perspective by His Majesty King George III.'[13] In addition to this single securely attributable piece there is a large group of architectural drawings at Windsor, which appear once to have been kept with the even larger corpus of drawings by the architect William Chambers (1726-96) in that collection. However, the handling of the wash and the subjects of the drawings distinguish them from Chambers's own work, and it is almost certain that they are the work of George III himself. It is known that Chambers gave lessons to the young Prince George during the last years of George II's reign, when he was employed as architect to Augusta, Princess of Wales. Chambers complained that 'my hands are full of work, but my pockets are not full of money. The prince employs me three mornings in a week to teach him Architecture; the buildings and other decorations at Kew fill up the remaining time.'[14] For his pains he received an annual salary of £50 from the Prince and of £100 from Princess Augusta. With the passage of years it is difficult to disentangle the respective roles of Kirby and Chambers in tutoring the Prince on architectural matters. In their official capacities after 1761 the older man, Kirby, was clearly subservient to Chambers, who as Joint Architect to the Office of Works depended on Kirby as the man on the spot at Kew and Richmond, where Joshua and his son William were Joint Clerks of the Works. When Chambers's sumptuous volume on *Kew* appeared in 1763, three of the plates depended on drawings by Kirby.[15] Whether the Prince's architectural drawings, which consist of a series of individual studies of each of the classical orders (16 drawings), another series of drawings of temples (49), and a third (considerably larger) of domestic architecture, were made under Kirby's or under Chambers's supervision is not known. It can be stated with certainty, however, that the drawings depend to a large extent on published works, including those by Kirby and by Chambers. None of the drawings is dated, but as some depend on Chambers's

George III received lessons in both perspective and architecture during his teens. There are numerous architectural drawings by the King at Windsor. It is unlikely that such grandiose constructions as this were ever intended to be built.

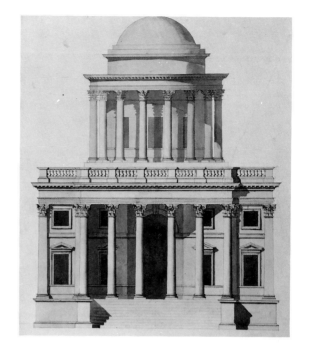

This design for a temple by George III is very close to the Temple of Victory *(built in 1759) at Kew, as illustrated in William Chambers,* Plans . . . of Kew *(1763), although the order is here Doric, not Ionic.*

Treatise, published in 1759, and others on his *Kew*, published in 1763, it is likely that they date from around this time. It should also be noted that the series of drawings of the Orders may well have been made with the assistance of an instrument called the 'Architectonic Sector . . . constructed upon new principles', as described by the King in a lengthy essay in the Royal Archives.[16]

In a letter to a friend dated January 1761, Horace Walpole wrote: 'The King and Lord Bute have certainly great propensity to the arts. Building, I am told, is the King's favourite study.' Ten years later, in the dedication to Desgodetz's *Ancient Buildings of Rome*, the publisher and architect George Marshall noted that 'this splendid art may hope for your Majesty's protection by a more particular claim as it has long had the honour of your notice and attention. Other Princes could employ architects, your Majesty can direct them; other Princes have the pride of building, your Majesty has the science.' It is possible that the King's first architectural work (as distinct from the labour of copying other people's designs) was carried out before his accession. According to Henry Angelo, whose father taught fencing to George III's children, 'a small temple, erected in Kew Gardens, which is much admired, and is engraved in the folio works of Sir William Chambers is said to have been entirely the design of the late King, whilst Prince of Wales.'[17] Angelo goes on to note that 'the old gate entrance from St James's-park to Carlton-house gardens, the two piers of which were lately standing, were also erected from the design of the same august personage.'

During the building works at Buckingham House, purchased for Queen Charlotte in 1762, the King was evidently involved with many of the details concerning design, and in particular the internal arrangements, alongside the architect William Chambers. Shortly after his accession, George III appointed a new Surveyor General to oversee the Board of Works (the predecessor of the Department of the Environment). He chose his friend and one-time equerry, Thomas Worsley (1710–78), who was himself a gentleman architect. Among the architectural drawings at Worsley's family home (Hovingham, Yorkshire), is a design by the King for a doorcase, which is extremely close to those in the 'Blue Velvet Room' as illustrated by Pyne.[18] The moveable furnishings of the new house also occupied the King's meticulous attention. When Lady Mary Coke saw the astronomical clock (destined for the new house) in Christopher Pinchbeck's shop in January 1768, she was told that 'the design

While William Chambers was transforming Buckingham House into a royal residence during the 1760s and 1770s he evidently received extensive advice from the King. The Surveyor General of the Board of Works, Thomas Worsley, was given this design of a doorcase in Buckingham House by his royal patron.

A rough ground plan of 'a Dorick Portico consisting of two Pilasters and two Collumns', made by the King on a piece of paper that formerly accompanied some military records. The date on the wrapper indicates that he remained actively interested in architecture into the 1770s, by which time pressing affairs of state might well have distracted him from such pursuits.

[was] partly His Majesty's and partly Mr Chambers his architect.' The following year Matthew Boulton reported that he was awaiting 'the King's design' for the blue-john eight-day clock, destined for Queen Charlotte's drawing room at Buckingham House. Once again the final design was doubtless mainly the responsibility of Chambers, but the King wished to be involved too.[19] During the 1770s George III was certainly very closely concerned with plans for hanging his collection of paintings in his own apartments and those of the Queen at Buckingham House. One drawing for this project is entirely in his own hand, while others include notes and alterations in his handwriting. A group of architectural designs by the King, mainly on a small scale and unassociated with specific projects, can also be dated to the 1770s.[20] In 1770 the foundation stone for the new Royal Palace at Richmond had been laid. Although William Chambers was to have been the architect for this

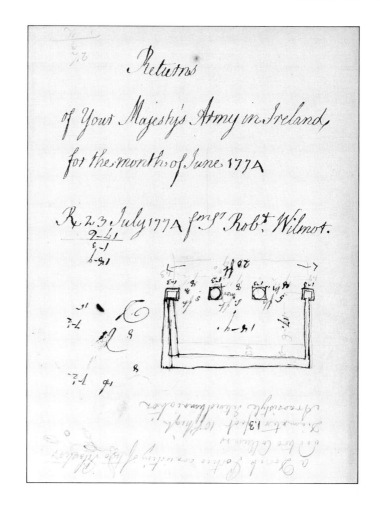

grandiose (and abortive) project, the King would doubtless have had a major interest in the design details. Mrs Papendieck records that 'In this year, 1769, we remained late in the season at Richmond, as his Majesty was greatly occupied in digesting plans with Sir William Chambers for a new palace at Richmond.[21]

George III gradually realized that many of his greatest pleasures – family life, hunting, farming, tree planting – could be enjoyed better at the old Royal Residence at Windsor than anywhere else. The castle had been virtually abandoned since the reign of Queen Anne, but following the return of the Royal Family to Windsor in the late 1770s, and the ensuing building works and alterations there, the King was again active in his architectural projects. Benjamin West's abortive schemes for a 'Chapel of Revealed Religion' and the series of pictures to illustrate the 'Institution and Progress of the Order of the Garter' were both said to have depended on the King's 'talents for drawing'. During the 1790s George III was much concerned with improvements in and around Windsor Great Park. These included the designing (and building) of a modest house for a labourer named Bradley, which was later illustrated in the journal made by Nathaniel Kent for the King. In his last years there are continuing references to the King's practical interest in architecture. Joseph Farington quotes a statement by the King (reported by Benjamin West) in his diary entry for 16 January 1800: 'I am a little of an architect and think that the *Old* School (meaning that of Lord Burlingtons period which had more of magnificence) is not enough attended to, – that the Adams's have introduced too much of neatness & prettiness, and even, added His Majesty, Wyatt inclines rather too much that way.'[22] In the following year work began on James Wyatt's so-called Castellated Palace at Kew, which was never entirely finished and was demolished three decades later. For us it is therefore another project of a King who surely understood more about architecture than any other occupant of the English throne, but who saw none of his more grandiose plans to completion.

In spite of his early lessons from Goupy in the drawing of landscapes and figures, George III's surviving works suggest that he was not particularly active in any art except architecture and design. However there are two series of landscape drawings at Windsor associated with him. They probably depend on his instruction from Joshua Kirby, from the mid-1750s. The first series, consisting of eleven drawings, evidently dates from before the accession and was gathered together by Queen Charlotte in 1809, at the onset of the King's final illness.[23] The

Two series of landscape drawings by George III as Prince of Wales also survive at Windsor. These are mainly of idealized subjects, but they include a view of Syon House, the seat of the 1st Duke of Northumberland, a senior member of the Royal Household. The view was taken from the gardens at Kew, the home of George III's mother, the Princess of Wales.

second series, consisting of more accomplished studies in black and white chalk on blue paper, are probably a little later in date. The fact that one of the drawings includes in the background a view of Syon House, the seat of Sir Hugh Smithson (later 1st Duke of Northumberland) and his wife Elizabeth (*née* Percy), provides a nice parallel with the pieces presented to that family by Queen Caroline and her daughter Princess Caroline, noted above. Elizabeth Percy was appointed one of Queen Charlotte's ladies of the bedchamber in 1761, while her husband served as lord of the bedchamber from 1753 to 1763 and as Lord Chamberlain to Queen Charlotte from 1762 to 1768. In her diaries Elizabeth noted that the King 'was fond of Architecture and Drawing in both of which he was a great proficient himself'.[24] The drawing of Syon could well be related to an oil painting entitled *An Evening View of Kew Ferry* contributed by Joshua Kirby to the exhibition at the Society of Artists in 1767.[25] According to a writer in the *London Chronicle*: 'It is assumed that a picture [probably that mentioned above] in the exhibition of paintings at Spring Gardens is the sole production of a very great personage, and introduced into the catalogue under a feigned name.'[26] Two years later the *View of Ockham Mill in Surrey*, also contributed by Kirby to the Society of Artists, was likewise said to be by the royal hand, although the figures were by George Stubbs (1724-1806).[27]

In view of his mother's close association with Kew Gardens, the King might also have been expected to be interested in botany, but this was not to be. In February 1768 the naturalist Peter Collinson wrote to William Bartram, the first truly American botanist: 'I wish the King had any taste in flowers or plants, but as he has none, there are no hopes of encouragement from him, for his talent is in architecture.'[28] By the 1780s the hopes for a royal botanical enthusiast were amply rewarded, for Queen Charlotte (1744-1818) had assumed a passionate interest in 'botanizing' and was soon to be joined in this pursuit by some of the princesses. In 1784, Lord Bute dedicated his *Botanical Tables* to the Queen and four years later she sent him a specimen from 'an Herbal of Impressions on Black Paper', doubtless based on Mrs Delany's floral cut-outs, which she had begun to make with the assistance of William Aiton, Jean André de Luc (her Reader), and the Princess Royal.[29] The volume of drawings by the Princess Royal at Windsor contains several plant studies dated between 1782 and 1784. Some of these are clearly copied from the plates in books such as John Miller's *Illustrations of the Sexual System of Linnaeus* (published in 1777), while others appear to be studies from actual plants. The *Crinum pendulum* drawn by the Princess on 5 July 1784 had only recently been introduced to England and no illustration of it had been published at the time (Plate 20).[30] During the 1790s the Queen (and Princess Elizabeth) received lessons in drawing and painting flowers from the Kew draughtsman Francis Bauer (1758-1840), so that by the end of the century it could be stated, that 'There is not a plant in the Gardens of Kew . . . but has either been drawn by her gracious Majesty, or some of the Princesses, with a grace and skill which reflect on these personages the highest honour.'[31] Queen Charlotte's correspondence with her brother Charles, Prince of Mecklenburg-Strelitz, included (in 1790) requests for special colours (obtainable from Nuremburg) in order to paint engravings of plants and flowers in gouache. The Queen's Reader, de Luc, added 'La Reine s'amuse a peindre des Fleurs, ou plutôt les Plantes, d'après Nature.'[32] Queen Charlotte evidently worked in oils as well as watercolour, for 'A mahogany box for oil colours and painting implements' was included in her posthumous sale.[33]

This 'botanizing' (of which very little has survived) took place both at Kew and at Frogmore, the house in the grounds of Windsor Castle which had been purchased by the Queen in 1790 and which thereafter served the purpose of a 'Petit Trianon' or private retreat for her and the princesses. The family life of King George III and Queen Charlotte with their fifteen children (born between 1762 and 1783) is charmingly evoked in the

writings of Mrs Delany, Fanny Burney, Queen Charlotte herself, and many others besides. Although the boys were soon
provided with separate households, the girls were all expected
to keep close to their mother, who depended on their presence
particularly after the King's first serious illness in 1788-9, and
during his final decline following the death of the last-born,
Princess Amelia, in 1810. Only three of the six daughters
married. Charlotte Augusta Matilda, the Princess Royal (1766-
1828, married to the Hereditary Prince of Württemberg in
1797), gave birth to a still-born child in April 1798. Princesses
Elizabeth (1770-1840, who in 1818 married the Hereditary
Prince of Hesse-Homburg) and Mary (1776-1857, who in 1816
married her cousin the Duke of Gloucester), only escaped from
their mother's protection (and domination) after any possibility
of child-bearing had passed.

The pattern of life at Frogmore was described by Princess
Elizabeth in July 1791: 'Mama sits in a very small green room
which she is very fond of, reads, writes and botanizes. Augusta
and me remain in the room next hers across a passage and
employ ourselves much in the same way. Of a Saturday my
younger sisters have no masters, so they also come down.'[34]
Three years later, on 24 April 1794, a full day's activity at
Windsor was described in the Queen's diary:

> This Morning the K^g went a Hunting the Dutchess of York
> and Sophia went out on Horseback with L^{dy} Charlotte Bruce.
> Some of the Princesses walked to Frogmore and some stayed
> at home. I wrote and was bysy till 11 when I also went to
> Frogmore, returned from thence by 2. Dressed, saw S^r
> George Howe then Mr de Luc who read to me till we went
> to Denery after caffe we all went to Frogmore returned from
> thence by ¼ after 10. then went to Supper to retire by 11.[35]

Sadly, very little of the Queen's handiwork has survived.
According to W. H. Pyne, whose *History of the Royal Residences*
(1819) contains many contemporary references to royal artists,
Queen Charlotte drew throughout her life, from her childhood
at Mirow (near Neustrelitz) to her extreme old age.[36] Among
the items connected with George III and his family which are
on view at the Dutch House, Kew Gardens, is a careful pencil
study of old buildings, which was apparently drawn by the
Queen in 1768. A more finished piece is suggested by the invoice
for 'framing and glazing one drawing of the Queen's in a rich
carv'd and gilt frame, and plate glass before the drawing'.[37]

Although George III's wife, Queen Charlotte, was evidently the guiding spirit behind the artistic work of their prolific daughters, very few of her drawings and paintings have survived. This study of a child holding a piece of paper inscribed 'God save the King' was given to 2nd Earl Harcourt in the 1790s.

Two landscapes painted in gouache by Queen Charlotte still hang in Windsor Castle.[38] The drawings at Windsor gathered together within an old paper band inscribed '7 Drawings by Her Majesty', are clearly copies of a master's work, demonstrating the construction of figures by geometric means.[39] But they are so close to a group of drawings by Princess Elizabeth at Homburg that it is hard to believe that they are not by the same hand. It should come as no surprise to discover that Queen Charlotte gave away many of her drawings. On 23 May 1796 she despatched three to the 2nd Earl Harcourt, advising him to burn them after looking at them. Queen Charlotte added that she had 'never attempted to do a stroke of a Figure till last December'.[40] The charming watercolour of a girl (somewhat reminiscent of Gainsborough) which is still at Stanton Harcourt may have formed part of this gift.

The Queen's passion for drawing, and particularly for copying great tracts of manuscript and printed works, continued into her seventies. When she was offered assistance with a copy she planned of 'The Advice of James II to his son', she declined saying, 'I am accustomed to such work; I have 400 pages of extracts which I have [made] from various works.'[41] The Queen's manuscript copy, and three other large volumes similarly copied by her between 1812 and 1815, are preserved in the Royal Library at Windsor. Where possible, the facing pages would be ornamented with appropriate engravings, or with drawn or printed copies of suitable subjects. Closely associated with this work was the establishment of a private printing press at Frogmore for the use of the Queen and her daughters. The press published six works between 1809 and 1817, under the direction of the Frogmore librarian Mr Harding,[42] and was sold (with quantities of unused paper, bookbinding equipment, etc.) after the Queen's death.[43]

Queen Charlotte was also closely involved in the interior decoration and furnishing of her various apartments. Her combined interests in music, art and needlework are displayed in Benjamin West's portrait of the Queen in the company of her eldest daughter, dated 1776.[44] Soon after joining the Royal Household (and specifically the Royal Nursery) in the following year, Mary Hamilton described the (no longer extant) Upper (or Queen's) Lodge at Windsor in the following words:

> The Queen has 7 or 8 rooms furnished in a style of elegant simplicity, beautiful paper hangings, light carved gilt frames for looking glasses, worked chairs and painted frames, every room different. Curtains of fine white dimity with white cotton fringe – one set of chairs are knotted floss silk of different shades sewn on to imitate flowers . . . N.B. Her Majesty had done a great deal of the knotting herself, & every Lady in, & some out of the family who could knot well, can boast of having done some.[45]

In 1786 the Queen sent some of her knotting to Lady Harcourt, hoping that 'in examining it closely, you will discover every knot to be the Tie of Friendship of your affectionate Friend – Charlotte'.[46] There is still at Frogmore a box containing fragments of the Queen's knotting and some unused reels of thread. In 1789 the Queen noted in her diary how she and the Princesses were taught to paint on velvet at Windsor by Monsieur Trottier (12 and 23 November 1789). On 17 November Queen Charlotte wrote, 'I finished my 1st Chair to Day after L^{dy} Westmorelands pattern.' Presumably the chair was covered with painted velvet, although no examples of this work have come down to us. Horace Walpole mentions an unusual subject for royal needlework in a letter of 1796: 'Sir Joseph Banks has carried Lysons to Kew with drawings of all his discoveries at Woodchester. They made great impression, and he is to send patterns of the mosaics for the Queen and Princesses to work.'[47]

The artistic products of Queen Charlotte's daughters are inevitably closely related to those of their mother, who ensured that they stayed at court and continued to work alongside her for much of their lives. The following description was written, by the King's dear friend Mrs Delany (1700-88), in November 1785, but the scene must have continued fairly unchanged for many years thereafter: 'I have been several evenings at the Queen's Lodge [Windsor], with no other company but their own most lovely family. They sit around a large table, on which are books, work, pencils and paper . . . the younger part of the family are drawing and working &. &.'[48] During the following two years the princesses held drawing and painting classes at Buckingham House, for the entertainment of themselves and others. The equipment for these sessions doubtless included the '2 large mahy drawing boards made to their order' supplied in 1787 for £1 11s 6d.[49]

A large number of different artists are noted as having taught the royal children. Joshua Kirby, who had instructed their father in his youth, resided at Kew from 1759 until his death in 1774. The possibility that his works were known in the Royal Nursery is raised by the knowledge that he contributed a *View of the Monk's Kitchen at Glastonbury* to the Society of Arts in 1770, while one of the two surviving works by the young Prince Ernest, Duke of Cumberland (1771-1851), is of the same subject.[50] Paul Sandby (1731-1809), the 'father of watercolour painting', is listed as Prince George's drawing master in the subscription list to Gandon's *Vitruvius Britannicus* (vol. IV), published in 1771. Although nothing by the Prince of Wales himself has survived from this association, there is at Windsor a group of small land-scape studies in gouache by the younger princes, dated around 1780.[51] Among the portfolios and albums of drawings at Greiz (GDR) which previously belonged to the prolific Princess Elizabeth, is a group of studies by Paul Sandby, who may also therefore have taught the princesses.[52] Another artist, John Alexander Gresse (1740-94), is described as drawing master to the younger princes and princesses from 1778 to 1793.[53] Like the other royal drawing masters at this time, he did not work on a salaried basis, but received annual payments which varied from £2 17s (in 1778) to £67 5s 9d (in 1789). W. H. Pyne described his style as 'in the early manner of Paul Sandby, correctly outlined with a pen, and tinted with colours'.[54] Gresse's master, Giovanni

Battista Cipriani (1727-85), had also apparently given some lessons to the Royal Family.

The influential early watercolour painter Alexander Cozens (1717-86) taught the younger princes (William and Edward) from 1778.[55] His quarterly payments varied from just over £22, for his lessons to Prince Edward (later the Duke of Kent) during the three months up to 5 July 1779, to £4 14s 6d for his lessons to the same pupil six months later. Cozens held his appointment until the time of his death in April 1786,[56] although Prince William (later King William IV) probably ceased to be Cozens's pupil on his entry to the navy in mid-1779.[57] It is interesting to note that Dr John Fisher (1748-1825), a notable amateur draughtsman and future bishop of Salisbury, was appointed preceptor (or tutor) to Prince Edward in 1780. Mary Hamilton mentions that Fisher gave drawing lessons to Princess Elizabeth during the summer visit to Eastbourne in the year of his appointment.[58] An etching of Kew Green signed 'Edward 1785' has a certain historical value for the topography of the area, in which the princes frequently stayed during their childhood.[59]

The King's drawing master, Joshua Kirby, was a close friend of another Suffolk artist, Thomas Gainsborough (1727-88), and was doubtless responsible for his introduction to the Royal Family.[60] Gainsborough worked for the King from 1781 until his death, painting portraits of most of the Royal Family, including each of the princes and princesses. According to Angelo (and then Pyne), 'Her majesty took some lessons of Gainsborough, during the then fashionable rage for that artist's eccentric style denominated Gainsborough's moppings.'[61] Queen Charlotte had an important collection of Gainsborough's drawings. Her posthumous sales in 1819 contained 22 of his studies, presumably including ten of his much acclaimed drawings in coloured chalks.[62] In 1789 it was stated in *The Morning Herald* that 'The PRINCESS ROYAL has copied those [drawings by Gainsborough] in the Queen's possession in a most successful stile; and indeed those *sketches* are the first lessons for *effect*.'[63]

It is possible that Gainsborough actually taught the royal children, as well as supplying models for them to copy. He may have been the teacher involved in the princesses' painting sessions in London in the winter of 1786-7 mentioned above.[64] In the present Royal Collection there are no examples of works by the Royal Family demonstrating the direct influence of Gainsborough, however the drawing of a shepherd girl by Queen Charlotte, probably presented to Lord Harcourt in 1796, is clearly dependent on his style.[65] Although the Princess Royal was said to have copied Gainsborough's drawings, the only one of her surviving works that is dependent in any way on that artist is her etched portrait of Prince Octavius dated March 1785, which derives ultimately from the painting of September 1782.[66] The Prince died, aged only four, in May 1783. According to an inscription on a copy of the print in the British Museum,[67] Princess Charlotte copied a drawing of the painting by her master, Gresse. This print was evidently presented by the Princess Royal to the royal governess, Lady Charlotte Finch, in the year it was made. The direct influence of Gainsborough is instead found in the work of 'The Muse', Princess Elizabeth, one of whose watercolours at the Gothic House, Bad Homburg, is a fairly close copy of a drawing by Gainsborough of a landscape with farm cart.[68] A watercolour by the Princess entitled *The Wood Girl*, representing a child with a bundle of faggots on her head, is likewise very reminiscent of a group of late drawings by Gainsborough.[69] Princess Elizabeth's soft-ground etching of a woodboy by a gate is in a very similar style.[70] The example in the British Museum is in its original wrapper inscribed: 'A present from H.R.H. the Princess Elizabeth brought here by M.ʳ Harding April 16 1812. designed and etched by Her Royal Highness'. (Edward Harding was Queen Charlotte's librarian at Frogmore.)

In connection with art lessons of 1786-7, which are said to have involved all the princesses, it is worth turning briefly to the fourth of George III's daughters, Princess Mary. Although she is shown holding a drawing of a child in Beechey's portrait of 1797, few artefacts by her are known today.[71] However, during her late seventies she contributed no fewer than sixteen works to the Patriotic Fund exhibition in aid of the victims of the Crimean War, which were shown alongside the juvenile paintings of the children of her niece, Queen Victoria (see p. 218, n. 8).

Another royal art teacher was Richard Cooper (1740-1814), who 'drew classic scenes, in black chalk heightened with white in a peculiar style of richness and effect'.[72] On 3 April 1794, when the Court was in London, Queen Charlotte noted in her diary: 'We saw Mr Cooper the Drawing Master with a very fine Drawing of his own.' Following the invention of lithography by Aloys Senefelder in 1798, and the introduction of the new technique to England in 1800, Cooper was one of the earliest English artists to produce his own lithographs. A lithograph by Princess Elizabeth in the British Museum is inscribed 'R. Cooper invᵗ', and is evidently dependent on one of his compositions.[73] An article in the *Gentleman's Magazine* for March 1808

Prince Octavius, the eighth son of George III, died at the age of four in May 1783. The previous September he had been portrayed by Gainsborough. The Princess Royal's etched portrait of the Prince, dated March 1785, apparently depended on an intermediary copy of Gainsborough's picture by her drawing master, Alexander Gresse.

This watercolour by Princess Elizabeth incorporates a number of elements from a landscape study by Gainsborough, who was in receipt of royal patronage during the 1780s. It is possible that he gave lessons to the princesses, as well as to the Queen.

This landscape by Thomas Gainsborough, dated to the early 1760s, appears to have been the pattern on which Princess Elizabeth's watercolour was based. It may have been part of the important collection of drawings by Gainsborough formed by the Princess's mother, Queen Charlotte.

mentions a flower piece by the Princess among the lithographs recently published (by Vollweiler). If Princess Elizabeth's experiments with lithography were assisted by Richard Cooper, according to Henry Angelo her attempts with the mezzotint medium were made 'under the gratuitous instruction of Mr

Matthew Wyatt'.[74] The American artist Benjamin West, who was much patronized by George III during the last three decades of the century, appears also to have taught the princesses. The etchings by the Princess Royal of female personifications of the Five Senses appear to be copies of lost designs – perhaps made specifically for this purpose – by West. The date on these prints (1784) falls within the period (*c*.1780-1809) during which the artist rented a house in Park Street, Windsor, ensuring his regular attendance on the Royal Family while they were at Windsor.[75]

Specific subjects were taught by people such as Russen (or Ruston), a Fleming, who specialized in drawing heads, hands and feet on a large scale in black chalk;[76] Biagio Rebecca, who 'assisted in many a tasteful work and playful scheme projected by her Majesty'[77] and showed the Princesses how 'to draw the human figure', as well as teaching Princess Elizabeth 'the art of etching on copper'; Miss Black, who specialized in 'painting in crayons';[78] Mrs Cook 'who taught in a peculiar stile' at Brighton, and was later supported by Princesses Mary, Augusta and Sophia;[79] 'Cook from Bath', who was observed by Farington giving lessons to the Queen and Princess Elizabeth in August 1804;[80] Peltro William Tomkins (1760-1840) described as Drawing Master (but better known as an engraver), who assisted the princesses (and particularly Princess Elizabeth) in various ways with their handiwork; and Mlle Montmoullin, who specialized in fancy needlework, beadwork and the netting

Another of George III's artists, the American-born Benjamin West, provided the models for a series of etchings of the Five Senses by the Princess Royal. The Sense of Hearing is illustrated in this print, dated 1784.

of silk purses. Francis Bauer has already been mentioned in connection with his lessons to the Queen and Princess Elizabeth from *c*.1790. Another botanical artist, Margaret Meen, is noted in Queen Charlotte's diary for 8 December 1789: 'I drew with Miss Mean from 10 till one.' The surviving work by this artist includes an elaborate flower painting in the Victoria and Albert Museum, which served as the model for a very similar flower piece by Princess Elizabeth in the Royal Collection (Plate 21). The Princess's copy is dated 14 November 1792, and may be related to a payment in Queen Charlotte's nursery accounts for £22 12*s* to 'M. Meen – Drawings' on 23 March 1792.[81] Princess Elizabeth continued to correspond with Miss Meen following her marriage: a letter from the Princess to her has survived in the Royal Archives.[82] A possible use for the Princess's drawings and watercolours of flowers is suggested by the following entry in Farington's diary for 9 February 1794: 'Breakfasted with Wyatt, who shewed me several paintings of flowers in watercolours by the Princess Elizabeth painted for the Queen & intended for screens.'[83]

Throughout their long-drawn-out artistic training, the princesses must have benefited considerably from the collections of drawings and engravings formed by each of their parents. While the King's collection was available for study in his newly equipped library at Buckingham House, the Queen's was latterly kept at Frogmore House, until its dispersal following her death in 1818. A large proportion of the surviving work of the princesses consists of recognizable copies after drawn or printed works. Indeed the eldest daughter, the Princess Royal, often seems to have gone to some trouble to disguise her pen drawings as etchings: they are described as etchings in early inventories of the Royal Collection. The Princess's dated drawings range from 1777 to 1816. Following her botanical work in the early 1780s (noted above), in the mid-1780s she etched a drawing of a head adorned with richly decorated armour by Giulio Clovio[84] and copied the dramatic engraving (of 1775) entitled 'Richard II' by John Hamilton Mortimer (1741-79).[85] A drawing of 1794 is derived directly from one of Hollar's illustrations to Ogilby's Aesop.[86] Other designs are clearly dependent on engravings by (or after) earlier artists such as Barlow, Berchem and Silvestre.[87] Farington noted a total of sixty drawings by the Princess Royal hanging at Frogmore.[88] In his description of the house two decades later, Pyne observed that the walls of the Princess Royal's closet at Frogmore were adorned with 'several drawings, in pen and ink, of wild animals in imitation of the etchings

LEFT: Plate 1. *The Princess Royal: Prince Arthur as Henry VIII, 10 February 1853.* This charming watercolour was presented by the twelve-year-old Princess to her parents for their wedding anniversary. It shows her brother, aged 2½ years, in the fancy dress that he had worn on 11 January 1853. A few years earlier, Prince Alfred had worn the same costume.

BELOW: Plate 2. *A. E. Corbould, who taught the royal children from 1852, filled the left-hand half of each page in a sketch-book with figure studies, often of a comic nature. The Prince of Wales would then copy Corbould's drawing on the remainder of the sheet, and add watercolour. The future Edward VII was thirteen when he drew this figure, inscribed* 'I know my position, – Sir!'

BELOW: Plate 3. *One of William Leighton Leitch's 'painted lessons', made to show his royal pupils how to shade different colours*

RIGHT: Plate 4. *The skyline of Florence has often attracted royal artists. Queen Victoria's study was made during her visit to Italy in 1887.*

RIGHT: Plate 5. *Part of Princess Louise's honeymoon was spent in Florence (in 1871), when this view was probably made. The Princess revisited Tuscany on a number of occasions thereafter, and her visits often coincided with those of her mother.*

ABOVE: Plate 6. *The Prince of Wales first visited Florence in 1985, and was the guest of Harold Acton at his villa 'La Pietra' to the north of the city. Like Princess Louise, he was attracted by the varying shades of terra-cotta from which the roof tiles are made. This watercolour was painted on a sheet of the Prince's crested writing paper.*

LEFT: Plate 7. *The future Queen Mary lived in Florence with her parents and brothers from late 1883 to mid-1885. This view was taken from the north side of the Ponte Vecchio, looking down the Arno to the Ponte S. Trinità.*

ABOVE: Plate 8. *The Queen's holidays in Germany were often taken with other members of her family. In 1862 the Princess Royal, now Crown Princess of Prussia, travelled to Coburg with her children to be with her mother, and also painted Doris Notting in her colourful costume.*

LEFT: Plate 9. *Queen Victoria's sketch of Doris Notting, wet-nurse to her grandson, Prince Henry of Prussia, was made during a visit to Coburg in October 1862*

BELOW: Plate 10. *At the end of October 1862 the Crown Prince and Princess of Prussia travelled through Italy to North Africa. This sketch by the Princess was made 'In the Harem of the Bey of Tunis' on 27 October 1862. She was shown into the harem by the Bey's wife, Princess 'Lilla Bembey'. In a letter to the Queen, the Crown Princess described the dress of the Princess (shown to left of centre) and her girl attendants: 'some of the most lovely girls I ever saw, eyes, mouths, noses and hair quite beautiful – but all in the same odd dress as herself'* (Dearest Mama, *pp. 119-20).*

ABOVE: Plate 11. *The costumes worn in the different parts of Germany attracted the attention of the Princess Royal as much as they did her mother. This study was made at the Neues Palais, Potsdam, in 1860, and was sent home to the Princess's parents.*

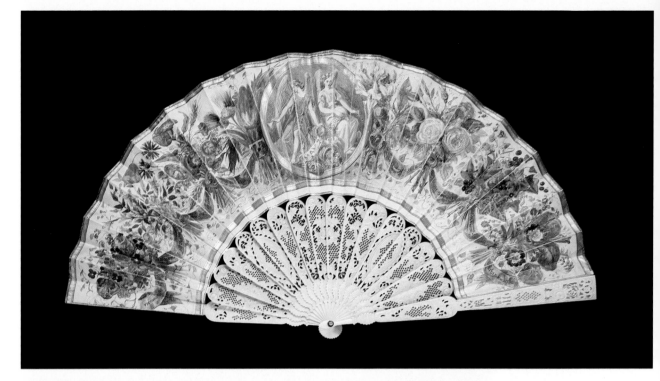

ABOVE: Plate 12. *The young Princess Royal painted this fan for her mother's birthday in 1856 (see illustration page 23). Each letter of the Queen's name supports a group of flowers beginning with that initial letter, while the names and birthdates of her children are inscribed on the swags between the flowers.*

LEFT: Plate 13. *Christmas 1858 was the first one spent away from England by the Princess Royal, who had married the previous January. Her combined Christmas and New Year offering retains a distinctly English character.*

The plate entitled 'Richard II' from J. H. Mortimer's Works, *published in 1778, was copied in pen and ink by the Princess Royal in 1786. This was one of a number of drawings 'in the style of etchings' by the Princess which formerly hung in the Queen's house at Frogmore.*

of Ridinger which were executed with the spirit and freedom of an able professor, by the Princess Royal'.[89] Thirty-eight of these drawings survive, in their original frames, at Windsor. Their indebtedness to works such as the *Entwurf einige Thiere* by J. E. Ridinger (Augsburg, 1738), is clear. A group of drawings by the Princess dated 1808-10, in the Staatsgalerie, Stuttgart, demonstrate that her copying activity did not cease with her marriage.

Princess Augusta (1768-1840), who never married and appears to have drawn and painted only in her early years, made etchings (dated 1785) after drawings by Leonardo (or members

*The unparalleled group of
drawings by Leonardo da
Vinci that has been part of
the Royal Collection since
the seventeenth century
provided other models for
Princess Augusta Sophia.
When etching her monogram
lower left in this print she
failed to reverse the 'S', and
repeated her signature
correctly elsewhere.*

*George III's second
daughter, Princess Augusta
Sophia, copied this figure of
a Geometer from a drawing
by the Venetian
eighteenth-century artist
Piazzetta, that had recently
entered the Royal Collection.*

of his studio) in the Royal Collection. An example of one such copy in the British Museum is inscribed 'etched after Leonardo da Vinci by H.R.H. Princess Augusta and given to Lady Cardigan'.[90] Like her elder sister, Princess Augusta copied the engravings of J. H. Mortimer. Her drawn 'Head of an Oriental' dated 1784 is directly dependent on Mortimer's print entitled 'An Aga of the Janizaries' (published 1779), and was in its turn used as the basis for Princess Augusta's etching of 1785.[91] She also made a series of copies, dated 1785 and 1786, after the heads by Giovanni Battista Piazzetta (1683-1754) which had recently been acquired by King George III.[92] The Princess's portrait by Sir William Beechey, exhibited at the Royal Academy in 1797, shows her with an open sketchbook before her, and a classical bust at her side.[93]

The most prolific of the royal sisters, Princess Elizabeth, also began her artistic career by copying (or even tracing) items in the Collection: a drawing by Domenichino, the study of Jonah attributed to Raphael (see p. 12), a group of landscapes by Marco Ricci, and so on.[94] And just as Queen Charlotte spent many an empty day copying vast sections of text, so did the princesses. Princess Elizabeth's copy (made in 1837) of the report of 'Christian IV of Denmark's visit to England to his sister Anne Consort of England', is at Bad Homburg, where she ended her days. Her account (dated 1837) of *L'Histoire de la Duchesse d'Ahlden*, concerning George I's estranged wife, is in the Royal Library (Plate 23), as is her copy of a book composed by Mrs Banks entitled 'Some account of the parts which the Queens of England and other royal and noble ladies have formerly been permitted to take in the processions and other public ceremonies of the Order of the Garter', made in 1832. Princess Mary, by whom no other works appear to have survived, copied an extract of a history of England from Henry II to George II, and passed it to her mother for the addition of appropriate illustrations. The finished product, dated 25 October 1808, is also at Windsor.

But if the greater part of the artistic activity of the princesses was far from original so far as design was concerned, in its application and quantity it was sometimes remarkable. The Princess Royal, described as a charming and talented girl by the novelist (and one-time courtier) Fanny Burney (1752-1840), and much loved by her father the King, moved to Germany following her marriage in May 1797 to the Hereditary Prince of Württemberg. After the accession of her husband as Duke seven months later (he was to become King in 1806, thanks to

Napoleon), the Princess moved into the Palace at Ludwigsburg (north of Stuttgart), and there set about the decoration of the ducal apartments. At least two sets of seat furniture worked by her survive at Ludwigsburg, some of which may be identical with those mistaken by Napoleon during his stay there in 1805 for the finest 'Lyons embroideries'.[95] In 1802 and 1803 Princess Charlotte was in correspondence with her father concerning chairs upholstered with her own penned velvet, but eventually decided that it would not be possible to ship the chairs to England. We have two references to dresses embroidered by the Princess Royal: in January 1797 she wore a dress stitched with artificial flowers for the Queen's birthday, and her wedding dress was entirely her own work, 'and the real labour it . . . proved from her steadiness to have no help'.[96]

More remarkable than her needlework was the Princess's activity in association with the Ludwigsburg porcelain factory, immediately adjacent to the palace. The Princess eventually had her own kiln at Mathildenhof, in the grounds of the palace, where her hand-painted porcelain would be fired. She appears to have begun to work with porcelain soon after her arrival in Germany, for on 30 March 1805 the Princess offered her father 'a broth cup of Louisburg china made after my design',[97] and on 5 July of the same year, following the King's favourable reaction to the cup, she informed him that she would 'venture

LEFT: *Following her marriage in 1797 to the Hereditary Prince (later King) of Württemberg, the Princess Royal's skill as a copyist was given another dimension. During the first two decades of the nineteenth century she painted numerous designs on pieces of porcelain produced by the factory attached to her husband's residence at Ludwigsburg. The model for this stag was an engraving by J. E. Ridinger.*

RIGHT: *The plate from J. E. Ridinger's* Entwurf einige Thiere *(Augsburg, 1738) which was copied on to porcelain by the Princess Royal.*

to bespeak some flower pots after my design which I hope your Majesty will place in your palace'.[98] It is not known whether these gifts have survived, but a large number of pieces of porcelain decorated by the Princess are known: plates, cups and saucers, flower pots and stands (Plate 17), and flower vases. Most are signed (with her initials CAM) and dated by her on the base. The earliest date so far encountered on these pieces is 1811, which appears on a cup in the Royal Collection, and on a cup and flower pot at Ludwigsburg. Other items bear dates from 1812 to 1816. In addition to these independent pieces of porcelain there is a remarkable group of porcelain-mounted furniture, which once adorned the principal apartments at Ludwigsburg and is now divided chiefly between Ludwigsburg and Friedrichshafen. The traditional attribution of these plaques to the Princess Royal is borne out by the discovery of her signature (with the date 1815) at the back of one such plaque used on the top of a gueridon table. The flat porcelain plaques, which are sometimes oval or circular and sometimes rectangular or square in shape, are decorated in monochrome with subjects very similar (sometimes identical) to those found in the drawings 'in the style of etchings' described by Pyne at Frogmore. Their origin in engraved works is clear. What is new and original is the decoration of German furniture in this way, employing products of the local porcelain manufacture in a manner that is reminiscent of the use of Sèvres porcelain to decorate Parisian furniture in the second half of the eighteenth century. It may also owe something to the rather similar use of Wedgwood plaques on furniture: these were exported to both France and Germany during the late eighteenth and early nineteenth centuries.[99] Related to the Princess's use of her hand-painted porcelain to decorate furniture, is the employment of penwork plaques, incorporating very similar (chiefly floral) designs drawn on the wood by the Princess herself, in much the same way. Pieces of such furniture were sent by Princess Charlotte to her sister Princess Elizabeth and are still to be seen in the castle at Bad Homburg. Other pieces, particularly workboxes, were sent home to the Princess's unmarried sisters in England (Plates 18 and 19).

George III's third daughter, Princess Elizabeth, was even more active artistically than the Princess Royal. Fanny Burney described how 'in her fits of gayety, there bursts forth a vein of sportive ideas that would charm you, I am sure, into laughter by the hour.' Princess Elizabeth's apartments at the Queen's Lodge were 'the most elegantly and fancifully ornamented of any

Most portraits of Princess Elizabeth allude to her artistic talents. When J. P. Fischer painted her in 1827 she was shown at work on a botanical drawing, with Windsor Castle in the background. Nine years earlier she had married the Landgrave of Hesse-Homburg, but revisited England on several occasions.

in the Lodge, as she has most delight and most taste in producing good effects'.[100] Her oil painting of a view near the Ranger's Lodge, Windsor Great Park, is at Clarence House, while her copy of Edridge's miniature portrait of Lady Charlotte Finch (1725-1813), the royal governess, is at Windsor. One of the visiting cards that came to the British Museum in 1818 is that of the Countess of Macclesfield, inscribed as having been 'designed and etched by H.R.H. The Princess Elizabeth' in 1797.[101] The most remarkable aspect of her artistic output is indeed the number of printed and published works with which her name is associated. *The Birth and Triumph of Cupid* (1795),

This miniature portrait by Princess Elizabeth depicts Lady Charlotte Finch, governess to the royal children (particularly the princesses) from the 1760s. It is based on another miniature portrait in the Royal Collection, attributed to Edridge.

with 24 plates engraved by P. W. Tomkins from the Princess's silhouettes (rather than Lady Dashwood's as the title page modestly claimed), was reissued in 1796 (and 1822 and 1823) as *The Birth and Triumph of Love*, with two additional plates and poems by Sir James Bland Burges. In the same year Tomkins published prints from seven more of Princess Elizabeth's silhouettes, under the title of *The Birthday Gift or the New Doll*. It is more than likely that the publication of both *Cupid* and the *New Doll* were connected with the marriage of, and subsequent birth of a child to, her eldest brother, George, Prince of Wales, in 1795 and 1796 respectively. Princess Elizabeth was always touchingly fond of children. In her sixties she declared 'There is nothing I love more than children.'[102] But her own late marriage (in 1818, at the age of forty-eight) had deprived her of the prospect of motherhood.

In 1804, Princess Elizabeth's list of publications was continued with a series of 12 plates, engraved from the Princess's designs by W. N. Gardner and 'illustrated' with some rather questionable verse by Thomas Parke, which appeared under the title *Cupid as a British Volunteer*. The zenith of this output was the publication in 1806 of *A series of Etchings Representing the Power and Progress of Genius*, consisting of 24 plates which were both etched and designed by Princess Elizabeth, with a dedication to the Queen. In 1833, fifteen years after her marriage and transfer to Hesse-Homburg, these designs were reissued, redrawn for the Princess as lithographs by J. H. Ramberg and with German sonnets by Minna Witte, under the title *Genius, Imagination, Phantasie*. This work was dedicated to the Princess's brother Adolphus, Duke of Cambridge, Regent of Hanover (where the work was published), and was sold in aid of a charity much supported by Princess Elizabeth, to finance a crêche for the small daughters of working mothers in the city of Hanover. The copy of the English edition of *Genius, Imagination, Phantasie* (1836) sent by the Princess to her niece, the Princess Victoria, is still preserved in the Library at Windsor (illustrated p. 25).

In 1810 and 1816, H. D. Thielcke published in London two series of plates (from Princess Elizabeth's designs), with titles such as 'Father's Return', 'The Warrior's Tale' and 'Pylades and Orestes before a rose-decked urn'. A number of independent plates were also issued, based on her designs, while the Princess herself produced a number of single lithographs, mezzotints and etchings.[103] The subject matter of all these works can be more or less covered by the term 'fancy', but the designing hand was clearly her own. Her contemporaries, such as Pyne and Angelo, were at pains to point out that whereas the Princess Royal's (and Princess Augusta's) artistic products were mainly derivative, Princess Elizabeth 'was superior to the drudgery of copying'.[104] The serious nature of the Princess's artistic activity is confirmed by the inclusion of her name, with those of professional artists (such as her former master, Richard Cooper), in a list of exponents of the new art of polyautography (i.e. lithography) published in the *Gentleman's Magazine* in 1808.[105]

We have already noted how Princess Elizabeth's first publications were series of prints based on her cut-outs. When the draughtsman Henry Edridge (1769-1821) portrayed the Princess in 1804 it was not surprising that he showed her with a pair of scissors in her hand. Some of her silhouettes, cut from shiny black paper, are in the Royal Library at Windsor,[106] while others, cut from cream paper and painted within the outlines in brown wash, are preserved among her drawings and prints at

LEFT: *Between the years 1807 and 1817, Princess Elizabeth presented a number of individual silhouettes, cut out of shiny black paper, to her friend Sarah Sophia Banks, the only sister of Sir Joseph Banks. These were mounted by the recipient into an album which is now in the Royal Library.*

BELOW: *Silhouette cut by Princess Elizabeth for her sister-in-law, Princess Augusta, Duchess of Cambridge.*

the Gothic House, Bad Homburg. In an album made up by her sister-in-law Marianne, which survives with the Hesse-Darmstadt papers at Wolfsgarten, there is a ravishing butterfly painted on rice paper by Princess Elizabeth, cut around and mounted on a coloured ground, in such a way that even at the distance of almost two hundred years we have to look twice before confirming that the butterfly is not real (Plate 22). The posthumous inventory of the Princess's drawings and prints in the Darmstadt archives lists other albums of birds, butterflies (on rice paper), cuttings and pressed flowers, in addition to volumes containing sketches in Scotland and Hanover in 1834.[107] Some of these are now at Greiz. The Victoria and Albert Museum has recently acquired a firescreen of rolled and cut paper-work, presented by one of the Princesses (probably Elizabeth) to her physician, Dr Alexander Fothergill, in 1787.[108]

Other small items with which the Princess was personally involved are the sixteen-piece tea and coffee service of Berlin porcelain, decorated with the complete series of 26 subjects included in her *Birth and Triumph of Cupid*, and the fans made following George III's recovery in 1789.[109] Such work was as typical of the cultivated and capable eighteenth-century lady as was silhouette-cutting, drawing and painting.

Princess Elizabeth was active throughout her adult life in designing, working and supplying items of interior decor for the various royal residences. At Buckingham House the seat furniture of the Saloon was decorated with white cotton velvet, painted with flowers by the Princess. The Queen's Breakfast Room was described in 1802 as having brown and maroon curtains painted in imitation of cut velvet by Elizabeth. Unfortunately no visual record of her work in these rooms has come down to us, for they had been refurbished by the time of Pyne's *Royal Residences* (1819). The same was luckily not the case at Frogmore, however. Pyne's plates (and accompanying text) relating to both the Red and the Black Japan Rooms show the extent of the Princess's involvement with the decoration there. In both cases the walls were adorned with panels in imitation of red and gold lacquer. In the Red Japan Room 'the furniture was ornamented by the same tasteful hand'.[110] The possibility that some of the lacquer panels were transferred to Germany following the Princess's marriage, or that she decorated her apartments at Bad Homburg in a similar style, is raised by the survival there of eleven out of an original set of 32 lacquer panels, one of which is clearly signed 'Eliza'.

A rolled paper-work firescreen made by one of the princesses (probably Princess Elizabeth) for her physician, Dr Alexander Fothergill, in 1787.

Among the most popular series of engravings to be published from the Princess Elizabeth's designs was the Birth and Triumph of Love, *first published in 1795, but reissued in 1796, 1822 and 1823. The 26 plates, engraved by P. W. Tomkins, were used to decorate the individual pieces of this Berlin porcelain tea and coffee service.*

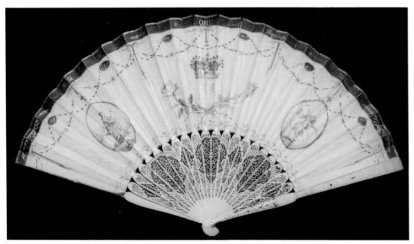

The King's recovery from his first serious illness in 1789 was celebrated by the production of a number of commemorative fans. The present one, painted by Princess Elizabeth, is inscribed 'Health restored to ONE and Happiness to Millions'.

According to that most informative diarist Joseph Farington, a 'long narrow room' at Frogmore had been decorated by Princess Elizabeth 'with painted flowers, & subjects of Children &c cut in paper, & finished by Tomkins. They all show ingenuity.'[111] The panels from this room, shortly to be reinstated at Frogmore, consist of flower swags, painted in oil and tempera in the manner of the artist Mary Moser (1744-1819), and two sets of decorative panels of which one set does indeed consist of paper cut-outs. During the early 1790s the Princess helped to design a number of the garden buildings at Frogmore: the Gothick cottage by the lake, the barn (or garden ballroom), the thatched Hermitage, and the octagonal Temple of Solitude (which contained a vault painted by the Princess). For her

Frequent allusions to Princess Elizabeth's handiwork are made in the text of Pyne's Royal Residences, *published in 1819. The Red Japan Room at Frogmore House, Windsor (depicted here by Charles Wild), contained lacquer panels and furniture decorated by the Princess.*

Princess Elizabeth's married home, the Schloss at Bad Homburg, West Germany, contains a number of lacquer panels of her own making. The central trunk in that to the left is inscribed 'Eliza'. The original context of the Homburg lacquer panels is not known. It is possible that they were removed from Frogmore House following Queen Charlotte's death in November 1818, seven months after Princess Elizabeth's marriage.

own bedroom in the south-east corner of Windsor Castle she designed an elaborate domed tent-bed with double festoons.[112] Other work by the Princess may include the charming murals of convolvulus and nasturtium around a bamboo trellis in the upper room of the Queen's Cottage at Kew (Plate 24). She was also apparently the mastermind behind the more ephemeral decorations made for the various fêtes at Frogmore, involving artificial flowers and festoons.[113]

Following her marriage to the eldest of the six surviving sons of Landgrave Frederick V of the tiny state of Hesse-Homburg, and particularly after her husband's accession as Landgrave in 1820, Elizabeth was allowed a free hand in decorating the old castle at Homburg which she described as 'my beloved and happy home'. At the time of her marriage, the British Parliament voted her an allowance of £13,000 per annum, which was considered a positive fortune at Bad Homburg and enabled the principal buildings to be modernized and adorned in a way that had not previously been possible.[114] A miniature portrait of the Landgravine in 1827 by Fischer shows her with a paint brush in one hand, and a flower in the other, while painting on the drawing board propped up before her.[115] From her correspondence with Louisa Swinburne in the years 1832-8 we learn of the Princess's continued application to drawing and 'work' into her late sixties. She described how in the evenings she would 'read and work till eleven . . . now I have taken up my drawing and am painting fruit with success.'[116] When the Princess wrote

Like her father, Princess Elizabeth was actively involved in the decoration of her residences and the design of garden buildings. This drawing by Howitt shows the 'Thatched Hermitage' at Frogmore. After her marriage, the Princess supervised the building of similarly 'primitive' structures at Homburg.

from Hanover in January 1834, she mentioned the name of her drawing master, Captain Stephens, who 'is so good-natured and draws so beautifully, that I am copying from him . . . and he proves there is nothing so fascinating as one's pencil'.[117] A contemporary description of the Princess's apartments at Bad Homburg, on the ground floor of the castle looking towards the Taunus mountains, noted that many of the hangings and much of the upholstery had been worked or painted by her, and that her studio contained her writing desk, easel and embroideries, in addition to her library.[118] Just as at Frogmore the garden and park were adorned by a number of tea and garden houses, so at Bad Homburg the Princess designed and built, with her architect Möller, a number of small buildings, including the still extant Gothic House.[119]

The daughters of George III were able to devote so much time to their artistic pursuits because there was very little else for them to do. The same was not the case with their brothers, who were all more or less active in public life and who might therefore have been expected to stop drawing after their drawing masters had left. However, the Prince of Wales was even more passionately interested in building and design, and in the fine arts in general, than was his father, and like him he took a personal interest in finished appearances. According to a note on a bill from William Gates, the cabinet maker, relating to furniture for the Prince of Wales, a pair of 'superb tripods or thermes' were made in 1780 according to the young Prince's design. The same must have been the case with other articles commissioned specifically for the Prince's lavish residences, Carlton House and Brighton Pavilion. Indeed in the British Museum there is a drawing dated 1818 by Prince George (now the Prince Regent) relating to decorative work in the New Music Room at Brighton, which was the responsibility of Frederick Crace, the recipient of the sketch. The Prince's small design for a fountain on the East Terrace at Windsor has also survived.[120] In the British Museum there is a juvenile costume study, made before 1783, 'by the Prince of Wales as a pattern for a masquerade dress in which he intended to have appeared for his Birthday',[121] reminding us of the trouble that the Prince took over his personal appearance, even at an early age.

In 1795 the Prince of Wales married Princess Caroline of Brunswick (1768-1821), to the relief of many, and more particularly of his own parents. That the marriage was a disaster is well known. What is less widely known is that Princess Caroline received lessons in carving and modelling from the young Italian

Although the future George IV was possibly the most important of all British royal patrons, we have very few works directly from his hand. This juvenile study was 'made by the Prince of Wales [before 1783] as a pattern for a masquerade dress in which he intended to have appeared on his Birthday'.

sculptor Peter Turnerelli (1774-1839), and that he had previously been employed to teach Queen Charlotte and her daughters at Windsor (1798-1801).[122] In Princess Caroline's portrait by Sir Thomas Lawrence dated 1804 she is shown, holding a modelling tool, in front of a clay bust of her father the Duke of Brunswick.[123] Turnerelli was probably introduced to the Royal Family by Sir Thomas Lawrence, who lived almost next door to him in Greek Street, Soho. Princess Caroline's only child, Charlotte, was portrayed beside a portfolio of engravings and was, perhaps inevitably, taught to draw and paint, particularly because her grandmother the Queen took so much interest in her upbringing. Her etching of a head of Hannibal, though crude, evidently enjoyed a certain popularity for it was reissued in the year of her death (1817), having been etched three years previously.[124]

Juvenile works exist at Windsor by Princes Edward, Ernest, Augustus and Adolphus, attesting to their thorough training under Sandby, Gresse and Cozens – and also, we assume, to the availability of an accomplished hand to complete a piece for presentation to a royal parent (Plates 15 and 16).[125] We have no works by Princes Frederick or William, but one of the latter's illegitimate daughters, Amelia (1803-58), made some interesting sketches of local scenes during her residence in Nova Scotia while her husband, Lord Falkland, was Lieutenant-Governor, from 1840 to 1846.[126]

Prince Edward's etching of Kew Green dated 1785 has already been mentioned. Five watercolours by the young Prince are

An etching of Hannibal, made by the young Princess Charlotte of Wales, the only child of the future George IV's unhappy marriage to Queen Caroline of Brunswick. The print was reissued following the Princess's death in 1817.

George III's fourth son, Prince Edward, Duke of Kent, was taught by Alexander Cozens and would also have received artistic advice from Dr John Fisher, his tutor from 1780 and a notable amateur draughtsman (and future Bishop of Salisbury).

Queen Victoria's mother, the Duchess of Kent, was born a Princess of Saxe-Coburg. She was responsible for the mural decorations in one of the rooms at the Rosenau, a country seat of the Dukes of Saxe-Coburg and the birthplace of her nephew, Prince Albert. This watercolour is by the local Coburg artist, F. Rothbart.

also at Windsor: three seascapes of 1781 and two landscapes of 1784.[127] During the 1790s he was chiefly resident in Canada, firstly as Colonel of the 7th Foot, and then as Commander of the British forces in Nova Scotia and New Brunswick. In Halifax Prince Edward was responsible for the construction of a number of interesting buildings, from Prince's Lodge (where he lived with his mistress, Madame de Saint-Laurent), with heart-shaped lake and circular peristyled music pavilion in the grounds, to St George's Round Church.[128]

When Prince Edward, Duke of Kent (1767-1820), finally married in 1818 he introduced another artist to the family. His wife, Victoria of Saxe-Coburg (1786-1861), had been married to Emich Charles, Prince of Leiningen, from 1803 until his death in 1814. During this time she painted and drew a number of more or less Italianate scenes (Plate 25)[129] and a highly accomplished view of their home, Amorbach.[130] In 1816 she painted (in oils) a pair of classical landscapes, which were presented to Queen Victoria by her uncle Leopold (the Duchess of Kent's brother) in 1836. In addition the Duchess was responsible for the mural decorations in one of the rooms of the Rosenau, which was the childhood home of her nephews Princes Ernest and Albert of Saxe-Coburg and Gotha.[131] By now, however, we have entered another century, and another chapter of our story.

3

Queen Victoria and Prince Albert

The Duchess of Kent gave birth to a daughter, Victoria, on 24 May 1819. Eight months later, on 23 January 1820, the Duke of Kent died after a short illness, leaving the Duchess a widow for the second time. Almost from the time of her birth, Princess Victoria was heir presumptive to the English throne. Naturally the Duchess's personal influence over the upbringing of the Princess was considerable. The notebooks recording the 'Daily State of the Princess Victoria's Studies' from March 1827 document a full timetable of lessons in a variety of subjects, with comments (as in a school report) by the teacher following each lesson. There were many elements of the 'Kensington system' which were unattractive, even cruel by today's standards, but the Princess's artistic education was not overlooked. Her first drawing lesson took place at 9.30 on the morning of Tuesday 4 December 1827, between lessons in religion and history, and poetry and general knowledge, both of which were taught by her Principal Master, George Davys, Dean of Chester. The drawing master was Richard Westall (1765-1836), whose lessons continued on a weekly basis until 1836. They took place on either Monday or Tuesday morning, and later on Saturday afternoon too, and were of one hour's duration. Westall was not paid for his services, but the Duchess (and later the Queen) supported his blind sister following his death (on 4 December 1836) to the extent of £100 p.a. In her Journal for 6 December 1836, Princess Victoria noted: 'Mamma told me that she had received the news that my poor, old, worthy drawing-master, Mr Richard Westall, died on the 4th, aged 71, in a state of great pecuniary distress . . . he was a very indulgent, patient, agreeable master, and a very worthy man . . . I have had every reason to be satisfied with him; he was very gentlemanly in his manners, and extremely punctual and exact in everything he did.'[1] Soon after, Princess Victoria copied another of Westall's

LEFT: *Drawing inscribed by the nine-year-old Princess Victoria on her mother's forty-second birthday. It copied one of the two figures in a study by Richard Westall, which had been made for that specific purpose.*

RIGHT: *Princess Victoria received drawing lessons from her ninth year almost throughout her long life. Her first master was Richard Westall, who provided a number of outlines for the Princess to copy, including the present one.*

drawings: 'Doge Marino Faliero taking leave of his wife: Plate traced from a drawing by the late Mr R. Westall, 1836.'[2]

Westall's comments on the Princess's work were normally 'Good' or 'Very Good', and only occasionally 'Indifferent'. At the time of his appointment Westall was in his sixties, an established artist and illustrator, but without other pupils. The Princess's lessons appear to have consisted chiefly of exercises in copying drawings by Westall himself: two volumes of the master's 'Studies for the instruction of Her Majesty' are preserved at Windsor. Those finished copies that were presented to the Duchess of Kent (the majority, one would assume) were pasted into an album by the recipient. On the first page is Princess Victoria's copy of a girl carrying baskets, with the date 17 August 1828, the Duchess's forty-second birthday. Victoria copied only part of Westall's drawing, but her study is a very competent piece of work indeed for a child who was not yet ten years old.[3]

Slightly less than a year later, on 12 August 1829, Princess Victoria presented a watercolour sketch of a child to her uncle, King George IV, who celebrated his sixty-seventh (and last) birthday on that day. The drawing was evidently later returned to the donor, for Queen Victoria lent it to an exhibition towards the end of her life.[4] Both the Duchess of Kent's and the King's birthday drawings were doubtless carried out well in advance, for in August the Royal Family were habitually away from London and on their summer excursions. During these annual visits to different parts of the country, Princess Victoria observed the scenery through which they travelled, the houses in which they stayed and the people they encountered. With time, and a few more lessons with Mr Westall, she was able to illustrate her diary jottings with little sketches – of the charade at Chatsworth in 1832, the stars of the ballets, operas and plays that so delighted her in the early 1830s, the French fishermen she encountered at Ramsgate in November 1836, or the gypsies camped near Claremont one month later (Plates 27-29). The various members of the Kensington Palace household, and visiting relations, provided other models to assist the Princess in her progress from a mere copyist to the first royal portraitist and pictorial chronicler.[5]

Princess Victoria spent much of the autumn of 1835 recovering from an illness at Ramsgate. She continued to draw and paint, and made this self-portrait of herself.

Throughout the 1830s Princess Victoria regularly exchanged drawings (see p. 24) and letters with her half-sister Feodora (1807-72), who had been her companion at Kensington until her marriage in 1828 to Prince Ernest of Hohenlohe-Langenburg. A volume of 'Miscellaneous Drawings by Princesses Victoria & Feodora' contains a large number of their early works.[6] Feodora's passion for art was doubtless an inspiration to her younger half-sister. She wrote to Princess Victoria from Stuttgart in March 1833: 'I take lessons in painting, and as we stay but so short a time here, every moment is precious to me for bringing on my drawing . . . If you are so fond of drawing as I am I almost pity you for I should like to do nothing else.'[7]

At the same time the Princess was receiving lessons in other relevant subjects. During a brief sojourn at St Leonards in winter 1834 she received instruction in perspective construction. She was also taught the more useful crafts of embroidery and dressmaking, albeit on a minuscule scale, by her devoted governess Baroness Lehzen, who was a profound influence on the growing Princess (and inevitably the cause of much jealousy following her marriage to Prince Albert: she was pensioned off to Germany in 1842). During the years 1830 to 1833, Princess Victoria and Lehzen dressed a total of 132 small wooden dolls, of which all but two survive in the Museum of London. The Princess's manuscript notes number and describe each doll in turn, and in most cases record precisely who was responsible for supplying the costume. The exquisite collection, in which each doll is dressed in a different way, was chiefly the responsibility of Lehzen, who made 56 of the costumes herself. She collaborated with the Princess on 14 other dolls, and Victoria

The young Princess Victoria was also taught to sew (and design dolls' clothes) by her governess, Baroness Lehzen. Between 1830 and 1833 they dressed 132 individual wooden dolls, of which a selection is shown here. The Princess clothed 27 of the dolls herself, and collaborated with Lehzen on at least another 14 of the costumes.

made 27 costumes without assistance. Although her needlework is crude when compared with Lehzen's, her fingers must have been nimble (and quick) to have worked on this tiny scale. One would assume that the Princess herself named the dolls, supplying such comic groups as a family resulting from the union between Mozart's Count Almaviva (a doll worked by the Princess) and the ballerina Marie Taglioni (worked by Lehzen). In the Royal Archives at Windsor are two slim volumes containing the collections of cut-out paper dolls belonging to Princess Victoria and to her playmate at Kensington, Victoire Conroy. Two of these are inscribed as having been painted or 'maid' (*sic*) by the Princess.[8] Her dolls evidently supplied a welcome outlet for her romantic ideas and her busy little mind, which must frequently have been stifled by the parsimonious and strait-laced life at Kensington.

Although there are occasional references to Queen Victoria's needlework throughout her long life – small items of clothing, such as slippers for Princess Alice, or 'muffiteers' for Prince Arthur in 1867[9] – her main artistic activity was drawing and painting. In addition to Westall's lessons, the Princess evidently received some tuition from the fashionable portrait painter George Hayter (1792-1871), who had held the appointment of 'painter of miniatures and portraits to the Princess Charlotte and Prince Leopold of Saxe-Coburg' since 1815. 'Uncle

Lady Lucy

Painted by Janet

Lady Maria

Painted by Princess
Victoria

Lady Caroline

Painted by
Janet

As well as dressing wooden
dolls, Princess Victoria also
painted and cut out a number
of paper dolls. The central
figure on this page, from the
book of 'Miss Victoria
Conroy's Paper Dolls', is
inscribed as 'Lady Maria
. . . Painted by Princess
Victoria'. The other two
dolls were painted by the
nursery maid Janet.

Leopold', the Duchess of Kent's brother, commissioned Hayter
to portray Princess Victoria in 1833, the year in which their
lessons seem to have begun. There are copies from Hayter's
drawings dated throughout this and the following year. One
such sketch was lent to an exhibition in the Queen's own
lifetime: 'Pen and ink sketch by Her Majesty The Queen when
13 years old, inscribed as follows, P.V.C. KP. March 8 1833,
from G. Hayter, presented to dear Lehzen from her very affectionate friend, Victoria.'[10]

Princess Victoria's journal frequently records the presentation
of gifts of books or other useful things, chiefly from her mother.
On 7 December 1833, her half-sister Feodora's birthday, 'Mama
gave me a book of beautiful outlines by Retzsch to Shakespeare's
Macbeth and another to Hamlet.' The extensive series of illustrations by Moritz Retzsch (1779-1857) were added to over the

years and provided admirably clear outlines for the Princess to copy.[11] Prince Albert's early drawings also contain copies from Retzsch, and in due course the royal children (particularly the boys) were introduced to his work too, thus encountering a vocabulary of gesture and facial expression that was very much more extensive than that found in the work of either Westall or Hayter.

This instruction equipped Princess Victoria not only to delineate and colour the main features of a figure or picture, but also to appreciate the qualities of the work of other artists. When Princes Ernest and Albert of Saxe-Coburg and Gotha visited England in May 1836, the Princess noted in her journal: 'I sat between my dear Cousins on the sofa and we looked at drawings. They both draw well, particularly Albert, and are both exceedingly fond of music . . . The more I see them the more I am delighted with them, and the more I love them.'[12] This single entry provides us with the first indication both of the love which was to unite Victoria and Albert for the next 25 years, and of their shared interest in art (and music), and in the drawings in the Royal Collection.

On 20 June 1837, following the death of her uncle King William IV, Victoria succeeded to the throne. Her accession was inevitably followed by an instant demand for portraits of the young Queen, and the journal entries for the early years of the reign note frequent sittings to painters and sculptors. Four days after the accession Hayter was appointed the Queen's 'Painter of History and Portrait'[13] and towards the end of the same year she 'Sat to Mr Hayter for a long while. Showed him some of my drawings which he praised and told me where they were in fault.'[14] The coronation took place on 28 June 1838, and was recorded by numerous artists, including the Queen herself and Princess Feodora.[15] The Queen's studies naturally depended on her skill at self-portraiture, which had occupied her from an early age.[16] Meanwhile she continued to make sketches of the members of her mother's family who came to stay, and found an additional willing sitter in her first Prime Minister, Lord Melbourne.

Unlike Queen Elizabeth I, who had ascended the English throne (in 1558) aged 25, Victoria, who became Queen at the age of 18, always hoped that she would marry. She had originally intended to wait a few years before so doing, but was evidently overcome by her feelings for Prince Albert and in October 1839 she proposed to him while he and his brother were again staying at Windsor. 'I told him it was a great sacrifice, – which he wouldn't allow . . . I feel the happiest of human beings.'[17] The marriage ceremony, which had long been dreamed of by the couple's Saxe-Coburg relations, took place in the Chapel Royal, St James's Palace, on 10 February 1840. Both bride and groom were twenty years old. Before the end of their initial blissful year together Victoria had given birth to the first of their nine children, 'Vicky', the Princess Royal (born 21 November 1840). During the course of the next four years three more babies were born to the young couple: Albert Edward ('Bertie', the future King Edward VII) on 9 November 1841, Alice on 25 April 1843, and Alfred Ernest ('Affie') on 6 August 1844. The births of the remaining five children – Helena (25 May 1846), Louise (18 March 1848), Arthur (1 May 1850), Leopold (7 April 1853) and Beatrice (14 April 1857) – were spaced rather more generously.

The Queen continued to sketch throughout these years and took particular delight in studying her small offspring. Indeed some of her most delightful work is contained within a large red album entitled 'Sketches of the Royal Children by V.R. from 1841 to 1859' in the Print Room at Windsor.[18] The Queen was inevitably forced to rest at home during the weeks leading up to her confinements. These enforced stays at Windsor or at Buckingham Palace must have been at least partly responsible for the adoption by the royal couple of a new pastime, the art of etching, on which they worked with great energy and dedication during their first four years together. Another factor was doubtless the ease with which personal gifts from the royal couple could thus be reproduced, as many times as was necessary, and then sent to their numerous friends and relations throughout Europe. In 1833, Princess Victoria had drawn a variant of Westall's composition of *Hagar and Ishmael*, and inscribed below the figures:

> I for Lady C. Jenkinson
> I for Foreign Bazaar
> I for Mrs Waldsen
> I for Dss Beaufort's Bazaar

For each copy the drawn outlines had to be gone around, in order to trace the design on to a fresh sheet of paper. The deep indentations on the Princess's original testify to her determined efforts in producing these copies.[19] Three years later she noted in her journal: 'Received . . . a very pretty little etching done by dear Uncle Leopold when he was laid up with his knee at

During the first years of their marriage Queen Victoria and Prince Albert would often draw and sketch their growing family. Sometimes the resulting drawings would be transferred to an etching plate and reproduced as prints. On 9 January 1845, the date inscribed on this etching (which shows the three eldest children), the Queen noted in her Journal: 'Such a thick fog again, and I did not go out but wrote and . . . etched, like yesterday and succeeded quite well. A late luncheon . . . and then did some more etching'.

Paris, from dearest Aunt Louise.'[20] The interest in etching was evidently strong in the Saxe-Coburg family, for in her journal Princess Victoria also records her receipt of a number of etchings (and drawings)[21] by Ferdinand of Saxe-Coburg, who in 1837 married Maria II, Queen of Portugal, and was a mutual cousin of the royal couple (see illustration p. 19). These gifts may well have spurred them into producing their own etched designs.

During the next ten years the Queen etched a total of 62 plates while Prince Albert etched 25.[22] Sometimes they would copy their own drawings on to the plate, alternatively one would copy a drawing by the other, or a piece by a contemporary artist (such as Landseer), or an Old Master (such as Stefano della Bella or Annibale Carracci), whose prints and drawings they had admired during their frequent visits to the Print Room at Windsor. Occasionally the design would be drawn directly on to the plate, with a spontaneity (and even abandon) which was proudly proclaimed in the inscriptions which the Queen added to her set of etchings (now at Windsor), and which accompany the etched inscriptions and dates applied to the plates themselves (for instance, *VR del Albert scult*, or *Albert del VR scult*).[23] In this activity the royal couple were helped by two professional artists, George Hayter and Edwin Landseer (1803-73), both of whom had been patronized by the Duchess of Kent during the 1830s.

Hayter was working on an oil painting of the *Marriage of Queen Victoria and Prince Albert* at the time of their first attempts at etching, in the summer of 1840. On 28 August the Queen noted in her journal: 'We spent a delightful peaceful morning, – singing, after breakfast, and etching together – our 1st attempt.' The annotations in the volume of etchings by Queen Victoria and Prince Albert which had belonged to Hayter [24] mention that in September 1840 the Queen's third plate was 're-etched & bit by GH', while the Prince's second plate was 'burnished by G. Hayter'. 'Worthy troublesome Hayter'[25] was evidently responsible for the acid biting of all the earliest etchings, but the Queen soon discovered that her dresser, Marianne Skerrett, could perform this task equally well, while in cases of difficulty the services of the London firm of Dominic Colnaghi could be enlisted. A printing press was set up by the firm of Holdgate at Buckingham Palace in 1840, but some plates were printed for the royal couple 'at the printing-office of Mr Brown, of Castle-Street, Windsor' in the autumn of the same year. This information is gained from the lengthy (and acrimonious) lawsuit brought by Prince Albert against William Strange, the publisher of a catalogue of 63 royal etchings in 1848. These etchings had been exhibited in London, without royal approval, but the ensuing lawsuit centred on the fact that a catalogue had been published of an artist's (in fact of two artists') work without the consent of the artist concerned. The Lord Chancellor's decision in favour of the plaintiff, Prince Albert, has ensured that an artist's rights over his own works are (according to English law) deeply embedded in the laws of copyright, with the case of *Prince Albert* v. *Strange* as the *locus classicus* of a judgement on such rights.[26]

By July 1842, the royal couple were in need of further instruction, and were able to call on the services of the Landseer brothers.[27] In 1836, Edwin Landseer had painted a portrait of Princess Victoria's favourite dog, Dash, as a gift from the Duchess of Kent on her seventeenth birthday,[28] and thus began a long association between the artist and the Court. He dabbled with etching himself, but his deaf eldest brother Thomas (1798-1880) was a professional engraver, having reproduced in engraved form the majority of Edwin's paintings. During the period 1841-4 no less than twelve of the royal couple's etchings are inscribed as having been based on designs by either Edwin or Thomas Landseer. At the time Edwin Landseer was at work on various royal commissions, notably the conversation piece entitled *Windsor Castle in Modern Times*. On 1 March 1843 the Queen noted in her journal:

> Albert sat to Landseer & I remained part of the time with him. Afterwards Landseer again gave us a lesson in etching, making us try various new points & showing us the great advantage of changing points for different stages of the work, – in which we have hitherto been very deficient.

In the following years the spate of royal etchings diminishes. Only seven plates are dated after 1843, and after January 1849 there were none at all. Lithography enjoyed a brief popularity in 1846, under the influence of the miniature painter William Ross and the supervision of his son-in-law Edwin Dalton. In February 1846 both Queen Victoria and Prince Albert worked on lithographic portraits of the Prince of Wales, after a watercolour by William Ross. Victoria noted: '[Albert's] lithograph as well as mine of Bertie, is finished & the proofs have just come. They are beautiful, & Albert's work not at all like that of an amateur.'[29] But the Queen's interest was already moving elsewhere, to the art of watercolour painting.

Richard Westall's lessons had included instruction in the use of watercolour for figure drawing, in the context of the linear style employed by that artist. Many of Princess Victoria's sketches of ballerinas and opera singers in the early 1830s are touched with colour. A tiny sketch of an earthenware jug, dated December 1833, is a particularly charming statement of her early skill with watercolour (Plate 26).[30] By 1846, Victoria evidently felt that she would like to do more than sketch her family and the people she encountered on her travels. Her 'Souvenir' or 'View Albums' consisted of watercolours recording different events or scenes witnessed on the journeys which she and the Prince made together. When no professional artist was on hand, a lady-in-waiting might be called upon to 'take a view', for the Queen did not feel sufficiently confident of her own draughtsmanship to do so herself. Charlotte Canning (1817-61), named after her godmother Queen Charlotte, served as Queen Victoria's lady-in-waiting from 1842 until 1855, when her husband was appointed Governor-General of India. Like her younger sister, Louisa Waterford, she was a skilled watercolourist and her talent was frequently employed by the Queen.[31] During the state visit to the French Royal Family at Château D'Eu in 1843, when Lady Canning was in waiting, she made the following entry in her diary:

> Sept 6. Another beautiful day. The Queen sent for me before breakfast to know whether I had drawn anything & to bespeak a sketch of the house from the avenue – the spot from which we first saw it as we arrived. The Queen had a paintbrush in her hand when I came in, & she owned she was trying to hide herself behind the curtain & to sketch the French soldiers who were serenading under the windows.[32]

Just over a year later, the Royal Family spent the summer holidays at Blair Atholl, which Lord Glenlyon (later the 6th Duke of Atholl) had placed at the Queen's disposal. On 16 September Lady Canning noted: 'There will be a great deal to draw here for the Queen wants views done for her in every direction.'[33] She went on to record that: 'The Queen had her first ride in the hills & she enjoyed it of all things. She had been sketching a little from the window & she wants to try & colour & has a great longing to draw some dirty children & I am to find these & begin, & she is to come quietly & look on & draw them when not observed.'[34] Five days later both Lady Canning and the Queen recorded the expedition up Glen Tilt and pronounced it a perfect subject for a picture, the Queen bemoaning the fact that she had not had the time to make such a picture herself. At the top of Cairn Chlamain (in Glen Tilt) the Queen paused to make a slight pencil sketch of the view, to which Lady Canning added stones in the foreground.[35] The Queen and Prince worked together on a view from their sitting-room window at Blair Atholl. The resulting picture, 'sketched by VR & coloured by Albert', also left room for improvement.[36]

It was to improve the quality of her painting that the Queen embarked on a series of twelve lessons (during the space of three weeks) in July 1846, two months after the birth of Princess Helena. Her teacher was the author and artist Edward Lear (1812-88), who had been brought to Queen Victoria's notice by the first volume of his *Illustrated Excursions in Italy* published earlier in the year. On 15 July 1846 she noted in her journal: 'Had a drawing lesson from Mr Lear, who sketched before me & teaches remarkably well, in landscape painting in water colours.' The lessons were begun at Osborne House on the Isle of Wight, which had been purchased by the royal couple as their southern retreat during the previous year. As with Westall, the instruction was initially conducted by way of copies, some of which survive at Windsor. On 17 July the Queen wrote: 'I had another lesson with Mr Lear, who much praised my 2nd copy. – Later in the afternoon I went out & saw a beautiful sketch he had done of the new house.' The following day: 'After luncheon had a drawing lesson, & am, I hope, improving.' A pencil sketch by the Queen, inscribed below 'New House at Osborne. VR copied from Lear. 18 July 1846' is among her drawings at Windsor.[37]

The Queen continued to sketch throughout the summer, which was spent almost entirely at Osborne, ending with a sailing expedition to Cornwall. But she felt the need for continued instruction in landscape painting and on 30 September 1846 received the first of many lessons from a slightly older artist, William Leighton Leitch (1803-83), whose instruction to the numerous members of the Royal Family continued until the time of his death. Queen Victoria and Prince Albert had been shown examples of Leitch's work by the Mistress of the Robes, the Duchess of Sutherland (1806-68), but probably owed their introduction to the artist to the faithful Charlotte Canning, who had herself received lessons from Leitch in the early 1840s. She may have been responsible for his presence at Blair in 1844, when he was asked to supply a series of views of the local scenery which would later be pasted into the Queen's albums alongside those by Lady Canning. Leitch's first lessons were

The Queen often drew the children of estate workers at Balmoral, such as the bare-footed Johnnie Fraser and Maggie Gow, shown here in September 1848.

at Osborne, but he was also called upon to visit Windsor, Buckingham Palace and (especially) Balmoral for the same purpose. His teaching methods are described in his biography. He began by explaining 'the elements of all art – the composition, of light, and shade, and of colour . . . He explained how all fine quality of colour was derived from a practical knowledge of the three, primitive colours, – yellow, red and blue',[38] and illustrated each theorem with painted examples (Plate 3).[39] The Queen's reported reaction was: 'This is wonderful, and I am delighted; but I am surprised that I have never had this explained before.' Leitch then prescribed half an hour's painting practice each day, and the pupil awaited her next lesson with eager anticipation.[40] By January 1847 the Queen informed Lady Canning in Rome: 'I have made great progress in my Drawing since I saw you, & I am sure you would be surprised & say as Leitch does: "I can hardly believe y[our] M[ajest]y has done these." He is an excellent Master & I recommend him whenever I can.'[41]

The Queen sketched and painted throughout the year, but her artistic talents were particularly exercised at Osborne, and during the annual visits to Scotland, from 1847 (Plates 30-34). She went out with her watercolour box almost every day of the holidays, noting the changing contours of the hills, the subtly changing colours of the heather, the sky and the water, and taking continuing delight in so doing. Following their delightful stay at Blair Atholl in 1844, the Royal Family waited three years

The royal children were sketched in many of their different costumes. Highland dress became the norm for both outdoor and indoor wear at Balmoral, where Prince Alfred was drawn in 1848. This watercolour was completed in February 1849.

before returning to Scotland. In the summer of 1847 they were lent a shooting-box at Ardverikie on the shores of Loch Laggan by the Marquis of Abercorn. Queen Victoria's painting activity at this time was to be recorded in oils by Landseer, for the Prince's Christmas present that year was Landseer's painting of *Queen Victoria sketching at Loch Laggan*.[42] In the following year the Queen acquired the leasehold of her own Scottish estate, at Balmoral, on the River Dee. The royal party arrived at Balmoral in mid–September, and thereafter the Queen's letters and journal positively buzz with her enthusiasm for the place: 'The Scenery all around is the finest almost I have seen anywhere. It is very wild & solitary, & yet cheerful and *beautifully wooded* . . . You can walk for ever; I seldom walk less than 4 hours a day & when I come in I feel as if I want to go out again. And then the wildness, the solitariness and everything is so delightful, so refreshing.'[43] During the holidays the Queen would draw, sometimes with, sometimes without instruction. The royal party would then travel south with their sketches and during the long winter evenings the Queen would produce finished watercolours from her jottings, or make copies to achieve different atmospheric effects.[44] At the beginning of the summer holidays in 1849, at Osborne, she 'Had a lesson with Leitch, who I am glad to say finds I have not lost much.'[45] The following May, Leitch was again at Osborne with the royal party. His watercolour of the entrance front of the newly completed house, dated 23 May 1850, was perhaps painted for the Queen's birthday the next day.[46] The genuine pleasure derived by Queen Victoria from the contemplation of nature during the holidays at Osborne and Balmoral is made clear in the following passage from her journal. After an afternoon spent painting at Osborne in August 1851: 'Sat out reading in the Lower Alcove. The evening was glorious & the sea & everything looked so beautiful. What is there more beautiful than Nature, "the autograph work of God"'.[47]

Leitch's talents as a teacher were questioned by another artistic member of the Queen's household, the Honourable Eleanor Stanley (1821-1903), who was maid of honour to Queen Victoria from 1842 to 1862. In October 1846, Miss Stanley wrote to her mother from Windsor and described her discussions with the Queen about her own drawings, and particularly her use of chalk. The Queen

was very sweet, and as she had nothing to draw upon but block sketch books, she was so condescending as to borrow my two boards and my desk . . . She seems very anxious to master the difficulty of colour, as far as mixing them and using them tolerably easily, but does not seem to have any ideas beyond that – of composition and light and shade, which Leitch will not give her, as it is there he is deficient; but I thought he explained the first beginnings of drawings and sketches very well yesterday.[48]

Elsewhere in her correspondence, Eleanor Stanley records life at Balmoral in some detail, with the sketching expeditions and ensuing discussions about the resulting views. In September 1854, Miss Stanley was working on a large sketch of Lochnagar, and a number of subsidiary studies. Queen Victoria 'was very kind and, by way of helping me with my foreground, sent me her "view album", as she calls it, in which were several drawings by Lady Canning, Leitch and others, which were a great help really and very pretty to look at besides.'[49] The Queen was so full of admiration for Miss Stanley's work that she later added a number of her watercolours to the albums.

Although Leitch continued to teach the Queen throughout the 1850s he enjoyed very poor health and frequently had to absent himself from Palace and Castle for many months at a time. During these periods the Queen would sometimes revert to copying the drawings or paintings of other artists, or to working up her own sketches into finished pieces. In the late 1840s and 1850s she was introduced to the paintings of two German artists, Philipp von Foltz (1805-77) and Carl Haag (1820-1915), both of whom had worked for her half-brother the Prince of Leiningen. Their sketches of Tyrolean or Italian peasants appealed to her love of the picturesque. In March 1849 the Queen recorded: 'I am busy copying that other picture by Foltz, of a Tyrolese Jäger, & dear Albert helps me, doing it much better than I can. I have but ½ an hour at the utmost before & after luncheon for drawing & painting.'[50] Carl Haag was formally introduced to the Queen in March 1853. The Queen saw (and copied) a number of his watercolours[51] before inviting the artist to spend the autumn at Balmoral with the royal party. Owing to the temporary loss of his painting equipment, Haag initially had to make use of the Queen's own materials.[52] After a successful six-week stay in Scotland, Haag came south with several unfinished royal commissions. His contact with the Royal Family continued through the following year, and during that summer he gave the Queen a number of painting lessons.[53] After one of these she commented that Haag was 'an admirable Master and has shown me more about the anatomy of the figure than anyone ever did before'.[54] In addition he taught her the rudiments of his elaborate technique of watercolour painting. Her mastery of this method is shown in the watercolour of 'Ciocara' at Windsor, inscribed 'after C. Haag, who touched up the face June 1859'.[55]

Leitch was at Balmoral again during the summer of 1861 with his son Richard Principal Leitch (*c.*1827-82), who sometimes deputized for his father in carrying out commissions and instructing the Royal Family. Leitch charged two guineas a day for the 24 days he spent at Balmoral teaching 'Her Majesty the Queen and their Royal Highnesses the Princesses' in September and October 1861.[56] But by the end of the year everything had changed, for the Queen's dearest Albert had died, on 14 December 1861. Thereafter each new sketchbook was carefully inscribed 'The 1st year of my misery', 'The 2nd year of my Great Sorrow', and so on, for the inconsolable widow continued to draw and paint.[57] Leitch was called back to Balmoral in both 1862 and 1863, and in the latter year he undertook to give a further series of lessons.[58] By now his pupils included several other members of the Royal Family in addition to the Queen. In a letter dated 30 September 1863 the artist wrote:

Work on the royal mausoleum at Frogmore began almost immediately after the Prince Consort's death in December 1861. The Queen paid frequent visits to her husband's burial place, and made this sketch of the new building in 1865.

I am exceedingly glad to tell you that the Queen has begun to draw again . . . To-day I went out with her Majesty and the Princess Louise [actually Princess Louis, i.e. Alice] of Hesse, and we had a drawing party out of doors. The day was fine although there was no sun. We got on very well, and the Queen was cheerful and enjoyed the work – chatting, and occasionally laughing at the little difficulties and draw-backs, and speaking also of auld lang syne in a very feeling manner, so that nearly two hours went by in the most interesting and delightful way imaginable.[59]

In a letter home the following week, Leitch described another outing during which the sketch begun at the end of September was to be completed:

I wish you could have seen us – her Majesty on a rough Highland pony with a Highlander to lead it; Lady Churchill walking alongside the Queen; the Princess Louise also trudg-ing along, and your husband walking alongside the Princess. When we got to our place of work there was another picture – Her Majesty sitting in the middle of a country road, with a great rough stone out of the river to put her paint box on; Lady Churchill holding an umbrella over the Queen's head, and I seated near her Majesty so that she could see what I was doing. The Princess Louise was on my right hand, sitting on a big stone, and working away at her drawing, and the Highlander the Queen's personal attendant, John Brown – with the pony in the background. Several people that passed did, I assure you, stare at the group. The Queen evidently enjoyed it very much. There was lots of talking and laughing, and nearly two hours passed away very soon – the Queen remarking how quickly the time flew when she was drawing.[60]

This was Leitch's last visit to Balmoral, although he agreed to teach the Royal Family in the south until 1865, when ill-health forced him to retire.[61]

The Queen's sketching activity continued, however. As the princes and princesses were all growing (if not grown) up, their childish antics no longer concerned her so much. The children – particularly the daughters – now filled a rather different role, frequently accompanying their mother on her sketching expeditions (Plates 8 and 9), even using the Queen's sketchbook. During the visit to Coburg in autumn 1860 the Queen and her

During Prince Albert's lifetime the Queen occasionally portrayed the Prince from nature, but was generally happier to copy an existing image by Hayter or Ross. After 1861 she was anxious to correct any faulty likenesses of the Prince. This drawing was made to assist Edward Corbould. The left-hand head deliberately exaggerated various imperfections in Corbould's portrait of the Prince, 'whilst the other head was to explain what HM desired done to a portrait of the Prince Consort'.

Edward Corbould, the drawing master to the princes and princesses from 1852, was commissioned to produce a memorial picture of Prince Albert in armour in 1862. The resulting image followed detailed discussions with the Queen.

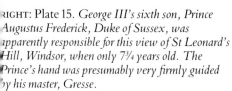

LEFT: Plate 14. *A note inside this gold snuff-box states that the ivory decoration was turned and carved by George III, with the help of a lathe (and a teacher) brought over from Paris for the purpose. An invoice dated 22 June 1769 for the lathe (£266 13s 4d), customs duties and transport costs from Paris (£21 14s 8d), and a gold snuff-box (£50), supplied by John Duval and Sons, has survived in the Royal Archives.*

RIGHT: Plate 15. *George III's sixth son, Prince Augustus Frederick, Duke of Sussex, was apparently responsible for this view of St Leonard's Hill, Windsor, when only 7¾ years old. The Prince's hand was presumably very firmly guided by his master, Gresse.*

BELOW: Plate 16. *Windsor Castle from the River Thames, painted by George III's fifth son, Prince Ernest Augustus, Duke of Cumberland, in his tenth year. In both subject-matter and technique (gouache) it shows the influence of Paul Sandby, whose follower J.A. Gresse was drawing master to the royal children.*

BELOW: Plate 17. *This flower pot, with detached base, was a product of the Ludwigsburg porcelain factory, in the grounds of the residence of the ruling family of Württemberg (and thus the home of George III's eldest daughter after her marriage in 1797). The painted decoration, based on a published design, was added by the Princess, who inscribed the base with her initials (C.A.M.) and the date, 1812.*

ABOVE: Plate 18. *Following her marriage to the Hereditary Prince of Württemberg, the Princess Royal sent home a number of boxes incorporating panels painted by her. The porcelain panel on the lid of this box was decorated with scenes copied from two engravings by J. E. Ridinger. The box was a gift to Princess Augusta Sophia. It later belonged to her great-nephew Sir Adolphus FitzGeorge, who bequeathed it to Queen Mary on his death in 1922.*

BELOW: Plate 19. *This penwork panel was set into the top of a workbox sent home from Germany by the Princess Royal*

ABOVE: Plate 20. *Queen Charlotte and her daughters frequently 'botanized', at Kew and at Windsor, either copying living specimens (as here), or recent engravings of plants and flowers in which they were interested. The Princess Royal's watercolour of a* Crinum pendulum *was made on 5 July 1784, shortly after the plant was first introduced to England.*

RIGHT: Plate 21. *Flower piece painted by George III's third daughter, Princess Elizabeth, in 1792. An almost identical still life is signed by Margaret Meen, whose work was purchased by Queen Charlotte.*

LEFT: Plate 22. *Silhouettes of various types were cut by Princess Elizabeth throughout her life. This South American Owl butterfly (of the genus* Caligo) *was made from a sheet of rice paper, painted to simulate the insect's wings.*

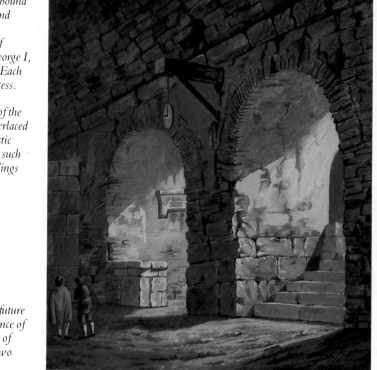

ABOVE: Plate 23. *Queen Charlotte and her daughters spent many hours carefully copying (and sometimes compiling) historical texts. These would then be mounted on to folio sheets, and bound up as large albums, illustrated with appropriate drawings and engravings. Princess Elizabeth's 'Histoire de la Duchesse d'Ahlden' (completed in Hanover, 1837), is the life story of Princess Sophia Dorothea of Zell, the estranged wife of George I, who was imprisoned (at Ahlden) for her alleged infidelity. Each page is adorned with a floral surround, painted by the Princess.*

ABOVE RIGHT: Plate 24. *The main room on the first floor of the Queen's Cottage, Kew, decorated with a bamboo trellis interlaced with convolvulus and nasturtium. Princess Elizabeth's artistic activity extended from tiny silhouettes to decorative schemes such as those at Kew and Frogmore, and designs for garden buildings both in England and Germany.*

RIGHT: Plate 25. *This painting was made in Rome by the future Duchess of Kent while married to her first husband, the Prince of Leiningen. In 1811 it was given by her to Louise, Countess of Degenfeld, whose husband was guardian to the Duchess's two Leiningen children during their minority.*

married daughter, the Princess Royal, often drew together (Plate 37). On 29 September they went to the Rosenau, 'Vicky & I sketching the beautiful view of the Festung and Oeslau', while at Callenberg two days later 'we sat on the upper terrace, & Vicky & I began to sketch.' In the years immediately following Prince Albert's death the princesses also gave advice about the private (and public) memorials made in his honour. The Queen naturally had very firm views on this subject. Prince Albert's likeness for his imposing portrait in armour painted by Edward Corbould in 1863-4 was criticized by the Queen, whose own 'caricatured' head of the Prince, given to Corbould, is now in the British Museum.[62] The Queen was also at pains to guide and correct those engravers and printers that she employed to reproduce portraits of family and friends for private circulation. 'The engravers' proofs of these, always carefully scrutinised by the Queen, were never returned without some pertinent comment, sometimes illustrated by a drawing by the Queen upon the margin. "None but an artist could have made that suggestion" was a not uncommon remark of the engraver.'[63] After 1861, the Queen's sketches are concerned almost exclusively with the surrounding scenery rather than the companions who had occupied her so much during her early years. Her studies record private and uninterrupted moments in the life of the Queen Empress (e.g. Plates 4, 38 and 40). Few of them were ever mounted and framed for display:[64] they were the modest (but accomplished) accompaniments to the journal that she kept so meticulously from 1832 until the year of her death in 1901.[65]

Queen Victoria's drawings in coloured chalks (or pastels) were of a rather different nature to her sketches in pencil or watercolour. The fragility of the surface finish meant that they could not easily be kept in albums, but should instead be mounted and framed for hanging. In 1846 the Queen had suggested that Eleanor Stanley might teach her to draw in chalks, as she had already taught Lady Canning, but apparently nothing came of this plan.[66] Instead Edwin Landseer once again came to the rescue, and the Queen's works in this medium contain many copies of his work, or of studies by the Hungarian artist Karl Brocky (1807-55), dated 1850 and 1851. In her journal for 24 March 1850 Queen Victoria noted: 'Tried to draw with chalks. Landseer showed me how to, the other day in a few charming sketches, executed in 5 or 10 minutes. It is wonderful to see the effect he brings out with but a few touches.' Landseer's tuition (like Haag's) evidently included some study of human

The Queen fully realized the expressive qualities of a back view. Her granddaughter Princess Louise of Wales was drawn in January 1872, shortly before her fifth birthday.

anatomy. The royal couple 'looked over some fine anatomical drawings' by Landseer after dinner on 23 November 1850, and the following January the Queen noted: 'Made a successful sketch of a cast of a skull brought, by Sir Ed: Landseer. It will be a great help, & it is very interesting to study our wonderful anatomy.'[67] Shortly before this date the Queen had finished her copy of Landseer's chalk drawing of Archie and Annie Macdonald, the children of Albert's ghillie or 'jäger', John Macdonald. The previous December she had seen Landseer at work on his drawing in the Painting Room at Windsor, and she was at pains to note that when making her own copy the children were called in to sit to her.[68] In November 1850 the Queen and Landseer worked together on a coloured chalk portrait of Prince Alfred.[69] During the stay at Balmoral in September 1851 the Queen made studies in chalk of the stags shot by Prince Albert, and these were later retouched by Landseer.[70] The three volumes of photographs and drawings of stags shot by Prince Albert between 1851 and 1859 include over fifty studies by the Queen, in chalk and pen, of specific and identified beasts.[71] But she realized that her chalk drawings were not a success, and twenty years later wrote, 'I never could manage that well.'[72] (See Plate 35.)

The same was also unfortunately the case with oil painting, about which Queen Victoria wrote to her eldest daughter, the Princess Royal (now Princess Frederick William of Prussia), in April 1859:

> I hear you model and even paint in oils; this last I am sorry for; you remember what Papa always told you on the subject. Amateurs can never paint in oils like artists and what can one do with all one's productions? Whereas water colours always are nice and pleasant to keep in books or portfolios. I hope, dear, you will not take to the one or neglect the other![73]

The Queen omitted to mention that both she and the Prince had once worked in oils, as had her mother, the Duchess of Kent. As with the etchings, the key to Queen Victoria's early painting activity may lie with George Hayter. Shortly before her fifteenth birthday, she noted in her journal: 'At 3 Lehzen & I went to sit with Mama who was painted. In the course of the afternoon Mr Hayter made a sketch of *dear* Dash . . . in chalk on a pannel, and I painted it. *My first* attempt at oil colour painting! We stayed there till a ¼ to 5.'[74] Prince Albert and his brother Ernest are said to have begun to paint in Brussels, during visits to their Uncle Leopold while they were studying at Bonn University from 1836 to 1837. Prince Albert's paintings of a long-eared owl (dated 1836 and inscribed Op. III) and of a 'Scene from Götz von Berlichingen' (dated 1837) are in the Royal Collection. His dramatic, but frankly far from successful, 'Death of Count Mansfield' was presented to the Queen in November 1839 (three months before their marriage), and the two pictures of the 'Death of the Marquis of Posa' (from Schiller's *Don Carlos*) were painted for his young wife the following year.[75] According to the Queen, during the early years of their marriage the Prince was 'much taken up with painting'.[76] George Hayter noted in his diary that he supplied Prince Albert with a sketch of the death of the Marquis of Posa; it is possible, therefore, that the Prince's picture is largely based on Hayter's (lost) sketch. While Prince Albert was finishing work on the 'Marquis of Posa' pictures, the Queen was working on a figure of a kneeling nun in oils, 'Albert shewing me how to do it'.[77] But neither this picture nor the earlier head of 'Dash', has survived.

It was ten years before the royal couple returned to working in oils, and this time they turned for assistance to the German artist Franz Xaver Winterhalter (1805-73). He had been introduced to the Queen and Prince through their relations King Leopold I and Queen Louise of the Belgians, and from 1842 had carried out a vast number of royal commissions, ranging over a period of nearly twenty years: there are still over one hundred paintings by Winterhalter in the Royal Collection.[78] The portrait of Winterhalter in oils at Osborne is a particularly personal memento of the artist's royal associations. Although it is neither signed nor dated (perhaps because it remains unfinished), it presumably dates from the early 1850s, and is attributed in early inventories to Prince Albert. The following anecdote, first related shortly after Queen Victoria's death, would seem to suggest that the portrait is in fact by the Queen. Winterhalter was having difficulty in painting the Queen's portrait because of her constant activity. She is reported to have said:

'I know I am a bad sitter, but I never can keep still unless I have something to do', so the painter suggested that the Queen should paint him, while he was painting her. The idea found favour; canvas, paints, and brushes were sent for, and the Queen went to work . . . the sketch (a lifesize head) of Winterhalter was, moreover, a good likeness.[79]

This oil portrait of Winterhalter at Osborne is neither signed nor dated but is traditionally described as the work of Prince Albert, c. 1851/2. There is a possibility that it was instead painted by Queen Victoria.

On 23 June 1851 the Queen noted:

> After luncheon I took my 1ʳˢᵗ lesson in oil painting with good Winterhalter, which I was successful in, to his & my astonishment. I am doing a copy of the head of little Louise. I find that the drawing in chalks, has been of the greatest use. Albert was much pleased at the beginning I made.

Four days later: 'Painted with Winterhalter, who is so kind, & shews me everything so patiently, though at the same time, he is strict, which is such an advantage.'[80] The Queen presented her copy of Winterhalter's portrait of Princess Louise to the artist before his departure from England in July 1852.[81] He was apparently delighted with his gift.

In July 1851, Queen Victoria records making painted likenesses of two members of her household: Sarah, and Jane the nurserymaid. In November she returned to copying, selecting Landseer's painting of 'Lassie' as a model.[82] At the time both Winterhalter and Landseer were engaged on royal commissions, as well as providing instruction to the Queen and the Prince. The Queen noted: 'It is delightful to see 2 such great artists, so devoid of jealousy & so ready to aid one another.'[83]

The small group of surviving oil paintings by the Queen commences in August 1851 with her copies of the circular portraits of Princesses Amélie and Clothilde, the daughters of the royal couple's mutual first cousin, Prince Augustus of Saxe-Coburg and Gotha, which were based rather precisely on Winterhalter's recently completed portraits.[84] A few days later the Queen began work on a profile portrait of her third daughter, Princess Helena, who was five years old at the time. She worked on the picture for the following three days, and noted that Prince Albert thought it excellent.[85] A more ambitious project involved the depiction (from nature) of the scene from Kotzebue's play *Der Hahnenschlag* which was enacted by her six oldest children at Windsor Castle on Twelfth Night (6 January) 1852. The Queen made some preliminary sketches at the time, and for the next four months worked on the painting, with a considerable amount of assistance from the Prince. Thereafter (in early summer 1852) the Queen worked on a second picture of the same juvenile troupe, this time performing a Scene from Racine's *Athalie*, on the royal couple's twelfth wedding anniversary (10 February 1852), at Windsor Castle. Meanwhile, the Queen was at work on two more portrait heads, and on a copy of the picture entitled *La Simplicité* (dated June 1852) by Winterhalter's brother, Hermann. The portrait heads, both dated April 1852 and apparently sketched from nature, are of Archie and Annie Macdonald, the same children who had sat to Landseer (and the Queen) for a joint portrait in coloured chalks over a year before.[86]

The year 1851 was, of all years, Prince Albert's own. It saw the opening in London of the Great Exhibition, the vast display of the arts and industries of all nations which owed so much to the Prince's vision, enthusiasm and organizational powers. His multifarious interests and talents were constantly alluded to in the Queen's writings, as was his importance in encouraging the arts in his adopted country.[87] On the Prince's birthday in 1850,

When the royal children performed an arrangement of Kotzebue's play Der Hahnenschlag, *on Twelfth Night 1852, the Queen painted a record of it in oils. In the foreground are Princesses Helena and Louise, and in the background a procession led by Prince Alfred, with the Prince of Wales, the Princess Royal and Princess Alice behind. Queen Victoria records her work on the picture throughout January 1852. Prince Albert assisted her, particularly with the background. The painting was finally completed in May, and was placed in the schoolroom at Buckingham Palace.*

she noted the opinion of the sculptor John Gibson, who had just finished work on a bust of the Queen: 'He [Gibson] deplores the lack of taste in this country, but says that Albert has already done a great deal to improve art, & by degrees to raise the whole standard.'[88] Prince Albert was a tireless perfectionist, to an extent which sometimes defeated even the Queen. After his death she described how they used to select and order watercolours for the Souvenir Albums. The Prince 'was not satisfied if they were not really good wh. sometimes disappointed me – as I – stupidly – & unworthily – was more easily satisfied with mediocrity.'[89]

Prince Albert had included instruction in drawing in the timetable he compiled for himself during his fifteenth year.[90] His first master in art, as in most other subjects, was 'Rath' Florschutz, who acted as tutor to Princes Ernest and Albert from 1823 until the end of their time at Bonn University in 1838. The products of these early years consisted of boldly delineated (and sometimes highly coloured) scenes of military or political history (Plate 39), or personal caricatures. There were also more homely subjects, such as the drawing of Prince Albert's faithful greyhound Eos made in 1834, which served as the basis for the Queen's etching of six years later.[91] The highly competent profile portrait of his brother Prince Ernest, dated 1836, shows the thoroughness of Prince Albert's early artistic training.[92] Ten days after their wedding, Prince Albert showed his wife 'a portfolio of drawings which he had done when a child'.[93] Following his father's death in January 1844 the Prince revisited Coburg and found another collection of his early drawings at the Rosenau, the country seat of the Dukes of Coburg in which he had spent much of his childhood.[94] Prince Albert's talent for caricature (both enacted and drawn) was much exercised during his time at Bonn University. The mannerisms of one of his teachers there, Professor Harrlos, were therefore well known to the Queen before she was introduced to the professor during their visit to Bonn in August 1845,[95] as were those of Count Beusch ('the funniest, oddest man I have ever seen') whom the Queen had met five years earlier.[96]

After their engagement in October 1839 the Queen and Prince would sometimes draw and sketch side by side. Queen Victoria lovingly preserved a page of doodles made by her future husband on the back of a concert programme on 17 October 1839.[97] These contrast very strikingly with the somewhat overworked oils which were the product of the same years. Prince Albert's pen and pencil sketches from this period (which included copies of drawings in the Royal Collection) were often etched, either by him or by the Queen. The rather hard illustrator's outline of these drawings is quite distinct from his wife's more relaxed style. Only a small number of landscapes and watercolours by the Prince have come down to us, and these mainly date from the summer holidays from 1845 to 1847, at precisely the time, therefore, that Queen Victoria was herself receiving tuition in this medium. Several views of the Channel Islands were taken from on board the Royal Yacht in August and September 1846. After pasting Prince Albert's views into her albums, the Queen noted that (like many of her own watercolours) they were

The young Prince Albert also received drawing and painting lessons. This pencil portrait of his elder brother Ernest, made in 1836 during their time at Bonn University, is a skilful likeness by the sixteen-year-old Prince.

Queen Victoria and Prince
Albert became engaged on
15 October 1839. Two days
later the Prince attended a
musical evening at Windsor
Castle, and covered his
programme with doodles and
caricatures. The Queen
inscribed the sheet
accordingly, and treasured
it for posterity.

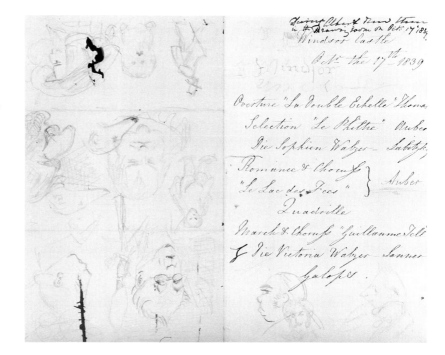

This pen drawing by Prince
Albert of the two eldest
children at play in January
1843 was later reproduced
as an etching, the joint work
of the Queen and the
Prince.

The drawing on the left side of this page was sketched by Prince Albert from his seat in a carriage during the summer holidays on the Continent in August 1845. The Queen inscribed the figure study at the right, which was drawn on the same occasion, as her own work.

'finished afterwards', when the royal party had reached dry land.[98] Many years later the royal couple spent some time on a new experimental process 'of painting in oil colours on the back of a photograph previously dipped in oil'.[99] Not surprisingly, no products of this brief interest appear to have survived.

The close attention which Prince Albert paid to the work of the artists who were in receipt of royal commissions often involved him in sketching out the overall design for a painting before the artist began work on it. When William Corden (1819-1900) was at work in 1848 on his portrait of Frederick William, Duke of Brunswick (killed at Quatre-Bras in 1815), for the Waterloo series at Windsor, he was assisted by 'sketches of uniforms and military details made by the Prince'.[100] According to the entry for this picture in the nineteenth-century inventory of the Royal Collection, it was 'composed by Prince Albert and Corden from a Minature [*sic*] of the Duke said to be a good likeness'.[101] In 1851, Winterhalter was commissioned to paint a group showing the Queen and Prince Albert with the Duke of Wellington and his namesake the young Prince Arthur, to be entitled *The First of May*. This was the eighty-second birthday of the Duke and the first birthday of his godson, as well as being the opening day of the Great Exhibition. The Queen noted that the original concept for the picture had been her own: 'but Winterhalter did not seem to know how to carry it out so dear Albert with his wonderful knowledge & taste, gave W. [Winterhalter] the idea which is now to be carried out.'[102]

The same 'beneficial interference' was involved in the Prince's dealings with the sculptors John Francis (1780-1861) and Thomas Thornycroft (1816-85). After the death of the Duke of Coburg at the beginning of 1844, Prince Albert commissioned Francis to make a posthumous bust of his father, on which work proceeded throughout February and March. The marble version of the bust (now at Windsor Castle) is inscribed 'BY J. FRANCIS UNDER THE GUIDANCE OF H.R.H. THE PRINCE ALBERT FROM RECOLLECTION 1844'. Prince Albert was evidently actively involved in the modelling of the bust of his father, and later of the figure of 'Eos'. By the second half of the nineteenth century it was normal practice for a well-established sculptor to employ assistants, specifically to translate the master's clay or plaster model into stone. This would be done by a 'pointer', who transferred the measurements from model to stone block, and drilled holes to the correct depth, and by a 'carver' and 'chaser'. The master would supervise the work, and apply the finishing touches.[103] In the case of the Prince's work, he acted as the master sculptor, modelling the likeness in clay, before handing it over to the professional (John Francis) for translation into stone or for casting in plaster or bronze. The Prince was evidently closely involved in the making of the clay model of his father's portrait bust. According to the Queen, the bust of the Prince's father 'is in fact [Albert's] doing, he having directed every line & feature & all the drapery, even working on it himself.'[104] Two days later the Queen noted that the precious bust had been dropped, 'and was broken into atoms, or rather more squashed into a lump!',[105] but Francis immediately resumed work and after a week the bust had been remade. On 12 March, Victoria noted: 'After prayers Albert put the finishing touches to the bust', and the royal couple witnessed the casting process three days later.

In July of the same year, 1844, Prince Albert suffered another loss, that of his beloved greyhound Eos. 'She had been his constant & faithful companion for 10 & ½ years & she was only 6 months old when he first had her . . . poor dear Albert, he feels it too terribly, & I grieve so for him. It is quite like losing a friend.'[106] In August Prince Albert made an etched copy of Landseer's drawing of the two dogs, Eos and Cairnach,[107] and two months later the sculptor Francis was at work on a model of Eos at the kennels at Windsor: 'It is for a statue to be put over her grave.'[108] The Queen explained that 'Albert directs everything and also works himself at it.'[109] The bronze figure of Eos was finally set in place the following September, at the

After the death of Prince Albert's faithful greyhound Eos in 1844 the Prince set to work on a life-size portrait statue to go over the dog's grave at Windsor. He collaborated with the sculptor John Francis in the production of the clay model, which was later cast in bronze. Another cast (illustrated here) was placed on the terrace at Osborne.

top of the Slopes in the Home Park, Windsor.[110] Another cast was later placed on the terrace at Osborne, and Francis exhibited a 'Model of Eos . . . executed for H.R.H. in bronze' at the Royal Academy in 1848.

In February 1840, Mary Francis (1809-95), the talented daughter of John Francis, had married a fellow sculptor, Thomas Thornycroft. The Prince commissioned works from both husband and wife. Thomas Thornycroft's large equestrian group of Queen Victoria was given pride of place at the Great Exhibition in 1851. It was later decided to publish this group as a bronze statuette, with the substitution of a feathered hat for the crown worn by the Queen in the full-size sculpture. The reduced version was shown to the royal couple at Windsor in November 1853. The sculptor recorded that the Prince 'suggested an improvement to which I assented, and taking a modelling tool, H.R.H. set to work'.[111] Some years later the Prince explained his fondness for sculpture to his eldest daughter, the Princess Royal, who had recently married and moved to Germany. 'That you take delight in modelling does not surprise me. As an art it is even more attractive than painting, because in it the thought is actually incorporated.'[112] When Mary Thornycroft was

Queen Victoria's set of orange-blossom jewellery, made of frosted gold, with small enamelled green oranges and white porcelain blossom, was made to Prince Albert's designs for presentation to the Queen from 1839.

working on a bust portrait of Princess Alice in 1861, the Prince Consort assisted her by providing a 'caricatured' profile portrait, stressing her somewhat long and pointed nose.[113] This slight sketch is probably the last design that has come down to us from the Prince's hand.

Prince Albert was also active in providing designs for decorative metalwork. He devised the charming set of enamelled orange-blossom jewellery which he presented to the Queen from 1839. The original orange sprig brooch (an engagement gift) was followed by a circlet (for their sixth wedding anniversary) and earrings.[114] A grandiose gilt centrepiece, incorporating miniature portraits of four of the royal dogs, was made to the Prince's design by Garrard Jewellers in 1842. Ten years later the massive table fountain depicting 'Arabs leading Horses to Water' was made by the same firm, under Prince Albert's direction.[115]

It was appropriate and only natural that Prince Albert should also have been closely involved with the design of the various royal residences. The first project with which he was intimately involved was probably his father's mausoleum at Coburg,

Osborne House on the Isle of Wight was largely Prince Albert's creation. With the London builder Thomas Cubitt, he worked painstakingly on new designs for the house from the time of the purchase of the estate in 1845. This pen and ink sketch was made by the Prince in 1849.

This design for a new house on the Osborne estate appears to be entirely in Prince Albert's hand.

'erected by the whole family, after Albert's & Ernest's designs, in the Italian style'.[116] While it was being built in the 1850s, Prince Albert was hard at work on plans for the newly acquired country retreats at Osborne and Balmoral. Early in 1845 it was reported that 'The Prince makes plans with Mr Cubitt' (Thomas Cubitt, the London builder) for a new house at Osborne,[117] and Prince Albert's design for a lodge to Barton Farm, on the

Osborne estate, has survived in the British Museum.[118] With A. H. Humbert (1822-77), the architect of the mausoleum for the Duchess of Kent (and later of that for Prince Albert himself) at Frogmore, the Prince is said to have designed the new church at Whippingham, near Osborne, built 1854-5. At Balmoral the architect was William Smith from Aberdeen, but the Prince was again involved in every last detail of the design so that by 1856, when building work was almost complete, the Queen could report that '*all* has become my dearest Albert's *own* creation, own work, own building, own laying out, as at *Osborne*; and his great taste, and the impress of his dear hand, have been stamped everywhere.'[119]

4

THE NEXT GENERATION

Prince Albert's meticulous, almost obsessive, concern with all that went on around him was doubtless a contributory factor to the illness leading to his early death in December 1861. With the Queen and their mentor Baron Stockmar (1787-1863), he devised a comprehensive plan for the education of the royal children, which included the teaching of drawing and painting. The princesses – particularly Victoria, Alice and Louise – were more responsive to the royal couple's encouragement of and interest in the arts than were the princes. At the time of her father's death the Princess Royal (1840-1901) was already established in her own home, following her marriage in 1858 to Prince Frederick William (1831-88), son of the Prince of Prussia, while Princess Alice was engaged to be married to another German princeling, Prince Louis of Hesse. The correspondence of the two eldest daughters reveals the extent to which they (and their mother) continued to value the opinion of their father. The Queen turned to the Princess Royal for help as 'you know his taste. You have inherited it.'[1] For each of the memorial projects instigated by the Queen during the months after her 'great loss', the Princess Royal acted either as the initial inspiration and designer, or as the mentor on whose artistic judgement the Queen depended.

As her parents' eldest child, exceptional care had been taken over the Princess Royal's upbringing. By the age of three she could speak both English and French fluently, and soon thereafter had mastered German as well. Her first drawing and painting lessons were from the artists who taught (and painted for) her parents:[2] Leitch, for instance, instructed her in landscape painting. In April 1852, however, the illustrator and water-colour artist Edward Henry Corbould (1815-1905) was appointed drawing master to the princes and princesses, a position which he occupied until 1866 at least. He became touchingly attached to his royal pupils, and faithfully preserved their juvenile artistic efforts. The majority of their works outside the immediate circle of the royal family can indeed be traced back to Corbould.

In 1853, the year after Corbould's lessons began, his impact on the Princess Royal's paintings can clearly be seen. The meticulous watercolour portrait of her third brother, Prince Arthur, in Tudor dress is dated 10 February 1853 and was evidently a wedding anniversary present to her parents (Plate 1).[3] The Queen described the gift as a 'beautiful sketch almost entirely by herself, of little Arthur as "King Hal" from

Corbould's pencil drawing, dated September 1835, was the model for the romantic scene painted by his pupil, the Princess Royal, 'expressly' for her future husband, Prince Frederick of Prussia, in 1853.

Nature',[4] and it is not difficult to identify the guiding hand of Corbould. Princess Victoria's gifts for the Queen's birthday that year do not appear to have survived. The proud mother commented at the time: 'Vicky's drawing of a Christ's head is wonderfully done & the little sketch of herself, in her riding dress [is] very nicely drawn & coloured.'[5] In July 1853 the Princess Royal, then aged only twelve, drew and coloured a charmingly romantic drawing and inscribed it 'to my dear good Fritz'. Prince Frederick William of Prussia had first met the Princess in 1851, when he had visited London with his father to see the Great Exhibition. He was evidently smitten with the

A romantic scene drawn by the twelve-year-old Princess Royal two years after her first meeting with Prince Frederick William of Prussia in 1851. It was copied from a drawing by her teacher, Corbould, and is inscribed 'to my dear good Fritz, as a souvenir of his very loving English sister'. The couple did not become formally engaged for another two years, and were married in January 1858.

Princess Royal, and his father returned to England in 1853 to discuss a possible marriage alliance with the Queen. The Princess Royal's drawing, which is now part of the Hesse Archives at Fulda, is a touching document to her own early affection for the Prince.[6] Elsewhere in the same collection is Corbould's original outline drawing on which the Princess's watercolour was based.[7]

The Princess Royal and Frederick William became formally engaged in September 1855, by which time both Britain and Prussia were involved in the Crimean War. The Patriotic Fund for the dependants of the soldiers fighting in the Crimea, which had been set up in 1854, looked for assistance wherever it could find it. In April 1855 an exhibition of paintings by amateur artists was staged at the Bond Street premises of the picture dealer Ernest Gambart. Such was the success of the exhibition that in early May it was transferred to Burlington House, Piccadilly, where it remained on view for a further two months. Revenue from admission fees and catalogue sales was passed on to the Patriotic Fund, as were the proceeds from the sale of the exhibited works. 'Under the sanction of her Majesty, drawings by members of the Royal Family' were included in the exhibitions.[8] The Prince of Wales contributed 'The Knight', which fetched 55 guineas. The artefacts of Prince Alfred and Princesses Alice and Helena (then aged 11, 12 and 9 respectively) were sold for 30 guineas apiece. But pride of place went to the Princess Royal's large finished watercolour entitled *The Field of Battle*, which was purchased for 250 guineas. The painting was originally to have shown a wounded Greek warrior attended by a maiden, but at Corbould's suggestion the warrior was transformed into a British grenadier.[9] Permission was given for the painting to be published in chromolithography, and the resulting prints sold for one guinea each, also in aid of the Patriotic Fund.[10] (See illustration p. 26.) The *Illustrated London News* had described the Princess's painting as 'by far the best drawing in the room . . . The composition is artistic, the sentiment poetic, and the execution spirited.'[11]

Prince Albert personally tutored the Princess Royal for one hour each day during the period of her engagement. The bond between father and daughter was extremely close: after Prince Albert's death the Princess Royal declared: 'I am but beginning life and the unerring judgment on which I built with so much confidence for now and for the future is gone! Where shall I look to for advice?'[12] Following her marriage she reminded the Queen of her drawing of the balcony scene in *Romeo and Juliet*, 'which dear Papa helped me with so kindly, – do you remember – one day when you came back from the Drawing room Papa washed out the sky with a sponge?'[13] Her lessons (including those with Corbould and Leitch) continued to form the well regulated pattern of the Princess's days.[14] There are watercolour sketches of Osborne, Balmoral and Aldershot, and costume studies made during the Royal Family's private sailing trip to Normandy in August 1857. One of the Princess Royal's gifts for the Queen's birthday in 1856 was a fan, the field painted with flowers and allegorical figures by the donor (Plate 12).[15] The following August, Princess Victoria painted a watercolour view of the Solent from the terrace at Osborne, during the course of a lesson with W. L. Leitch, her mother's sketching teacher for the last ten years.[16] In 1857 another of the Princess's watercolours, entitled 'The Wise and Foolish Virgins', was published in chromolithography.

On 11 January 1858 the Princess Royal inscribed a fine pencil drawing 'for Mr Corbould the Last Time' (see p. 31).[17] Two weeks later the Princess was married, and found herself abruptly transferred to a very different domestic setting. On 5 March she wrote to her father from Berlin: 'I confess I could not live as the rest do here, in busy idleness, without rest, without work, doing no good, and at the end of the day – knocked up and tired – the next morning a headache!'[18] Shortly after her arrival in Germany the previous month Princess Victoria had confided to her mother: 'I dare not talk of painting it brings back to me a thousand recollections of pleasant hours, of which now nothing but the recollection remains, oh how my heart aches sometimes at the thought of all I have left behind.'[19] Feelings such as these, expressed rather too frequently during her years in Germany, did little to endear her to the Prussians, who grew to consider her influence on her husband, the charming but inactive 'Fritz', nothing short of malevolent. In her efforts to dispel her unhappiness, the newly married Princess busied herself in various ways, and her letters home make constant references to work in hand. (See also Plate 13.) Occasionally the Princess illustrated these letters with drawings to acquaint her mother with details such as the layout of her rooms at Berlin,[20] or the seating arrangements at Princess Alexandrine of Prussia's confirmation service.[21] The Princess Royal's watercolour of her boudoir in Berlin (dated 1858) was given to Helen Paterson, the Princesses' Dresser.[22] Soon after her arrival in Germany she acquired a new drawing teacher, Carl Gottfried Pfannschmidt (1819-87), but he was often engaged on work

*In 1858 the Princess Royal
sent home this view from her
new boudoir in Berlin.*

away from Berlin or Potsdam, where Prince and Princess
Frederick William were chiefly resident. In November and
December 1861 she was hard at work on drawings intended,
pathetically, as her father's Christmas presents. 'Having no Mr
Corbould to direct me they will be but poor productions and
not fit to be seen by the side of those of my sisters.'[23]

During these early years in Germany highly finished watercolours of the 'Finding of Moses' or 'Romeo and Juliet' are
interspersed with sketches of the christening of the first child,
William (the future Kaiser), early in 1859, views of Coburg

The Princess Royal portrayed her first child, the future Emperor William II, on numerous occasions, just as the small Princess had herself been sketched by Queen Victoria.

during a visit in September 1860 (which coincided with Queen Victoria and Prince Albert's own holiday there), and scenes from an extensive trip to Italy and North Africa in autumn 1862 (Plates 10, 11 and 42). The Princess Royal lent her mother a group of sketches from this holiday in January 1863. They were '*merest sketches* but as the names are written underneath you will see what they are. I have *merely kept* them as *souvenirs* as they are much too bad for anything else.'[24] Meanwhile, in spite of her mother's advice to the contrary, Princess Victoria had been active in painting pictures in oils, explaining that she hoped 'to improve myself by so doing – the oil painting will be of great use to my water colour painting, it is therefore that I do it.'[25] Her early instruction from Corbould, who handled watercolour paint in a very similar way to the oil medium, meant that the division between the two techniques was less distinct for the Princess than for her mother. However, she frequently bewailed the fact that because there was no studio at Potsdam her oil painting was confined to their residence at Berlin.

The Princess Royal returned to England for a brief visit in May 1859, and may have had further lessons with Corbould at this time.[26] During her stay in London, the Royal Family went to a performance of Shakespeare's *Henry V* at the Princess's Theatre.[27] The Princess Royal quickly worked up her sketches made on this occasion into a finished watercolour of 'The Attack on Harfleur', presented to the Queen as a late birthday present on 1 June, the eve of her departure for Germany.[28] Once home in Berlin she worked on another scene from this play, 'The Entry into Harfleur', and this too was presented to her parents.[29] Two years previously, as an unmarried girl, the Princess had been amongst the royal party which had attended the performance of *Richard II* at the same theatre. In retrospect, she declared: 'I do not know when a thing made such an impression on me.'[30] At the time, the performance had inspired her watercolour of 'The Entry of Bolingbroke into London', which was a birthday gift to the Queen in May 1857.[31] This must have been based on a number of preparatory sketches, similar to one (entitled 'Scene during the Tournament, Richard II') which the Princess Royal gave to Corbould at Osborne in May 1857.[32] At the end of 1859 the Princess wrote to ask her mother for the loan of her Theatrical Album, which contained (and still contains) the watercolours and photographs of theatrical performances to which the Queen had been since 1852.[33] The watercolours, which were commissioned by the Queen, are chiefly by Corbould and the Swedish artist Egron Lundgren (1815-75).[34] They were presumably therefore matters for discussion during royal drawing lessons, particularly because the princesses had also been present at the performances to which the watercolours relate. The album of Princess Victoria's drawings and watercolours entitled 'Souvenirs of Richard II, given at the Princess's Theatre, 1857',[35] may therefore date from 1857 or from 1859. But in no case are her pictures precise copies of those in her mother's album. There are always significant differences.[36] (See also Plate 41.)

In January 1861 the incapacitated King Frederick William IV of Prussia died, to be succeeded by his brother (who had ruled as Regent since 1858) as King William I. As the eldest son, 'Fritz' was now Crown Prince of Prussia. In autumn 1863, the Crown Prince and Princess revisited Coburg and again coincided with a visit which Queen Victoria was herself making (Plate 8). Another visitor from England at this time was the watercolour painter William Callow (1812-1908), who had taught various members of the Orléans family in France during the 1830s and 1840s, and continued his tuition in their exile at Claremont in the 1850s (see pp. 20-1). He had encountered the English Royal Family at exhibitions in London in the 1850s and the opportunity of inviting Callow to Potsdam for a brief series of lessons was eagerly seized on by the Crown Princess. Callow describes his visit, and his abrupt reception by the Prussian courtiers, in his autobiography.[37] On the first day of lessons, 3 September 1863, he had been told to report at the Neues

Palais, Potsdam, at 8 a.m. He sketched with the Crown Princess in the grounds before breakfast, and then moved on to the nearby palace of Sans-Souci and the Belvedere for more painting. After dinner (at 3 p.m.) there was a sketching expedition to the Ile des Faisans, which involved a crossing by punt. On the following day rain forced Callow to paint indoors. Princess Victoria added a figure (intended as a self-portrait) to his watercolour of a vista through a series of reception rooms in the Palace.[38] Callow left soon after, but returned to Berlin in 1874 and was invited to join the Crown Prince and Princess on a sketching expedition. Thereafter 'I had the honour of dining with them. The Princess showed me some of her paintings and sketches in oil, which were excellent.'[39] The Crown Princess's oil painting of Sans-Souci in the Royal Collection is dated 1874 and probably dates from Callow's visit (Plate 44).[40]

During their visits to Scotland, Queen Victoria's sons-in-law were expected to wear Highland dress. The Princess Royal's study of 'Fritz' was probably made in September 1863.

By 1872 the Princess Royal's family was complete. She gave birth to a total of eight children, four boys and four girls. The fourth child, Sigismund (1864-6) and the sixth, Waldemar (1869-79) did not live to adulthood. Throughout these years the Crown Princess attempted to keep up with her painting and drawing, but there was rarely adequate time. In April 1867 she informed her mother:

> I have quite lost the habit I had of scribbling on bits of paper for amusement. I paint a large oil picture now and then when I can give all my attention to it – and do that in a studio which is lent me – and when I get Home I have too much to do ever to make me feel inclined to draw.[41]

Nevertheless, the Princess found time to paint a portrait of her second son, Prince Henry (1862-1929), for her mother in August of the same year.[42]

Following the early success of the Princess's contribution to the Patriotic Fund, there are a number of references in the 1860s and 1870s to her contributions to charity exhibitions, and to the publication of her paintings for charitable purposes. In May 1864 she was at work on a series of four pictures of soldiers specifically intended for reproduction in lithography (by Carl Süssnapp) in aid of the Crown Prince's Fund on behalf of those wounded (or widowed) during the recent war against Denmark. The lithographs could be acquired at three Thalers for the set, or one Thaler for individual prints. Her chamberlain, the dramatist Gustav Pulitz, described the series in a letter to his wife in July 1864:

It is a memorial to the victory of Düppel [on 18 April 1864, after which the whole of Schleswig was ceded to Prussia], and represents 4 soldiers each belonging to a different arm of the service. The first is shown before the attack in the morning; the second is waving the flag at noon; the third, wounded,

In 1864 a set of four lithographs were published in aid of the Crown Prince's Fund for the victims of the recent Danish war. The prints reproduced pictures made specifically for this purpose by the Crown Princess. In each case a single soldier was represented, at various stages of the conflict.

LEFT: Plate 26. *This study was made by the fourteen-year-old Princess Victoria at Kensington Palace. The simplicity of the subject (a glazed earthenware jug) recalls the severe economic measures undertaken by the Duchess of Kent to maintain her court.*

ABOVE LEFT: Plate 27. *Marie Taglioni, the creator of romantic ballet, was Princess Victoria's idol in the 1830s. On 8 July 1834, after a morning ride (on 'my pretty new horse Taglioni') the Princess went to the opera and saw part of* Anna Bolena, *followed by the ballet* Le Pouvoir de la danse ou la Nouvelle Therpsichore *'in which Taglioni again danced most beautifully and looked very lovely . . . I was very much amused indeed.' Thereafter the Princess made a series of studies, adding little dabs of watercolour for the flowers on the hair and dress.*

ABOVE RIGHT: Plate 28. *On 26 December 1833 Princess Victoria was taken to the Drury Lane Theatre to see Mr Ducrow performing as St George in the 'grand Christmas spectacle called St George & the Dragon'. She worked up this sketch of 'The combat between St George and the Dragon' at home in Kensington Palace. In her journal she had commented that Mr Ducrow 'acted uncommonly well & rode beautifully . . . The horses were beautifully trained; & Mr. Ducrow's fight with the dragon, on horseback, was quite beautiful; the horse reared almost erect & never started or shied at the fiery Dragon which came flapping & biting about him.'*

RIGHT: Plate 29. *At the end of their summer holiday in 1835 the Duchess of Kent and her daughter stayed in Ramsgate. In early October the Princess succumbed to typhoid and spent the next three months recovering. She received a gift of paint brushes from 'dear Aunt Louise' in early November, and soon felt well enough to draw and paint again. Her subjects included 'several funny little French boys running about' near the harbour.*

ABOVE: Plate 30. *Queen Victoria's first lessons specifically in watercolour painting took place at Osborne House in 1846. Two years later, under the continuing instruction of W. L. Leitch, she made this sketch of the house from the valley footpath.*

ABOVE: Plate 31. *The view from Osborne across the Solent was frequently drawn and painted by the Queen and her children. This study was made in August 1848.*

LEFT: Plate 32. *The shadows of varying colours and hues on these rocks on the sea shore were sketched by Queen Victoria, in September 1848, according to the principles laid down in Leitch's illustrated lessons. The Queen recorded in her journal 'taking another walk down to the sea. – Had a lesson from Leitch.'*

LEFT: Plate 33. *The six eldest children of Queen Victoria, drawn by their mother in the garden at Osborne, June 1850.*

RIGHT: Plate 34. *After spending the first part of their summer holiday at Osborne, the Royal Family would move north to Scotland. This view, from Craig Gowan along the Dee towards Abergeldie, was taken in 1848, the year of the Queen's acquisition of the lease of the Balmoral estate.*

BELOW: Plate 35. *The Queen was taught to draw in coloured chalk (or pastels) by Edwin Landseer. In this drawing she portrayed Jane Mackenzie at Balmoral, on 22 September 1851.*

ABOVE RIGHT: Plate 36. *During the summer holidays in 1856, the Royal Family spent a week in the Royal Yacht* Victoria and Albert, *sailing along the south coast of England. The Queen recorded the costume of women seated in a boat on the river Tamar (not the Dart, as noted in the inscription). In her journal she observed 'The Women about Saltash & along the river wear picturesque linen bonnets'.*

BELOW RIGHT: Plate 37. *During the Royal Family's visit to Coburg in the autumn of 1860 the Queen made a number of sketches. The Rosenau, shown here, was Prince Albert's birthplace.*

ABOVE: Plate 38. *The Queen's sketching activity continued practically unabated after the Prince Consort's death. In October 1864 she painted this moonlit view from her window at Balmoral.*

ABOVE: Plate 40. *Queen Victoria frequently walked in the gardens of Frogmore House (in the Home Park at Windsor), the site of the mausoleums of both her mother and her husband. She made this sketch of summer foliage in 1867.*

BELOW: Plate 39. *Prince Albert's early sketchbooks are full of military subjects, whether independent uniform studies or battle scenes such as the present one. It is dated 1832, the year in which the twelve-year-old Prince began his studies at Bonn University.*

LEFT: Plate 41. *The Princess Royal was greatly moved by the performance of* Richard II *which she attended with her parents in 1857. This sketch was one of a large number made by the Princess as a record of the play.*

BELOW: Plate 42. *The Crown Prince and Princess of Prussia would frequently spend their summer holidays in the newly-acquired region of Schleswig-Holstein. This harvesting scene was painted by the Crown Princess (i.e. the Princess Royal) at Niblum in August 1865.*

BELOW: Plate 43. *In 1877 the Princess Royal sent her mother this portrait of a Nubian named 'Mohammad', whom she had painted in Berlin. His dramatic features were further intensified by back-lighting.*

ABOVE: Plate 44. *This oil painting of Sans-Souci, in the grounds of the Neues Palais, Potsdam, was painted by the Princess Royal in 1874, probably during the visit of the artist William Callow. It was sent to the dealer Algernon Graves in London by the Princess, to be sold in aid of one of the German charities.*

BELOW LEFT: Plate 46. *This title-page was illuminated by Princess Alice for her husband, Prince Louis of Hesse, in 1865. Similar decoration was applied by the Princess to sacred and profane texts from the mid-1860s.*

BELOW RIGHT: Plate 47. *In 1875, Princess Alice (in Darmstadt) began to receive lessons from Ruskin (in Oxford), who would let her have drawings to copy and would then make notes on the reverse of the copies intended to assist and inspire her work. Ruskin's comments were invariably too effusive to be of any great help to the Princess. Of this watercolour he wrote: 'the colour of the lower four petals are excellent, and the foreshortenings all as good as can be.'*

ABOVE: Plate 45. *The seventeen-year-old Princess Alice became engaged to be married to Prince Louis of Hesse in November 1860 and commemorated the event in this charming watercolour. Owing to Prince Albert's death, the wedding did not take place until July 1862.*

BELOW LEFT: Plate 48. *Princess Alice kept a chronicle of the main events in the lives of herself and her husband from 1862 to 1871. A vellum page would be devoted to illustrations of the year's events, as recounted in the beautifully calligraphed accompanying text. During 1869, the subject of the present page, Prince Louis and his brother-in-law 'Fritz' of Prussia attended the opening of the Suez Canal (on the left), while Princess Alice and her sister, the Princess Royal, stayed in Cannes (on the right).*

BELOW RIGHT: Plate 49. *By the following year, 1870, the tone of Princess Alice's 'Hauschronik' had changed dramatically. The names of the major battles of the Franco-Prussian war occupy the upper part of the page. Below, to the left, one of the military hospitals set up by Princess Alice is shown, while her short-lived second son Prince Frederick lies on his mother's lap, lower right.*

RIGHT: Plate 50. *Princess Louise, the most professional artist among Queen Victoria's daughters, continued to paint throughout her life. This page is from a small group of studies made during a cruise down the Nile in 1906.*

BELOW: Plate 51. *A door in Rideau Hall, Ottawa, that formerly led into Princess Louise's 'blue parlour', painted with a branch of foliage by the Princess. As the official residence of the Governor-General of Canada, Rideau Hall was the home of the Princess and her husband, the Marquess of Lorne, Governor-General from 1878 to 1883.*

ABOVE: Plate 52. *This painting entitled* Battlefield, Crimea *by the Prince of Wales is reminiscent of the painting of* The Field of Battle *by the Prince's elder sister, Victoria, contributed to the Patriotic Fund exhibition in the same year, 1855 (see p. 26). However, the Prince's pictures were always more linear and less assured, recalling the careful guidance provided by his teacher Corbould.*

LEFT: Plate 53. *Prince Alfred, Duke of Edinburgh, received a series of drawing lessons from Alfred C. Snape of Gosport from 1858 to 1860, presumably intended principally to equip him to make sketches in his naval log (see pages 5 and 6). This watercolour of sailing boats on the Solent, with Osborne House in the middle distance, was a birthday gift from the thirteen-year-old Prince to the Queen in 1858.*

ABOVE: Plate 54. *Towards the end of the nineteenth century, after Leitch's death in 1883, a change is apparent in the Princess of Wales's watercolours. In common with her nieces, the Edinburgh and the Connaught girls, she drew still-lifes, invariably on long, narrow sheets of paper or drawing boards.*

LEFT: Plate 55. *Like each of her sisters-in-law the Princess of Wales (later Queen Alexandra) received lessons in watercolour painting from Leitch. In the autumn of 1863 he reported that 'her Royal Highness takes to the drawing with great heartiness, and gets on exceedingly well'.*

BELOW: Plate 56. *This carefully composed page is from the Princess of Wales's album recording a Norwegian cruise in 1893. It consists of watercolours and photographs, together with an account of the cruise, in every case the work of the Princess herself.*

is listening to a hymn in the afternoon; while the fourth, victorious with a laurel wreath, stands in the evening at an open grave . . . The conception shows real genius, and it is carried out most artistically.[43]

The Crown Princess realized there would be no point in attempting to sell the prints in England, for 'who would buy one of those inhuman monsters who butcher women and children', but she would send the Queen a set if she liked.[44] At the time of the exhibition in 1870 at the New British Institution, London, in aid of the Destitute Widows and Orphans of Germans killed during the Franco-Prussian War, the Crown Princess undertook to act as patron, and to distribute the funds resulting from the venture. On this occasion her own exhibits were a pair of oils entitled *St Elizabeth distributing alms* and *The Church Door*, a watercolour called 'Widowed and Childless', and lastly 'Little Anglers', painted inside a shell valve. The first three items were sold by lottery, and the shell painting was purchased by the Rajah of Kolapore.[45] Princess Louise also sent several works to this exhibition (see p. 150).

There was evidently a fresh bout of painting activity during the 1870s. In 1872 the Crown Princess sent Queen Victoria three still life paintings of fruit, which are in the Print Room at Windsor:

> They are Copies after magnificent sketches done at Venice – by one of our rising Artists here called 'Knillee' . . . I admired them so much that I asked him to lend them to me, & have tried very hard at copying them for you, . . . I will also give Fritz a portfolio of the sketches I did this Autumn while we were at Wiesbaden – just to show you. They are very inferior I know as Landscape is *not* exactly my line.[46]

Kaiser William II mentioned his mother's lessons with Knillee in his autobiography, and recalled visits to his studio.[47]

During the 1873 summer holidays, spent on the island of Föhr off the west coast of Schleswig-Holstein, the Crown Princess had a few lessons from the local artist Christian Karl Magnussen (1821-96), 'for one can always learn, and I find his hints normally very useful'.[48] At around the same time Heinrich von Angeli (1840-1925) began teaching the Princess to paint in oils. She had first encountered the artist at the great International Exhibition at Vienna, and thereafter invited him to Potsdam both to paint and to teach. He was so successful in the latter that even the Crown Prince began to draw. Early in 1874, following Winterhalter's death the previous year, the Crown Princess told her mother that von Angeli: 'really is the first portrait painter alive now – and universally admitted as such in Germany'.[49] Two years later she presented the artist with a meticulous watercolour copy of Holbein's oil portrait of the German merchant Georg Gisze, which was then (as now) in Berlin (illustrated p. 15).[50] The following year, in a long letter to her mother about the pleasure which her painting brought her, the Princess wrote:

> Of course it is of the greatest imaginable value to me to watch G. [*sic*] von Angeli paint! If I could have a few regular lessons from him I know I should get on, he is the best master living! I write down notes for myself of all I see him do, of the colours he uses & the way he goes to work, – and of the remarks he makes & I refer to these when I work on alone.[51] . . . Painting in oils is my happiness and delight and if only I had a proper *atelier* and good light – the right models at hand and regular lessons, I should in 2 or 3 years perhaps be able to do something tolerable.[52]

In the spring of 1875 the Crown Prince and Princess visited Italy. This trip included a prolonged stay in Venice, where they encountered the German painter Anton von Werner (1843-1915):

> He records that the Princess drew and painted with real industry, now sketching the unequalled treasures of the past, now studying the effects of light or shade on the canals or in the square of St Mark's. The painter was astonished not only at the Princess's powers of technique, but also at her artistic sympathy and feeling. She seemed to know intuitively what would make a fine sketch.[53]

On a subsequent visit to Italy, in the winter of 1879-80, the Princess painted 'a little Italian *contadino* . . . with the vigour and boldness of an accomplished artist'.[54] In 1880 this portrait was submitted to the exhibition of the Institute of Painters in Watercolour, of which the Crown Princess had recently become a member.

A number of oil portraits of members of the Princess's immediate family were made in the 1870s. In her sitting room at Friedrichshof there are large paintings of Prince William

(1859-1941), and Princesses Charlotte (1860-1919), Victoria (1866-1929) and Margaret (1872-1954). The last is dated 1876. In the Royal Collection there are other portraits of Princesses Victoria (dated 1878) and Charlotte (dated 1879), in addition to the head of Prince Henry (dated 1867) noted above. There is also the half-length portrait of the Crown Princess's niece, Princess Marie of Edinburgh (later Queen of Roumania, 1875-1938), which she sent to Queen Victoria in September 1881, during a visit to the Isle of Wight. She regretted

> It does not do the lovely Child justice in any way – & I am afraid I have not got the likeness! The painting is very rough, and to make it presentable I ought to have had 3 more sittings, but you know how great the hurry was . . . Besides the light in my round drawing room was *very bad* for painting – out of doors wd. have been so much better but the weather prevented that.[55]

The Crown Princess had earlier sent her mother a remarkable portrait of a Nubian, which now hangs at Osborne House, although the artist evidently expected it to be taken to Scotland (Plate 43).[56]

> The man who sat to me was indeed splendid, I wish you could have seen him, he is as tall as Cowley & much broader, only 24, and *just* come from Algiers with a painter called Prof. Gantz [?] – who only paints oriental subjects. – I was so struck when I saw this man that I thought I wd. try & do a study for you, but it is alas nothing but a mere big sketch & very hasty . . . The man is called 'Mohammad'.[57]

The Crown Princess described how she 'worked away sometimes 4 hours at a stretch to get it done; sitting with an umbrella over my head to shade my eyes – as my model sat with his back to the window'.[58]

In the course of the following year the Crown Princess's brother, Prince Arthur, became engaged to be married to Princess Louise Margaret of Prussia, a first cousin of the Crown Prince. During the negotiations leading up to the marriage Prince Arthur's private secretary, Sir Howard Elphinstone, visited the Crown Princess at Potsdam. Elphinstone and the Crown Princess shared a common interest in art. He wrote home to his wife:

Seeing the Princess paint has made me long to imitate her and to have a couple of hours daily . . . The Princess Royal has kindly promised to paint a picture for us, for our dining room in the future house . . . She several times said that she would like to dress you up as a Puritan, or North German peasant girl, and draw your picture, as those dresses would suit you to perfection, and make such a pretty picture.[59]

During this visit Sir Howard painted one of the rooms at Potsdam. As with Callow's Potsdam interior of 1863, the Princess added a figure to the finished picture, on this occasion a portrait of Sir Howard, seated sketching.[60] Early the following year Sir Howard reported that the Princess 'has finished the picture for the hall [of Prince Arthur's house] at Bagshot, and very clever it is'.[61] He also 'saw her drawing another huge skeleton figure. This time the side view, to obtain correct knowledge of the muscles. She is most patient in her work and her memory is wonderful, this drawing will prove of the utmost use to her.'[62]

The Princess Royal painted a number of still lifes or landscapes as gifts for family and friends. A large still life was destined for the dining room of her eldest daughter Charlotte, following her marriage in 1878.[63] A pair of decorative views of the castles at Windsor and Kronborg (Queen Alexandra's first home) were sent to England in 1881. They were intended as overdoors for the Prince of Wales's new dining room at Marlborough House. The Crown Princess wrote: 'I am much disappointed with the result though they have given me no end of trouble. I only hope they will be good enough to be put up in that lovely room.'[64] An article on the Princess's paintings in the German magazine *Gartenlaube* for 1885 included illustrations of three recent works: a female portrait, a view of Pegli near Genoa dated 1879, and a still life entitled 'Perishableness' dated 1882.[65]

During the 1880s the Crown Prince developed cancer of the throat so that by the time of his father's death in March 1888, he was terminally ill. He ruled as the Emperor Frederick III for only three months, himself to be succeeded by his eldest son, Prince William, 'Kaiser Bill'. The Empress Frederick (as the Princess Royal was now known) soon decided to leave Berlin for the freedom of the Taunus mountains to the north-west of Frankfurt. She knew the area well already, from her frequent visits to nearby Bad Homburg, previously the home of another English Princess, the Landgravine Elizabeth. She acquired an estate at Kronberg, and during the next decade built herself a vast country house in the style of Norman Shaw. The Empress called her new home 'Friedrichshof', Frederick's court. It was designed (by the Berlin architect Ihne) to the Empress's specific requirements, adorned with her painted decoration, and served as a perfect showcase for her extensive art collection and library. Among the pictures that still adorn the walls of the house are numerous examples of her own handiwork, both in oil and watercolour, dating from her last years. At Friedrichshof she surrounded herself with friends and companions – including artists such as Hermann Corrodi – and continued to paint.[66] She travelled extensively in Europe throughout her life, whether to visit her family in England and elsewhere, or for the sunshine and relaxation of the Mediterranean. There was an added incentive to 'go south' after 1889, when her third daughter Sophie married Prince Constantine, later King of the Hellenes. The Princess Royal made frequent visits to Paris, either incognita or in high Prussian state. During a much-publicized and not entirely successful trip in 1891 she was entertained by a number of artists, including Bonnat, Detaille and Carolus-Duran. In October 1898, while staying with her mother at Balmoral, she drew some pastel portraits of the gillies. She also 'did a beautiful head of Dr Storey', the Principal of Glasgow University, who had been invited to preach at the Castle.[67] As the century was drawing to a close, the Empress Frederick became aware that she had contracted the same fateful disease that had killed her husband. Queen Victoria died (aged 81) on 22 January 1901. The Empress Frederick outlived her by a mere 6½ months, and died (aged 60) on 5 August 1901.

Throughout her life, but especially during the early years of her marriage, the Princess Royal was active in both sculpture and design. And like each of her siblings she was taught to sew, working a quilt for the Queen in 1858 and two cushions for the Blue Room at Windsor (in which the Prince Consort died) in May 1864. Another minor application of her artistic talents was apparently fostered during a visit to England in the early 1870s, when 'she took lessons in painting on pottery from a lady artist resident in Chelsea.'[68] Her first lessons in sculpture probably took place in England. Following her marriage she had modelling lessons from Hugo Hagen (1820–71), the chief assistant and pupil of the recently deceased Christian Daniel Rauch (1777–1857), from whom Queen Victoria and Prince Albert had acquired various pieces.[69] In the four years between her marriage and Prince Albert's death a number of pieces of her own sculpture (usually casts, rather than originals) were sent home by the Princess, in the hopes that they might be approved of (or at least accepted) by her parents. During 1860 the correspondence mentions a small group of the Princes in the Tower, a profile of Countess Lynar, some bas reliefs, and a bust of Prince William (born the previous year). The latter, which was sent as the Queen's Christmas present, was to be placed against a dark background and should not be lit from both sides as (she informed her father), 'it is not well done . . . it was a difficult business as I could never have him for more than 10 minutes at a time at most and then he was screaming almost all the time.'[70] The following spring some painted bas reliefs were despatched. Prince Albert showed them to the Italian sculptor Carlo Marochetti (1805-67), and they received his approval. The Princess asked her mother to ensure that 'dear Papa will place them in a good light to look at them as so much depends upon that. I know there is a great prejudice against painted sculpture and an objection usually raised is that it is a corruption of taste. I own I cannot share this opinion. I think nature shows that this is a mistake & that form & colour ought to go together, the ancients thought so too.'[71]

In June, Prince Albert received the Princess Royal's bust of her mother-in-law, the Queen of Prussia, with a request that he 'show it to Winterhalter as he was there while I was working at it and Winterhalter's advice was of the *greatest* use to me'.[72] Since the end of 1860 the Princess had been working on a bust of the Empress Charlotte of Russia, one of her husband's aunts, which had been commissioned by the Prince Regent following the Empress's death that November. The bust was to be made 'from recollection, with only 2 little photographs and a Lithograph of Winterhalter's Picture for Guides, – it was not easy I can assure you but it is finished, and I think has succeeded pretty well'.[73] The 'very beautiful piece of sculpture – a female figure pouring water from a ewer' mentioned in Leitch's biography as a gift from the Princess Royal, may also have been produced at around this time.[74]

After the shattering news of Prince Albert's death the Princess's abilities were much employed.[75] Before two weeks had elapsed she wrote promising to send the Queen two sketches for 'the dear Mausoleum of which you speak'.[76] Three days later she informed her mother: 'Tomorrow I shall see Mr Gruner – I shall explain all my ideas to him and I shall give him my sketches which I have had corrected by our first architect here.'[77] She agreed with the Queen that the mausoleum should be in the style of that at Coburg (partly designed by Princes Albert and Ernest), and hoped to be allowed 'to contribute in some measure to beautifying it'.[78] The Prince's effigy, recumbent on a sarcophagus, was to be in the centre of the mausoleum. Baron Marochetti was chosen to produce the effigy, according to a preliminary drawing by the Princess Royal. After examining photographs of the Baron's figure, she commented: 'It is just what I imagined it when I drew the very imperfect sketch at Osborne.'[79] The Princess Royal was also responsible for the original conception for Theed's group of the Queen and Prince in Anglo-Saxon dress, which is now somewhat incongruously placed in the ambulatory of the mausoleum (1863-7).[80] In early 1863 she was at work on her own bust of 'darling Papa': 'It is a work which completely engrosses me and about which I feel very nervous as, if it should fail, it will be a great disappointment.' She wished that the Queen was there to give advice, as Professor Hagen never saw the Prince 'so he can hardly judge the likeness'. The Princess Royal's work was based on the earlier busts by Theed and Marochetti. She considered that 'though both are full of valuable truths; Marochetti's is the better work of art but the other is much more like.' She hoped that the Queen would order it to be sculpted in marble (by Hagen) for her to keep in Prussia.[81] When Queen Victoria received the photographs of the Princess's bust at the end of March 1863 she made various corrections before returning the prints to Berlin. A plaster cast was despatched to England the following spring and, as the original scheme for the commissioning of a marble version did not materialize, at Christmas 1864 the Crown Prince and Princess themselves presented the Queen with a marble bust of the Prince Consort, based on the Princess's model.[82]

The Princess Royal was also closely involved in plans for the conversion of 'Wolsey's tomb house' at the east end of St George's Chapel, Windsor Castle, into the Albert Memorial Chapel, as a place of pilgrimage for the public. Her views were crucial in the decision to show the Prince in medieval armour on his cenotaph inside the chapel. The likeness of the Prince in this effigy, which was the work of the French sculptor Henri de Triqueti (1804-74), was partly dependent on Princess Victoria's own bust of her father.[83] The walls of the chapel were to be adorned by medallion portraits of each of Victoria and Albert's children by the English sculptor Susan Durant (1820/30-73). When Miss Durant visited Germany in September 1865 to model the Princess's medallion, the two artists got on so well that there were even discussions about setting up a joint studio. In the event, she merely received some fresh tuition in sculpture.

Some years later the Crown Princess turned to the German sculptor and painter Reinhold Begas (1831-1911) for additional tuition, and for the use of a studio.

Apart from her designs for the mausoleums for her father (at Frogmore in the 1860s) and her husband (at the Friedenskirche, Potsdam, in the late 1880s), and the building of Friedrichshof soon thereafter, the Crown Princess had few opportunities to exercise her architectural interests, although her award of a gold medal at the Brussels exhibition in 1876 for the design of a barracks hospital may have been one of many such projects. Two world wars and the collapse of the German empire have ensured that few records of such activity have survived. But at her death the Empress Frederick was widely acknowledged for her philanthropic work, for her stimulation of interest in the arts, for her encouragement of artistic education in Germany, and for the very high quality of her own painting and sculpture.

Queen Victoria and Prince Albert's second daughter, Alice (1843-78), was born in April 1843, and was thus three years younger than the Princess Royal. When the latter wrote home from Germany in November 1861, bewailing the fact that because she had no drawing master her Christmas gifts that year 'will be but poor productions . . . by the side of those of my sisters', she must have been thinking principally of Princess Alice's work. There are drawings and paintings by Princess Alice from her tenth year throughout her comparatively short life. Her early works show clear signs of the influence of the royal drawing master: indeed, Corbould's model for her watercolour of a couple crossing a river on horseback has survived in the archives at Fulda. It is inscribed 'Matter for Reflection' and is signed and dated 21 November 1856, 'For H.R.H. Pr. R's birthday'.[84] The Princess Royal evidently lent the drawing to her younger sister soon after receiving it, for Princess Alice's copy was presented to her mother as a Christmas gift the following month. Two years later Princess Alice's finished watercolours begin to be proudly inscribed 'Composition', indicating that the design was thought out by her, based on some literary model. The semi-circular watercolour of 'Lear and Cordelia' at Windsor, presented to Prince Albert for his birthday in 1858, is one of a series of compositions taken from Shakespeare's *King Lear* which the Royal Family had seen performed at the Princess's Theatre, London, in 1858[85] with Charles Kean in the title role. A similarly highly worked watercolour of the 'Separation of the Dauphin from Marie Antoinette in the Temple' was given to her parents by Princess

Alice at Christmas 1858. Her pen drawing of 'La fuite. Marie Antoinette et le Dauphin', dated Balmoral, 18 October 1858, was presented to Mme Rollande, the French governess.[86] A comparatively small number of actual sketches have survived by Princess Alice. Her drawing (also for Mme Rollande) of 'Arthur quand il a mal à la tête' (Arthur when he has a headache), on 5 January 1859,[87] shows her ailing eight-year-old brother. A month later, Princess Alice sketched her mother enrobed for the opening of Parliament.[88] In the same year the wedding anniversary was remembered with a composition based on Schiller's *Das Lied von der Glocke*, and the Queen's birthday with a composition from *Hamlet*.[89] For New Year's Day 1860, Princess Alice painted various subjects (see p. 23) including 'Beethoven composing his moonshine [*sic*] Sonata', for the Queen's birthday 'Dame Cicely the Nut Brown Maid', and for Prince Albert's three scenes from *Enid*.[90]

In June 1860 the Queen had included Princes Louis and Henry of Hesse, the sons of Prince Charles of Hesse and nephews of the reigning Grand Duke, among her house party at Windsor for Ascot Races. Princess Alice and the elder Prince, Louis (1837-92), were evidently attracted to one another and in November the same year they became engaged. Both the Queen and Prince Albert were delighted, not least because it was rightly considered unlikely that the Hesse family would act in such a proprietorial manner towards Princess Alice as the Prussians had towards Princess Victoria. The Prussian King insisted that she request permission for every excursion out of Berlin and this was often withheld. Queen Victoria was increasingly resentful of her lack of control over the Crown Princess's movements, and the choice of husbands for her younger daughters was at least partly determined by consideration of how much access she would have to the girls after their marriages.

At around the time of her engagement Princess Alice painted a symbolic composition incorporating the arms of Britain and Hesse, with St Cecilia and a group of angels making music (Plate 45).[91] The wedding was the subject of discussion throughout 1861. Meanwhile the regular flow of works from the Princess's brush continued. The 1861 wedding anniversary gift was a watercolour showing (somewhat prophetically) a memorial to her parents, topped by four young angels and the words 'God Bless You', with Britannia standing by and a female figure chipping away at the stone. More watercolours of dramatic subjects such as scenes from *Romeo and Juliet* or Boucicault's *The Colleen Bawn* were painted, presumably on the basis of considerable preparatory work which does not appear to have survived.[92]

Towards the end of the year Prince Albert's health began to cause concern and Princess Alice became her father's chief nurse. Following his death on 14 December she assumed an extraordinary degree of responsibility, for the Queen appeared unable to take any important decisions, except in so far as these concerned memorials to her beloved husband. Like her younger sisters, Princess Alice composed her own memorial piece, on the theme of the phrase 'Why seek ye the living among the dead? He is not here. He is risen!'[93] This was inscribed with the date 14 January 1862, exactly one month after the Prince's death. But a more substantial piece of work was represented by Princess Alice's design for the octagonal base supporting William Theed's bust of the Prince Consort at Osborne. This incorporated cherubs' heads and interlacing flower swags, carved in high relief. Theed claimed that the delay in his completion of the base (which had taken twelve months to execute) was due to 'the minuteness of execution' required by the Princess's elaborate design. The base was finally installed in the entrance hall at Osborne on 13 February 1864.[94]

Prince Louis arrived from Germany to assist and support his fiancée as soon as he could. The plans for their wedding were inevitably delayed, and the ceremony finally took place at Osborne on 1 July 1862. From the start it was evidently understood that Princess Alice would return to England regularly, and as she and Prince Louis were constantly short of money they were not unwilling to be supported in this way. Their first child, Victoria, was born at Windsor in April 1863.[95] The same year William Leitch described the sketching expeditions at Balmoral, when the Hesses were again among the guests. Princess Alice went out with her pen or her watercolour box on numerous occasions during these holidays. In one of her albums at Wolfsgarten there are two studies dated October 1863, inscribed 'Louis in the Highlands', showing 'dear Louis' in authentic Highland dress.[96] His sketch of a scene at the 'Black Snake', dated October 1863, is at Windsor.[97] In the following year Prince and Princess Louis visited England earlier (in July and August), for their second child was expected in November. While there the Princess again sketched with Leitch and made charming watercolours at Osborne of her first-born, Victoria (aged 1½), and of the black servant William Jeroe Koedjo.[98] In 1865 the visit was again an autumn one. The sketches Princess Alice made during the royal party's ascent of the Sluggan on 6

Like her elder sister, Princess Alice delighted in drawing members of her family. The eldest child, Victoria (shown here on the lap of her father), was born at Windsor Castle in April 1863. By the following January, Princess Alice could inform her mother that 'Baby says "Papa", "Mama", and yesterday several times "Louis" . . . she gets on her feet alone by a chair, and is across the room before one can turn around.'

October were used as the basis for an oil painting for the Queen's Christmas present that year. On 5 December the Princess informed her mother (from Darmstadt): 'Yesterday I was painting in oils, and I copied my sketch of the Sluggan, and, if it be in any way at all presentable and fit to give, I will send it to you. I hope it won't be very Chinese, for our sketches had a certain likeness to works of art of that country.'[99]

Many further visits were made to England and Scotland. However, by now their new house (the Neues Palais) at Darmstadt was nearing completion, and Princess Alice was beginning to become deeply involved in the educational and philanthropic life of Hesse. The design of the new house had been very largely the Princess's concern. In March 1866 she wrote to her mother to request that: 'dear Papa's and your blessing rest on our new home . . . it reminds me a little of Osborne, of Buckingham Palace, a little even of Balmoral. Could I but show it to darling Papa! If I have any taste, I owe it all to him, and I learned so much by seeing him arrange pictures, rooms, etc.'[100]

Although there are many fewer works of art by Princess Alice than by the Princess Royal, those that do exist sometimes record intimate moments of family life. Little Victoria is shown seated on Prince Louis's lap in January 1864. Women in different national costumes are depicted, and journeys chronicled. The

Ernest, the eldest son (and fourth child) of Princess Alice and Prince Louis of Hesse, was drawn by his mother during his eighth year at the family's summer residence, Kranichstein.

growing family is sketched in pen and pencil, the eldest son and heir perched by a table at their summer retreat, Kranichstein, in 1875, or in a sailor suit holding the hand of his sister Alix, the future wife of Nicholas II and the last Tsarina.[101]

Highly finished watercolours, depending ultimately on Corbould's example, continued to flow from Princess Alice's brush after 1861. During her engagement she painted a number of different versions of 'The Lady of the Lake', of which the final one was presented to the Queen for her birthday in 1863.[102] A scene from Tennyson's *Princess* was painted as late as 1867. By now, however, Princess Alice had embarked on another interest, that of manuscript illumination. There is a group of illuminated pages by her at Wolfsgarten (Plate 46). Richly ornate designs, incorporating much gold leaf and considerable inventiveness in the decoration, as well as meticulous handling of the paint, are concerned with prayers, biblical texts, passages from Tennyson, or formal pages of address. They are obviously related to the most remarkable monument to Princess Alice's artistic abilities, the 'Hauschronik' of Prince and Princess Louis from 1862 to 1871 (Plates 48 and 49).[103] The main events of each year covered by this volume are shown as vignettes, combined on a single sheet of vellum, set out, drawn and painted by the Princess with the greatest confidence and competence. These events are then described in the illuminated text on the following pages. The penultimate illustration shows the dark clouds of the Franco-Prussian war, a ward in one of the military hospitals set up by Princess Alice, and the more familiar role of the young mother, nursing her second son (and fifth child), Frederick William (born in October 1870). Princess Alice apparently failed to complete the Hauschronik, perhaps because there was now no time to combine the very meticulous, almost miniaturist painting technique with the hospital rounds and care for family and home.

In 1874 a new interest appears: the painting of fruit and flowers in watercolour. A group of these paintings, bearing dates from February 1874 to July 1875, is contained in another volume at Wolfsgarten.[104] Each sheet bears a single spray of flowers, or a single flower, and on the back of several there are notes in English from someone who was at the time evidently fulfilling the role of Princess Alice's distant drawing master (Plate 47). With the help of some letters among the papers of the Princess's younger brother Prince Leopold, Duke of Albany (1853-84), it is possible to identify the hand as that of John Ruskin (1819-1900), the author and art critic and, from 1869, the first Slade Professor of Fine Art at Oxford University. Prince Leopold had encountered Ruskin during his years at Oxford, and corresponded with him from time to time thereafter.[105] On 31 May 1875, Ruskin recorded that Princess Alice

eagerly asked me to 'lend' her some drawings for her children. So of course I asked if I might make them for her and give them to her, and of course she was good enough to be pleased; and then I asked her to tell me what she would have and she said 'a water-lily' and some tree stems. And I think I shall do one for her that she'll like. For she verily knows what drawing is.[106]

The occasion of his meeting with the Princess is explained as the formal institution of the Ruskin School and Art Gallery in his diary entry for the following day: 'June 1st 1875. Tuesday, Oxford. Yesterday with Princess Alice over galleries and signed deed of gift to them, Princess and the two princes, Louis and Leopold, for witnesses.'[107]

Two months later Ruskin wrote to Prince Leopold to report that he had received Princess Alice's drawings, and praised them effusively:

The drawings are in truth of extreme beauty, showing not only very high natural gifts for art, but an energy and patient industry which would be singular and admirable in any woman . . . I confess to being almost mortified that there remains so little for me to show to her Royal Highness . . . it cannot but be some days before I am able to return the drawings with such notes as Her Royal Highness expresses her gracious wish that I should make on them.[108]

The drawings were to be returned on 6 September 1875.[109] The following March what must have been a further consignment of Princess Alice's drawings was being discussed. In each case Ruskin seems to have sent the Princess some of his own drawings, in addition to applying his comments to the back of her own work that he was returning. Ruskin's last letter concerning this interchange suggests that Prince Leopold (or Princess Alice) had criticized the length of time that Ruskin had held on to her drawings before returning them to Germany. No further exchanges are recorded thereafter.

By now however Princess Alice was receiving lessons from someone rather closer at hand. In December 1875 she informed her mother: 'I am working hard – with the assistance of Col: Macbean who gives me lessons – at a watercolour for you – I had finished one, but he would not hear of my sending it to "Her Majesty" as not good enough. He is a wonderful artist – an oldish gentleman – a thorough Highlander & Presbyterian & I fear in not good circumstances.'[110]

Princess Alice's last years were fraught with tragedy. Prince Frederick, shown as a baby in the 1870 Hauschronik page, died after falling from a window in 1873. Princess Alice was naturally distraught, but devoted herself to continuing a normal family life for the remaining six children, five girls and one boy. Domestic economy, in the true meaning of those words, prevailed at Darmstadt. The Princess made many of the children's clothes herself, and sometimes gave the Queen a piece of embroidery rather than a painting for her birthday or Christmas gift.[111] This example was followed by her daughters. The second child, Ella (1864-1918), wrote to Queen Victoria at Christmas 1877 and informed her that: 'for Mama each of us made a frock, pinafore, petticoat and 2 shifts for a poor child, we put a pocket handkerchief into the pocket of the frock because we thought the child who got it would like to find it their [sic]. It took a long time to make them.'[112]

After her early encounter with death, and the responsibilities that were then immediately thrust upon her, Princess Alice became a serious-minded and admirably dutiful mother figure.

But just as Prince Albert's own overwork may have hastened his path to the grave, so may Princess Alice's. She worked unstintingly in the hospitals, the educational institutions and on other charitable causes throughout the 1870s. After the death of Prince Louis's uncle, the Grand Duke Louis III, in 1877, and his accession as Grand Duke Louis IV, her duties naturally increased. In November 1878 the entire Grand Ducal family, with the exception of Ella and initially Princess Alice herself, contracted diphtheria. Princess Alice nursed them safely through nights of high fever and panic, but on 16 November the youngest child, Mary, died. Three weeks later, just as the rest of the family were finally recovering, Princess Alice herself contracted the disease, and she died on 14 December 1878, aged only 35, exactly 17 years after the death of her father.

Queen Victoria and Prince Albert's third daughter, Princess Helena (1846-1923), subsequently undertook to edit Princess Alice's correspondence with her mother and the resulting volume was published in 1884. In spite of her own daughter's claims,[113] Princess Helena was probably the least prolific of Queen Victoria's daughters. Her juvenile works show the continuing influence of Corbould, who coached her to produce highly competent (and brightly coloured) copies and compositions from c.1860. There are scenes from *Henry V*, and illustrations of poems by Wordsworth and Mrs Norton.[114] William Leitch records Princess Helena among his pupils at Balmoral in

An illustration of Mrs Norton's poem 'The Arab's Farewell to his horse', composed and painted by the third daughter, Princess Helena, for presentation to her father at what was to be his last birthday, 26 August 1861.

1862, and her Christmas gift to the Queen in 1861 (a watercolour of the Dee near Balmoral) already shows the results of his teaching.[115] In 1866, Princess Helena married Prince Christian, the second surviving son of Duke Christian of Schleswig-Holstein. Her husband was persuaded to establish the family home in England, so that Princess Helena could continue to minister to her mother's needs, and during the following years they lived happily first at Frogmore House and then at Cumberland Lodge, Windsor, and also at Schomberg House, Pall Mall. While their five children were growing up, Princess Helena seems to have briefly resumed her painting activity. A watercolour of the Cuillin Hills, Skye (dated 1881), and an oil painting of a bridge over a river (dated Christmas 1883), still hang at Osborne House.[116] But Princess Christian's chief contribution lay in her wide-ranging philanthropic and social work. She was closely involved in the provision of training for nurses, and the setting up of nursing homes. In addition, in 1872 she became the founding President of the School of Art Needlework (later the Royal School of Needlework), 'to supply suitable employment for poor gentlefolk', in the restoration of old embroideries and the making of new.

When Mary Severn portrayed Princesses Helena and Louise in 1858, she showed the elder child pointing to the drawing being carried out by her sister, who was two years her junior. Princess Louise (1848-1939) was active as a painter and sculptor throughout her long life. The sixth child and fourth daughter of Queen Victoria, she evidently benefited from Corbould's lessons at an early age. There are copies of drawings and engravings in the late 1850s and 1860-1 and a small view of Osborne House, presented to the German governess, Fräulein Bauer, in May 1858.[117] Pictures inscribed proudly as 'Compositions' date from 1861. Princess Louise's Christmas gift in that year to the recently widowed Queen Victoria was a watercolour of 'David and Goliath'.[118]

Prince Albert's death inspired at least two elaborately symbolic pieces, haunting works by a girl only fourteen years old. The first (for the Queen's wedding anniversary in February 1862) shows a sleeping figure (presumably the Queen), with a vision of her reunion with the Prince in an ethereal haze above. The second, given to the Queen for her birthday in 1862, is another bedside scene, showing the sleeping Queen accompanied by two of her daughters, and above a group of three angels with the words 'Blessed are they that mourn, For they shall be comforted'. The first anniversary of Prince Albert's

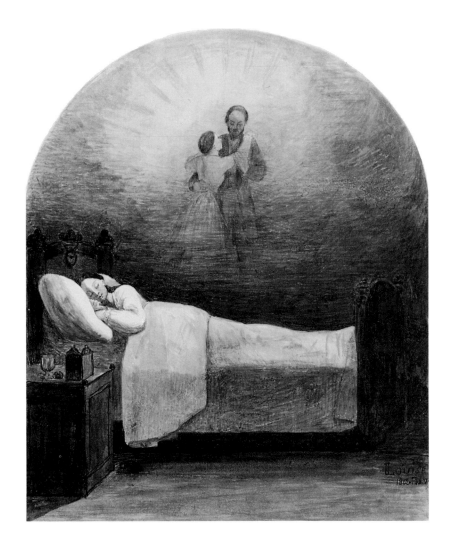

Queen Victoria's fourth daughter, Princess Louise, was only 13 years old at the time of her father's death. For her mother's wedding anniversary the following February she painted this haunting image of her parents' ethereal reunion.

death was commemorated by Princess Louise with a picture of Mary Magdalen and an angel outside the open tomb. The text, from Matthew 18: 6, is the same as that used by Princess Alice for her own memorial piece. It was presumably a 'set work' for the princesses: in some way the imaginative and artistic talents of her children were intended to soothe the grieving Queen. A further memorial piece in which Princess Louise was apparently involved was the Queen's christening gift for Prince Albert Victor (1864-92), the eldest son of the Prince and Princess of Wales, born on 8 January 1864. This was to be a silver centre-piece, showing the Prince Consort as an armed knight standing on a plinth, at the three corners of which were female person-ifications of the Cardinal Virtues. The main figure was modelled by Theed, with the assistance of Corbould, but less than a month after the child's birth the Queen recorded that 'Louise has also been helping, and shows great taste.'[119] Two drawings by Princess Louise of 'Hope' and 'Charity', dated 5 February 1864, are presumably connected with this project.[120]

Corbould's influence over Princess Louise's work continued throughout the 1860s. Her Christmas present to the Queen in 1867 was a highly finished dramatic depiction of 'The Wreck of the Blanche Nef'.[121] In one of the albums of the Princess's work preserved at Windsor there is a charming series of pencil drawings, presumably dating from this time, depicting the four seasons. Her designs for the scenery used in the charade 'Band ditty', performed at Osborne in January 1868, were also doubt-less ultimately inspired by Corbould – 'helped by suggestions from Mrs Theodore Martin'. The drawing master's instruction can still just be detected in the design for a fan decorated with skating scenes, on which the Princess was at work in 1870-1.[122]

With her mother, brothers and sisters, Louise also received lessons from William Leighton Leitch, whose inspiration can clearly be seen in her early views of Scotland.[123] In January 1863 the Princess told Prince Arthur that she was having lessons every day from Mr Leitch.[124] Later the same year we have the artist's own account of a sketching party at Balmoral, with Princess Louise 'trudging along' beside him until they reached their place of work. She was then described 'on my right hand, sitting on a big stone, and working away at her drawing'.[125] Her copy of Princess Alice's sketch 'Upset on Alt-na-Guithasach Road, October 1863', and a charming picture of 'Hallowe'en at Balmoral' in 1868, are in one of the Queen's albums at Windsor.[126] Among Princess Louise's papers in the Royal Archives is a small sheet with five tiny drawings by Leitch, and the following text (illustrated p. 11):

> Mr Leitch presents his most respectful compliments to The Princess Louisa [sic] & Likes Her Royal Highness's drawing very much indeed. Mr Leitch has taken the liberty of sketch-ing a form or two of composition on the opposite page & should feel exceedingly happy if The Princess Louisa could find time to practice them a little now & then as Mr Leitch is quite sure The Princess would find the practice very usefull as well as very amusening [sic] – Osborne Augst 9th 1864.[127]

The following year Princess Louise sketched the pontoon bridge across the Thames at Datchet.[128] In a volume of the Queen's

This watercolour sketch by Princess Louise of herself (on the left) and the Queen warming themselves in front of the fire at Alt Dourie Cottage in October 1865 was inserted into one of the Queen's albums of sketches. On 26 October 1865 Queen Victoria noted in her Journal: 'At ¼ p. 12 drove . . . up behind Invercauld . . . it came on to rain heavily, so that we got off & drove to the small tea house beyond Invercauld, where we established ourselves in the kitchen, made a good fire & took our luncheon.'

'Sketches from Nature – 1862 to 1866' is a charming watercolour of the interior of Alt Dourie Cottage, dated October 1865 and inscribed 'Louise del'.[129] An oil painting of a ruined castle on the Rhine was an additional Christmas gift from Princess Louise to her mother in 1867. The Queen described it as a 'lovely picture'.[130]

In August and September 1868, Princess Louise accompanied the Queen (who travelled incognita as the Countess of Kent) to Switzerland (and specifically to Lake Lucerne) for the summer holidays. Her sketches made at this time are often demonstrably taken from the same position as her mother's.[131] The style is similar (as the teacher was the same), but the handling of paint as yet not quite so assured. The following summer the Princess took her oil paints to Balmoral, and recorded the view from the Prince Consort's sitting room. She noted the hour (nine o'clock in the evening) on the frame.[132] Princess Louise's correspondence also indicates that she was in touch with the ailing Edwin Landseer, who hoped that she would visit his London studio.[133] This contact, with the artist who had taught the Queen to draw in chalks twenty years earlier, seems to have led Princess Louise to experiment with this medium. In the autumn of 1870 the Queen's private secretary, Henry Ponsonby, described to his wife the Princess's work at Balmoral that autumn (where she was resting with a bad knee): 'She showed me two very pretty chalk heads of Duncan Stewart's child who comes here to sit for her. Really very well done and there can't be any help here.'[134] The parallel with Queen Victoria's chalk studies of John MacDonald's children is obvious.

While Princess Louise was at Balmoral, several of her works (with those of her eldest sister, the Princess Royal), were included in the exhibition at the galleries of the New British Institution in aid of the German war wounded. The chalk portrait of a 'Canadian lady' was presumably also in the technique inspired by Landseer. Princess Louise's most notable contribution to this exhibition was thought to be a night scene on a battlefield, with two Sisters of Charity tending the wounded in the foreground. The subject was clearly reminiscent of Princess Victoria's *The Field of Battle* of 15 years earlier. The title of Princess Louise's picture was *In Aid of Sufferers*.[135]

The following March, at the age of 23, Princess Louise was married to the Marquess of Lorne (1845-1914), son and heir of the 8th Duke of Argyll, whom he succeeded in 1900. Both Princess Louise and her husband continued to paint and draw throughout the remainder of their lives. Lorne, whose father was also a competent artist, evidently encouraged his wife in her artistic pursuits (Plate 5). He also introduced her into the 'greenery-yallery Grosvenor Gallery' world in which the Lornes moved so happily. Soon after arriving back at Inveraray (the Scottish seat of the Dukes of Argyll) following their honeymoon, Lorne wrote to tell the Queen that: 'Before long Louise will I hope send you some sketches of the views from the windows.'[136] In addition to sketching, much of the Princess's time in Scotland was spent in furnishing, arranging and decorating the various Campbell residences. She painted murals at Inveraray and Ben More Lodge, Mull, and designed decorative items for family use.[137]

The Lornes, who had no children, also spent a considerable amount of time in London, initially based at the family home, Argyll Lodge, Campden Hill. Louise sent her mother a charming watercolour study of the dovecote in the garden there in 1872.[138] In the mid-1870s the Lornes moved to Kensington Palace, and a studio was installed for the Princess next to their apartment. The historian and former American Minister to Great Britain, J. L. Motley (1814-77), had his portrait drawn by Princess Louise shortly before his death. He was delighted by the result and assured her that: 'I only know it was a great pleasure to me to sit to you.'[139] The Princess's artistic activity at this time is demonstrated by the jaunty embossed letter-

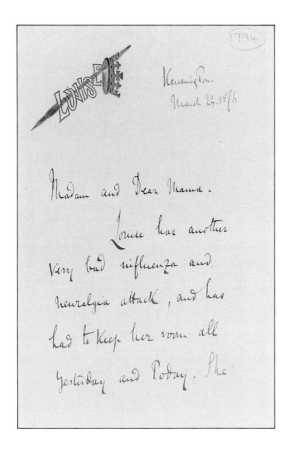

After her marriage to the Marquess of Lorne in 1871, Princess Louise moved with ease in fashionable artistic circles. One of her letter-headings showed a chalk holder supporting the letters of her name and a coronet. In this instance the paper was used by Lorne to inform the Queen ('Madam and Dear Mama') of his wife's indisposition.

heading she adopted, of a chalk drawing instrument threaded through the letters L O V I S E and supporting a coronet hanging vertically from it.[140] In 1877 she became an Honorary Member of the Old Water-Colour Society (renamed the Royal Society of Painters in Watercolour four years later) and frequently exhibited her work at their galleries.[141]

From 1878 to 1883 the Lornes were based in Canada, during the Marquess's appointment as Governor-General. Their drawings and paintings of those parts of Canada (and America) that they visited at this time are valuable pictorial records. Some of Princess Louise's sketches served as the basis for the illustrations to her article 'Quebec Pictures from my Portfolio', published in 1882.[142] Lorne's essay entitled 'Our Railway to the Pacific'[143] also contained illustrations based on sketches of Canada by both husband and wife. His book *Canadian Pictures* (1884) included a small number of his own sketches, but most of the plates were taken from drawings by S. P. Hall. Among the most interesting of Princess Louise's work are the sketches made during her

*Princess Louise's husband,
the Marquess of Lorne,
served as Governor-General
of Canada from 1878 to 1883,
during which time both
husband and wife were active
with their sketching
equipment. The Princess
caught her husband in
relaxed mood in this study.*

voyage through America to California, commencing in September 1882. She painted the mission churches of Monterey, Los Angeles and Santa Barbara. The following year her travels took her to Yuma, Tucson, Santa Fe, Kansas City, St Louis, Louisville, Richmond and Charleston, with a three-month stay in Bermuda.

In the Governor-General's official residence, Rideau Hall, Ottawa, Princess Louise established a painting studio, where she would work up her finished watercolours and oils. For outdoor work she designed a sketching box on wheels, with one side entirely of glass, in which she could paint in all seasons.[144] The years of Lorne's appointment to Canada coincided with a period of consolidation of the Canadian nation, following the end of the 'merely money-getting days'. With her strong sense of design and keen interest in art, Princess Louise realized that the time was ripe for developing Canadian popular interest in art. Through Lorne she worked towards the foundation of the Canadian Academy of Arts in March 1880. By the terms of its foundation each Academician (nominated by the Governor-General) would donate paintings that would form the nucleus of a new Dominion Gallery, now the National Gallery of

Princess Louise's work in oils was highly accomplished. This portrait of her friend the artist Henrietta Montalba (1856–93) was exhibited at the Grosvenor Gallery in 1882 and presented to the recently founded National Gallery of Canada two years later. The sitter was a successful sculptor, and was responsible for a bronze portrait bust of Princess Louise's husband, the Marquess of Lorne.

Canada. In the year of its foundation Lorne informed the Queen that Princess Louise was planning to send five items to the exhibition of the Canadian Academy in Ottawa: 'Two sketches of flowers, one of an old house in Kent, and two Portraits in pencil, of Libby my sister, and of Mr Motley, the late American Minister in England'.[145] Three years later Princess Louise presented her oil portrait of the artist Henrietta Montalba to the National Gallery of Canada.[146] Another portrait of this period (in watercolour, rather than oils) is that of Lorne's secretary Major de Winton, wearing a fur hat and heavy overcoat (see p. 32).[147] The door to Louise's 'blue parlour', painted by her with a branch of foliage, has survived in Rideau Hall (Plate 51).

*Study by Princess Louise
dating from the years around
the turn of the century, when
she was in touch with artists
such as Burne-Jones,
Leighton, Alma-Tadema
and Whistler. In July 1905
Sir Edward Poynter supplied
her with the name and
address of a suitable model
for life drawing.*

On their return home in 1883, and during her English visit in 1880-1 (following a serious tobogganing accident), the Princess re-established her contacts with the art world in London. She contributed articles to magazines under the pseudonym 'Myra Fontenoy', and allowed her paintings to be shown at various exhibitions: there were regular contributions to the Grosvenor Gallery.[148] A view of the Niagara Falls from the Canadian side was included in the Colonial and Indian exhibition in 1886.[149] The Walker Art Gallery, Liverpool, showed a number of her works in their exhibitions.[150] Princess Louise's work was also shown north of the border on numerous occasions: at the Glasgow International exhibition in 1888, the Royal Glasgow Institute of Fine Arts in 1903,[151] and at the Royal Scottish Society of Painters in Watercolour in 1893, 1910 and 1912.[152] She was lent drawings by Sir Edward Burne-Jones (1833-98),[153] and was supplied with the name and address of a suitable model by Sir Edward Poynter (1836-1919), who was both Director of the National Gallery and President of the Royal Academy at the time.[154] She was also in touch with Lord Leighton, Sir Lawrence Alma-Tadema and J. M. Whistler. With these associations Princess Louise was closely involved in the work of art schools and colleges, and in such organizations as the Ladies' Work Society and the National Trust. She had herself studied at the National Art Training School, later renamed the Royal College of Art. However, she was sensitive enough to appreciate how potentially explosive the promotion of such 'foolish luxury' as art might seem to the Radicals.

There are dated works throughout the 1880s, 1890s and 1900s. These include a pencil portrait of Queen Victoria dated 1881, that was later reproduced actual size in a supplement to *The Gentlewoman*.[155] A watercolour of the Church of S. Maria delle Salute, Venice, dated in the same year, reveals the refreshing effect of Italy on Princess Louise's palette.[156] In 1894 she supplied some charming illustrations to the ballad of *Auld Robin the Farmer* by Walter Douglas Campbell, a distant cousin of her husband. Princess Louise's watercolour 'An English Hebe' was presented to King Edward VII as part of the Coronation Gift from the Royal Watercolour Society in 1903.[157] Three years later she copied in watercolour, on a considerably increased scale, Samuel Cooper's portrait miniature of the Duke of Monmouth, also in the Royal Collection.[158] In the two albums containing sketches by Princess Louise in the Print Room at Windsor are a small group of studies made during a voyage down the Nile in 1906 (Plate 50).[159] They demonstrate both a

During her lengthy return visit to England from Canada in 1880-1, Princess Louise portrayed her mother, the 62-year-old Queen Empress.

continuing interest in life, and a high artistic competence, in one who was not only a Royal Princess, but also by now a Duchess and approaching her sixtieth year.

The element that singles out Princess Louise from her sisters is not her drawings and paintings but her serious and long-lasting interest in sculpture and modelling, in which she was active from her mid-teens. In the summer of 1863 her eldest brother, Albert Edward (later King Edward VII), wrote to ask: 'How are you getting on with Mrs Thornycroft [i.e. Mary Thornycroft, noted above]? do you find modelling very difficult?'[160] Later the same year he wrote to thank his sister for her birthday gifts:

I must also thank you very much for a very pretty carpet you have worked for me, which does your workmanship the greatest credit – the little statuette is really admirably modelled, & I strongly advise you to continue taking lessons with Mrs Thornycroft, as you certainly have great talent in modelling & may perchance become some day an eminent sculptor.[161]

The Princess's collaboration with Theed over Prince Albert Victor's christening present in 1864 has already been noted, but her association with Mary Thornycroft evidently continued for many years. Just as Mary's father, John Francis, had assisted Prince Albert with his sculpture in the 1840s, preparing and then carving (or casting) the bust of the Prince's father and the model of Eos, so Mary Thornycroft was called upon to provide materials, tools and assistance to Princess Louise. The bust of her seven-year-old sister Princess Beatrice, on which she worked in 1864, was carved in marble by Mrs Thornycroft at the cost of £50.[162] When it was presented for her birthday in May 1864, the Queen noted 'Louise's bust of Baby is charming and so like.' Three years later, Princess Louise was at work on a portrait bust of her younger brother Prince Arthur. Mrs Thornycroft supplied a box of clay (at £1), a team to transport the clay bust from Osborne to London, and three casts. Her charge for 'executing [the] bust in marble' was £47 5s.[163] The bust, another birthday present for the Queen (in 1867), was exhibited by Princess Louise at the Royal Academy in 1868[164] and was presented to the Royal Military Academy, Woolwich (of which Prince Arthur was a student), in the same year. A number of invoices from 1868 mention 'modelling clay tools', 'carving tools & hammer', or 'boxes of clay' supplied by Mrs Thornycroft for the Princess's use. In May the accounts mention '1 pair of Silver Compasses for H.M. The Queen', and another pair for the Princess, at £3 10s each: presumably these were similar to the measuring tools which Mary Thornycroft had when working on the portrait bust of Princess Alice seven years before.[165]

On Princess Louise's twentieth birthday, 18 March 1868, the Queen wrote to the Princess Royal to announce that Princess Louise 'is (and who would some years ago have thought it?) a clever, dear girl, with a fine strong character, and a very marked character [*sic*], – unselfish, – affectionate a good daughter and with a wonderful talent for art. She is now doing a bust of me, quite by herself, which will be extremely good.'[166] The bust mentioned in this letter was probably the last piece resulting from the long collaboration between Princess Louise and Mary

Thornycroft, a relationship which must occasionally have been somewhat vexing for the latter. An invoice dated 17 July mentions 'Eight journeys to Windsor in April', and 'Man's time travelling expenses, in moulding the bust of H.M. The Queen by Princess Louise', of which a cast was immediately sent to Osborne. The invoice for carving the bust in marble (which was settled by the Keeper of the Privy Purse, as before), amounted to £75.[167]

By this time the Princess had enrolled as a student at the National Art Training School at South Kensington, specifically to attend classes in modelling. Her fellow students included Henrietta Montalba, one of four talented artistic sisters with whom Princess Louise remained on friendly terms. Princess Louise had also begun to receive lessons from the Hungarian sculptor J. E. Boehm (1834-90), whose advice and assistance must have been crucial for the modelling and casting of her large-scale pieces. The Queen first met Boehm in January 1869 and immediately placed a number of commissions with him. Royal employment continued through the following years, and for the last decade of his life Boehm held the appointment of Sculptor-in-Ordinary to the Queen. The suggestion that Boehm should teach Princess Louise was made in February 1869 by the Queen's German Librarian, Hermann Sahl (who held this position from 1863 to 1887), and received the Queen's blessing. The Princess was Boehm's first pupil, and was only taken on because of her 'unquestionable talent for sculpting'.[168]

The Christmas following the start of Boehm's lessons, Princess Louise's gifts to her mother were three portrait busts, of her brothers Princes Arthur and Leopold[169] and of her cousin Princess Amélie of Saxe-Coburg and Gotha. The following May she was working on a bust of General Charles Grey, Mary Ponsonby's uncle. Mary's husband, Henry, reported to her how the librarian, Hermann Sahl 'went to the studio [at Osborne] where [Louise] is doing a bust of Uncle C. very good I hear, and [Sahl] corrected it making a pinch here and a job of clay there. When L returned not having asked him to criticize she was of course furious.'[170] In 1874 Princess Louise exhibited a bust of 'The late General Grey' at the Royal Academy,[171] which was presumably the outcome of these earlier labours and frustrations.

With Boehm's assistance, the Princess modelled another bust of her mother, and it was presented to the Royal Academy in 1877 as the Princess 'believed [it] to be better as a work of art' than her earlier bust presented eight years before. Princess

Princess Louise was active as a sculptress from her mid-teens, when she received lessons from Mary Thornycroft. This bust of Prince Leopold was made in 1869, shortly after the Princess's introduction to another sculptor, Boehm. It was presented as a Christmas gift to the Queen at the end of the year.

Louise added that she would be 'very glad if the bust could be placed in one of the Picture Galleries, and not, as before, in the centre of the Octagon Room, among the Sculpture'.[172] During the following year Boehm helped the Princess with a terra-cotta relief of 'Geraint and Enid', which was later exhibited at the Grosvenor Gallery.[173] In 1879 Princess Louise portrayed Boehm in a skilful chalk drawing which, following his sudden death, she gave to Boehm's pupil Alfred Gilbert (1854-1934).[174] The friendship between Princess Louise and Boehm was apparently of mutual benefit, for Boehm would ask her advice as often as she would request his. Very shortly before his death, in December 1890, the sculptor wrote to the Princess expressing the hope that it would be 'equally convenient to your Royal Highness to honour me with a call in the afternoon and to give me your valuable advice on the design I am just preparing.'[175] Princess Louise's visit coincided tragically with the sculptor's death: according to his obituary in *The Times*, she discovered his lifeless body.[176] Shortly thereafter the sculptor's son, Sir Edgar Boehm, presented some of his father's implements and 'a book of his most interesting sketches' to Princess Louise.[177]

After Boehm's death, Alfred Gilbert appears to have taken over his role as the Princess's aide and mentor in sculptural matters. In January 1892 the Queen informed the Empress Frederick that 'Gilbert the sculptor is Louise's great friend.'[178] The following year he helped Princess Louise with her figure of the Queen for Kensington Gardens. Such was his devotion that his neglected wife declared: 'I shall be very glad when that tiresome princess had finished her work.'[179] The Princess's full-size seated figure of Queen Victoria outside the east front of Kensington Palace had been commissioned as a gift to the Queen by her 'loyal subjects of Kensington . . . to commemorate fifty years of her reign', and was finally unveiled on 28 June 1893.[180] The friendship between Princess Louise and Alfred Gilbert lasted through his years of exile (following his bankruptcy in 1901) to the time of his death. When he was seriously ill in the Cromwell Nursing Home, London, in the summer of 1934, the Princess 'went constantly to the "Home", with flowers & fruit – & full of encouragement & hope & brightness, – & on the Evening before he "passed on" she was there, tho' he had been unconscious for some days. She came for the last sight of her old & valued friend.'[181] At his funeral in November, Princess Louise led the procession of mourners.

As the nineteenth century drew to its close, the Princess worked on more and more memorial projects, including a

Louise 1879.
Dec 12 1890

The move to Canada interrupted Princess Louise's sculptural work carried out under the supervision of J. E. Boehm, whom she portrayed in 1879. The second inscription in the lower left corner of the sheet records the date of Boehm's sudden death in December 1890.

number to close members of her family. At the end of 1897 she was at work on the wall monument in the church at Whippingham (near Osborne) to her brother-in-law Prince Henry of Battenberg (1858-96), who had died from fever contracted during the Ashanti expedition in South Africa.[182] The white marble sarcophagus and bronze screen in this chapel were the work of Alfred Gilbert. A few years later she designed the marble figure of a kneeling angel in St Mary Abbot's Church, Kensington, as a memorial to her brothers Prince Alfred, Duke of Edinburgh (1844-1900), and Prince Leopold, Duke of Albany (1853-84). In 1898 Prince Alfred, who as Duke of Coburg resided in the Palais Edinbourg, Coburg, had sent Princess Louise his 'order for Art and Science which I hope you will accept to wear. The only other Fürstlichkeiten [princely personages] who have accepted it are Vicky [the Princess Royal] and the Queen of Roumania [Prince Alfred's daughter, Marie].'[183] The St Mary Abbot's monument is clearly based on Boehm's monument to Thomas Baring in Micheldever Church, of around twenty years before.[184] Of more international importance was Princess Louise's monument in St Paul's Cathedral, to honour the soldiers from the Dominions who had died in the Boer War. This consists of a bronze group of the Angel of Salvation behind Christ on the Cross, supported by a large bronze bracket. Below is an inscribed bronze plaque signed and dated 1904.[185] Princess Louise's sculptural *oeuvre* represents a truly extraordinary output for a woman of gentle birth in the nineteenth century, let alone a Princess of blood royal.[186]

The serious artistic education of Queen Victoria and Prince Albert's fifth daughter, Princess Beatrice (1857-1944), was inevitably limited by the death of her father when she was only four years old. Nevertheless, she received lessons with the older royal children from Leitch, and was later taught by two other watercolour artists patronized by the Queen: N. E. Green (c.1833-99) and Benjamin Ottewell (fl. 1884-1937).[187] One of her watercolour boxes has survived.[188] The only work from Princess Beatrice's maturity in the Royal Collection is an undated watercolour of Scotch pines, which well demonstrates both her own competence and the enduring influence of W. L. Leitch.[189] It appears that most of Beatrice's work is now dispersed, so that any discussion of her art is no longer possible. Writing of the early 1880s her biographer stated that: 'Her own artistic work was a great comfort to her, and she spent much of her time at her water-colours. [A] visit to the Institute of Painters in Water-Colours [of which she was an Honorary Member] proved a fresh incentive to work, and some of her happiest hours were spent with paint and brush.'[190]

Princess Beatrice was seventeen years younger than the Princess Royal and was still a baby at the time of her marriage. In consequence she was more a contemporary of her nephews and nieces than of her elder brothers and sisters. By the time of Princess Beatrice's own wedding in 1885, a number of Princess Victoria's and Princess Alice's children were already married. Her husband, Prince Henry of Battenberg (1858-96), a first cousin of Princess Alice's husband, Louis, is commemorated in the sculpted memorial by Princess Louise at Osborne. Princess

Beatrice's own chief monument is the hand-written transcript of her mother's journal, which occupied her for thirty years following the Queen's death.

So much for Queen Victoria's extraordinarily active daughters. Although comparatively little has survived in the way of drawings or watercolours by her sons, the early education of the Princes included art lessons. The lesson timetable of Albert Edward, Prince of Wales (1841-1910), for 1849 included drawing lessons from 3.30 to 4.00 on Monday and Thursday afternoons.[191] The name of this first teacher is not known, but his place was taken by Edward Corbould in 1852. For his father's birthday that year the Prince of Wales drew the helmeted head of a knight and coloured in a printed map of Europe 'shewing table lands and plains'.[192] Corbould's teaching method is clearly revealed in the two volumes of figure studies, the covers embossed with Prince of Wales's feathers, which were used for his lessons with the Prince in the 1850s. The master's outline drawing occupies the left side of the page, to be joined by the pupil's copy on the right (Plate 2). Both drawings were then coloured in by the Prince, and an appropriate title was added. Just as Prince Albert's early drawings were chiefly of a military content, so were those by the Prince of Wales (Plate 52). One of his Christmas presents to his father in 1853 was a washed drawing of a bandaged male head – presumably belonging to a soldier wounded in action.[193] Two years later he contributed a drawing entitled 'The Knight' to the Patriotic Fund exhibition and sale. Later the subjects (and designs) were taken from literary works: illustrations by Retzsch were copied by the Prince, as they had been by his mother and father.[194] The Prince of Wales enjoyed working with a turning lathe in the winter of 1856 and made small items for his parents.[195] Among Prince Albert's birthday presents in 1858 was a watercolour of a seaport by the Prince of Wales. In the early 1860s Prince Albert Edward also drew a few not particularly commendable caricatures.[196]

In December 1861 the Prince of Wales was introduced for the first time to his future bride, Princess Alexandra of Denmark (1844-1925). The meeting, in the town of Speyer on the Rhine, had been arranged by the Princess Royal, who described it in some detail to her mother: 'I see that Alix has made an impression on Bertie, though in his own funny, undemonstrative way. He said to me that he had never seen a young lady who pleased him so much . . . I never saw a girl of sixteen so forward for her age: her manners are more like 24.'[197] Owing to the Prince Consort's death less than three months later, the wedding

This study of the head of a wounded soldier would today seem a curiously inappropriate Christmas gift by the twelve-year-old Prince of Wales to his proud father in 1853.

did not take place until March 1863. However, during the intervening months Princess Alexandra's education was taken in hand. The Queen reported to the Crown Princess that: 'dear Alix . . . is truly and laudably anxious to improve herself. She will read English with Mrs Bruce, write with Mr Ogg also with Mme. Hocédé, – and draws with Mr Leitch. All this she is most anxious for – as she wishes to be of real use to Bertie.'[198]

In the autumn following their wedding, the Prince and Princess of Wales joined the rest of the Royal Family in Scotland, although they stayed at Abergeldie (a nearby estate leased by the Prince Consort from 1849) rather than Balmoral. Leitch wrote home on 30 September and described how:

I have also been giving lessons to the Princess of Wales every morning these last nine days, and her Royal Highness takes to the drawing with great heartiness, and gets on exceedingly well. Abergeldie is two and a half miles from Balmoral, and when the weather is fine I generally walk there and back. It does me good; but of course when it rains and blows there is always a carriage at my disposal.[199]

One of the first results of these lessons must have been the Princess's watercolour of a family picnic – complete with camp fire – at Loch Muick, which was later pasted into one of the Queen's albums.[200] There are large numbers of watercolours by Princess Alexandra in the Royal Collection which relate to her lessons with Leitch, such as a series of apparent copies of originals by the master (Plate 56),[201] and several Scottish subjects including views of Abergeldie.[202] According to Leitch's biographer:

> His last pupil was the Princess of Wales, of whom he always spoke in terms of high admiration, and he continued to give lessons to her Royal Highness, at Marlborough House, long after all other teaching had been declined. The Princess was very kind to him, and frequently on the occasion of his giving a lesson would give him some little present. Her last act of kindness was a tribute to his memory, when, on his death [in 1883], she sent a beautiful wreath of white flowers to be placed upon his coffin.[203]

No paintings or drawings by Princess Alexandra dating from before her wedding have survived in the Royal Collection. However, there is a small oil painting of the Venetian Lagoon by her mother, Queen Louise of Denmark (1817-98) at Sandringham.[204] The Princess's surviving engagement books record lessons from a number of other teachers besides the ailing Mr Leitch. Henry A. Harper (1835-1900), who specialized in views of the Holy Land, taught the Princess from 1877 to 1888.[205] In March 1883 she had lessons from Edwin Buckman (1841-1930), and two months later received the first of many lessons from the Italian landscape artist Hermann Corrodi (1844-1905).[206] Other lessons were provided in 1886 by the prolific marine painter Oswald Brierly (1817-94),[207] who had been appointed Marine Painter to the Queen in 1874, and received a knighthood in 1885. William Cave Thomas (1820-c.1890) taught the Princess in 1887 and 1889, towards the end of his life.[208] The engagement books also record a lesson in illuminating and instruction in how to varnish a picture.[209] No oil painting by the Princess appears to have survived in the Royal Collection, but she was evidently active in this medium as well as in watercolour.[210]

As a result of these lessons, the Princess of Wales was able to record her travels not only with the camera (with which she was very proficient), but also with her watercolour brush. There

Princess Alexandra's moonlit scene was probably painted during her early years in England, before the influence of Leitch's watercolour technique had become too firmly impressed. It can be seen hanging high on the end wall in the photograph of the artist's painting room at Windsor illustrated opposite.

are views of the Near Eastern tour in 1868-9 both in her sketchbooks at Windsor and as finished works, framed and hanging on the walls at Sandringham House, Norfolk, which was the country home of the Prince and Princess of Wales from the time of their marriage.[211] Later voyages were made to see the Princess's parents in Denmark, her brother William (from 1863 King George I of the Hellenes) in Athens, her sister Dagmar (from 1866 wife of the future Tsar Alexander III of Russia) in St Petersburg, and so on. In August 1893 the Princess of Wales was on a cruise in Norway and (typically) made up an album to contain her photographs, watercolours and diary notes of the cruise (Plate 56).[212] Two years later she was again in Athens, and sketched the Acropolis.[213] Her visit to Venice in 1910, during the onset of King Edward VII's final illness, was only one of many such visits, resulting in a number of watercolour views of the lagoon.

In addition to making sketches of scenery and landscapes

A photographic record of the contents of Queen Alexandra's painting room at Windsor. The framed watercolours on the walls would all appear to be by the Queen. Some of her paint brushes are seen to the right of the door.

Princess Alexandra also became adept at drawing the various members of her family, which had grown to include two sons and three daughters before the birth of the short-lived Prince John in April 1871. The following autumn the Prince and Princess were as usual at Abergeldie, and a series of figure studies (in pencil) dates from this time.[214] The early summers would frequently be spent with the Queen at Osborne. The eldest son, 'Eddie' (1864-92), was portrayed by his mother in sailor's dress, perhaps en route to the Isle of Wight, in 1880.[215] A study of another of the children, the second daughter 'Toria' (1868-1935), survives from the summer holiday at Osborne in 1886.[216] Princess Alexandra's copy of J. R. Swinton's portrait of the aged Princess Augusta, Duchess of Cambridge (1797-1889) in 1881, has also survived at Windsor.[217]

Colour prints were made of some of Queen Alexandra's paintings. These include a three-quarter-length figure of a stooping friar, dated 1891,[218] and 'A view in Windsor Park', which still shows clear signs of Leitch's influence but was probably painted after his death. During the 1890s Princess Alexandra may have acquired a new teacher, because her works from this time – mainly still lifes involving single flowers, fruit or dead animals, on long rectangular pieces of card – have a distinctive character that is quite unlike her earlier work (Plate 54).[219]

Princess Alexandra was a lifelong collector of fans and, confusingly, her name is inscribed (as a mark of ownership) on a number which are also signed by the artists responsible for painting the leaves. However, among the large group of painted wooden brisé fans in the Royal Collection, it is more than likely that some are the work of the Princess herself.[220]

The Princess of Wales was not the only artist among Queen Victoria's daughters-in-law. A watercolour by William Simpson of the Glassalt Shiel (a keeper's lodge at the west end of Loch Muick) dated 1882[221] shows two ladies sketching in a boat. They have been identified as the Duchess of Edinburgh and the Duchess of Connaught, who visited the Shiel with the Queen in 1881.[222] The Duchess of Edinburgh was Marie (1853-1920), only surviving daughter of Tsar Alexander II of Russia, who in 1874 married Queen Victoria and Prince Albert's second son Alfred, Duke of Edinburgh. She was thus related twice by marriage to the Princess of Wales. Although no paintings by the Duchess appear to have survived in the Collection, there are some early works by Prince Alfred: an Italian landscape drawn in brown chalk, dated 25 December 1856,[223] a beached boat at Ryde, dated 25 November 1857,[224] and sailing boats on the Solent before Osborne, a birthday gift for the Queen the following year (Plate 53).[225] The subjects were appropriate, for Prince Alfred had been destined for the Navy from an early age. The Prince's log book 'Of the Proceedings of HMS Euryalus 51 . . . kept by Alfred N.C. [Naval Cadet] Commencing 31st of August 1858 ending February 28th 1860' is illustrated with views of the coastline from the ship, each one carefully signed by the young Naval Cadet (see pp. 5-6).[226] From late March 1858 Prince Alfred received drawing and painting lessons from Alfred C. Snape of Gosport.[227] Later he was taught by the German artist August Becker (1822-87), whose brother Ernest was Librarian to the Prince Consort.[228]

The other duchess shown at work in Simpson's watercolour was Louise Margaret of Prussia (1860-1917), who in 1879 married the Queen's third son, Prince Arthur, Duke of Connaught (1850-1942). As the daughter of Prince Frederick Charles of Prussia, she was a first cousin of the Princess Royal's husband, 'Fritz'. Once again, no works by the Duchess appear to have survived, but there are early works by the Duke both at Windsor and at Fulda.[229] From the time of his birth Prince Arthur was a favourite of the Queen's. For his parents' wedding anniversary in 1859 he composed a charming letter to accompany a watercolour of a fence.[230] Three years later, at the age of twelve, he

During his childhood and early youth Prince Alfred, Duke of Edinburgh, produced a number of landscapes drawn in black chalk or charcoal on oatmeal coloured paper and heightened with white, a technique that was very susceptible to dramatic lighting effects such as the present one.

Prince Arthur's drawing of an explosive shell was made in March 1867, during his time at the Royal Military Academy, Woolwich.

was sent to live at the Ranger's House, Greenwich, under the supervision of his Controller, Major (later Sir Howard) Elphinstone, himself a talented and prolific draughtsman.[231] But the Prince's holidays were spent with the rest of the Royal Family, and both he and his younger brother Prince Leopold naturally received instruction from W. L. Leitch at Balmoral.[232] In January 1866 the Prince was evidently receiving additional lessons from another artist, Aaron Penley (1807-70), the drawing master at the Woolwich Military Academy. He told his sister, Princess Louise: 'Mr Penley has quite recovered, he came here this morning to give me a lesson, and I told him that you had enquired after his health and he was greatly flattered'.[233] There is a small group of studies by Prince Arthur, inscribed with the initials R.M.A. (signifying the Woolwich Academy), at Windsor.[234] In 1868, while his mother and sister Louise were on their sketching tour in Switzerland, Prince Arthur was also attempting to paint nearby. On 8 September he wrote to Princess Louise from the Hotel der Jungfrau, Eggishorn, describing his holiday: 'I have been trying to make a few watercolor sketches but the result has been very disappointing as you can easily imagine however I intend to persevere.'[235] By now Prince Arthur had virtually completed his military training at Woolwich (1866-8). Whereas 'Affie' was to be a sailor, Arthur was to be a soldier, and was soon commissioned to the Royal Engineers. For both professions a rudimentary knowledge of draughtsmanship was required. In March 1867 he sent home a carefully shaded drawing of an explosive shell, an innocent still life study of one of the key weapons in the many conflicts which were to divide Europe during the remainder of the Prince's long lifetime.[236]

5

QUEEN VICTORIA'S GRANDCHILDREN AND THE TWENTIETH CENTURY

The quantity (and quality) of works by Queen Victoria and Prince Albert and their children described in the last two chapters was quite exceptional. By the early years of the present century (and particularly following World War I) the fabric of society which had nurtured and provided the context for the thorough artistic training of earlier royal personages was beginning to disintegrate. Thereafter it was no longer a natural part of a well-educated child's upbringing to receive lessons in drawing and painting. When in 1918 George V questioned the usefulness of painting (specifically still life painting) taught in schools, he was thus mirroring the changing place of art instruction as part of a general education – as well as revealing his own almost total lack of interest in art. His Minister of Education, the historian H. A. L. Fisher (1865-1940), pointed out that painting 'trains the powers of observation'. 'Perhaps', the King conceded.[1]

However, the majority of Queen Victoria's grandchildren were born well within the nineteenth century and therefore, like their parents and grandparents, most of them benefited from formal art teaching. The fact that their mothers were likely still to be receiving artistic instruction led to the same type of continuity as that seen in the work of Queen Charlotte and her children, and of Queen Victoria and hers. The sons and daughters of the Princess Royal, who was the first to be married (in 1858, to Prince Frederick William of Prussia), were all taught to draw. In May 1871, shortly before the Queen's birthday, the Crown Princess wrote to inform her mother that: 'The boys have done some drawings for you (*copies*) unfortunately they do not like drawing and have *no* taste for it . . . they never touch a pencil unless they can possibly help it (how different from us, as children we were *so* fond of scribbling).'[2] Nevertheless, in July of the following year, while the Crown Princess and her family were in North Friesland for their summer holidays, both she and her eldest son, William (1859-1941, from 1888 the Kaiser William II) received lessons from the local artist C. K. Magnussen.[3] Remarkably – in view of the numerous upheavals in Germany during the present century – the Prince's pencil drawing of Elena Hajens, made at the time, has survived in the Neues Palais, Potsdam.[4] Among the other drawings by Prince William in the same collection are a chalk study of an athlete, drawn at Cassel (where the Prince was educated) in May 1876, and two drawings dating from a visit to England in 1880: ships in the port of Sheerness and a British troop carrier passing the Needles.[5] A large black chalk drawing of the sculpted figure of an eagle, ready to strike out from its stone plinth, is inscribed 'Wilhelm von Preussen, 1895'.[6] The artist was by now Emperor of Germany, and relentlessly pursuing his policy of Prussian imperialism, of which the eagle was the principal symbol. The last two drawings of any note at Potsdam are related to two sculptural projects in which the Kaiser was evidently involved. Firstly, the statue to Admiral Raule ('the first Brandenburg Admiral') for the Marine Academy at Kiel, dated October 1900, and secondly the Achilles statue for the garden of the Kaiser's villa, Achilleion, on Corfu, dated 1908.[7] Ten years later, after World War I and the collapse of the German armed forces, the Kaiser was forced to abdicate and lived the remainder of his life in exile, in the Netherlands. Without any trace of irony he reproduced a watercolour sketch of himself by Queen Victoria as the frontispiece to his autobiography.[8]

Among the many German states to suffer under Prussian imperial ambitions was the Grand Duchy of Hesse. Kaiser William II's aunt, Princess Alice, had married Prince Louis of

A sketch of a British troop carrier passing the Needles, made by the future Kaiser during a visit to his grandmother in 1880. It was drawn on the back of an envelope containing the Prince's copy of a German sporting magazine.

Hesse in 1862. There is a pen drawing, dated 1880, of Schloss Auerbach (near Darmstadt) by their eldest child, Victoria (1863-1950), in the Royal Collection at Balmoral. After Princess Alice's early death, Queen Victoria encouraged her widowed husband and his children to spend their holidays in Britain, and got to know them well. Princess Victoria's drawing was presumably a gift to her grandmother during her visit (to Windsor and Balmoral) in the summer of 1880. In the Hesse family collection at Wolfsgarten there is a small sketchbook containing drawings and watercolours by the future Grand Duke Ernest Louis (1868-1937). Poignantly, the studies include copies made by the 17-year-old Prince of drawings by his dead mother. Two of these (studies of Victoria and Ella as children) were made four years before his own birth. Another, of a man called 'Ismarie' with a bandaged head, had been drawn in 1877, the year before Princess Alice's own death. Like his first cousin the Kaiser, Ernest Louis continued to sketch throughout his life and was a notable supporter of the Jugendstil, the German version of Art Nouveau. His sketchbook at Wolfsgarten contains coaching scenes, a sledging party in 1885, a curious subject of butterflies towing two ladies on a lily pond (inscribed Balmoral, 26 September 1885), and a scene in the officer's mess at Darmstadt (dated 1st February 1887).

In 1894, much to the delight of Queen Victoria, Ernest Louis married his first cousin Victoria Melita (1876-1936), the third child and second daughter of Prince Alfred, Duke of Edinburgh,

This sledging scene was sketched by the teenage son of the late Princess Alice and Grand Duke Louis IV of Hesse and the Rhine. Later, Prince Ernest was to become a notable supporter of the Jugendstil.

*The eighteen-year-old
Prince Ernest of Hesse
painted this scene in an
officers' mess in Darmstadt on
1 February 1887.*

and the Grand Duchess Marie. But the marriage was not a happy one, and ended in divorce after seven years. There are numerous drawings and paintings, in oil and watercolour, by Victoria Melita and her sisters at Langenburg, to which the contents of their family home in Coburg were transferred. The sisters' works share a common style: carefully arranged flowers or plants, sometimes with the addition of a symbolic sword or wreath, or other ornamental device, often in a long narrow format. There are also decorative objects such as ornamented eggs (inspired by their Russian mother), leather screens with embossed designs, and painted fans. A small group of the sisters' work survives in the Royal Collection, gifts to their grandmother, Queen Victoria. The eldest Edinburgh daughter, Princess Marie ('Missy'; 1875-1938), who had in 1893 married the future King Ferdinand I of Roumania, presented a stylized watercolour of tulips at Christmas 1897.[9] Another painting from the same year, of a single orchid with a bee, in a horizontal format, is so similar to some of the Princess of Wales's flower studies of the 1890s that it is very probable that they shared the same master.[10] One of 'Missy's' paintings at Windsor is a vellum sheet adorned with irises and stylized wheels, in an almost abstract pattern (Plate 57).[11] The names of Princess Marie's teachers are given in her autobiography: Fräulein Anna Messing taught her in the early days at Coburg, and later she and 'Ducky' (Victoria Melita) received lessons from Ruth Mercier, 'a remarkable flower painter' (who later also taught Princess Patricia of Connaught):

> My love of colour and instinctive feeling for line was a great asset; I never worked enough to be a real artist, but what I did produce had a certain originality . . . I developed my talent along certain lines with a tendency towards the decorative, acquiring a style of my own in which form and colour played the chief part . . .
>
> Ducky and I spent many happy hours painting together. In those days I was perhaps the better painter of the two, but in later life she became a real artist, whilst I laid down the brush for the pen.
>
> [At the age of 22 and 23] we decided each to paint a book for the other decorated with flowers and as text a selection of those poems and quotations most dear to us . . . we still treasure them immensely.
>
> My first book was painted on Japanese paper, but . . . later books [a wedding present for Pauline Astor and a gift to her husband] were painted on precious parchment, each page framed in silver and the whole book cleverly mounted on hinges so that when opened the pages lay quite flat.[12]

Princess Marie had at one stage been considered as a possible bride for her cousin George, the Prince of Wales's second son (and the future King George V). However, her father favoured a match with the Crown Prince of Roumania. The biographer of Prince George's eventual bride, Queen Mary, was very critical of 'Missy', who 'developed into a very theatrical personage, authoress of an extemely clever book of Memoirs', concluding that 'she would not have proved a satisfactory help-mate for Prince George'. A recent biography of 'The Last Romantic' has been more generous in her praise.[13]

The marriage in 1896 of the third Edinburgh daughter, Alexandra (1878–1942), to Prince Ernest of Hohenlohe-Langenburg (the grandson of Queen Victoria's half-sister, Feodora) provides the explanation for the presence of this 'royal art' at Langenburg. The castle there contains numerous examples of her artistic talents, whether in watercolour, pokerwork (for leather-

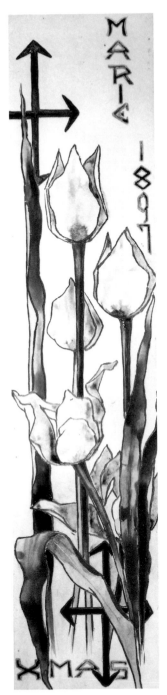

A Christmas gift to Queen Victoria in 1897 from her granddaughter, Marie, Crown Princess of Roumania.

covered screens, or wooden furniture), or in the coloured wax decoration of Easter eggs. The latter was evidently inspired by Alexandra's Russian mother, the Grand Duchess Marie, whose haughty manner led to her being called 'the most unpopular Princess in England'.[14] One of Alexandra's paintings, of irises and swastikas arranged in a similarly decorative style to the vellum painting by the Queen of Roumania, was presented to Queen Victoria in 1898.[15]

No works by the children of Queen Victoria's third daughter Helena, Princess Christian, have survived in the Royal Collection. In her gossipy autobiography, the fourth child (and second daughter) Marie Louise (1872–1956) describes a visit to Gibraltar in 1901, the year after her divorce from Prince Aribert of Anhalt. She befriended the Chief Justice, Sir Stephen Gatty, 'a wonderful person, full of interest and with a great feeling for art, and he was busily engaged in experimenting in the art of enamelling.'[16] The Princess 'became fascinated by this art, for, as you know, I have no talent for either painting or drawing, but colour appeals to me greatly.' Following her return to England, and with the assistance of Mr William Soper, Princess Marie Louise set up her own studio at the top of her house in Queensberry Place.

> Here I had a little furnace, my workman's bench, and rows of glass jars which contained the crystals which were to produce the various colours . . . I copied a great many pieces of Fabergé's jewellery, including a small pink brooch belonging to my sister. I brought her the two brooches, and taking up the one I had made (though she did not know this), she said, 'Of course, you cannot equal this: one can tell at a glance that it is Fabergé's' . . .
>
> One of my works was the clasp of the large ceremonial cope which the Bishop wears for the service of the Order of St Michael and St George (Plate 58). It was actually exhibited in the Royal Academy, and I am very proud to be the first member of the Royal Family to have exhibited there.[17]

Princess Marie Louise was wrong in thinking that she was the first member of the Royal Family to have exhibited at the Academy, for her aunt Princess Louise had done so in 1868, 1869 and 1874. The marriages of both Princesses Louise and Marie Louise were childless, which may provide some explanation for their continuing artistic endeavours. The same explanation cannot, however, account for the extraordinary quantity of drawings, collages and paintings in oil, watercolour and gouache that survive by Lady Patricia Ramsay (1886-1974), the youngest child of Prince Arthur, Duke of Connaught.

As the second daughter of a rather difficult mother, Princess Patricia was shy and withdrawn, finding more pleasure in the company of her painting tools than in social discourse. In February 1919, at the end of her thirty-third year, she married the Honourable Alexander Ramsay, a younger son of the Earl of Dalhousie: two days before her wedding she asked to relinquish her royal style and title, and was thereafter known as Lady Patricia Ramsay. The following December her only child, Alexander, was born, and the majority of her paintings (around six hundred in all) remain in his possession.

Lady Patricia continued to 'work' throughout her long life. In the 1950s she was described in the following terms by her first cousin, Princess Marie Louise: 'tall, beautiful, gifted, and a brilliant artist. Her paintings are rather modern – in fact, very modern – and sometimes I realise that I am not sufficiently "up" in the expression of modern art to appreciate all her pictures, though I know that they are brilliantly clever.'[18] With Lady Patricia's paintings we do indeed move away from the normal range of copies, or watercolour sketches made on outings, or even grandiose 'serious' oil paintings (as found in the Empress Frederick's *œuvre*), to a series of spontaneous expressions and subject pieces, using paint and colour with a delight and freedom which was often remarked on by her contemporaries – and with more sympathy than that voiced by Princess Marie Louise. At the time of the first of her one-man exhibitions, held at the Goupil Gallery, London, in May 1928, R. H. Wilenski devoted an article in *Apollo* magazine to a discussion of her paintings.[19] Wilenski described Lady Patricia as 'an amateur artist of genuine talent', and her pictures as:

> elaborate pictorial arrangements by an artist, long resident in the regions, and stimulated by forms and colours to seek to capture and record their appeal to her; they are not travel jottings but pictures evolved from perception and memory; and they are attacks in many cases on problems presenting pictorial difficulties which most professional artists would hesitate to undertake.

In addition to her three one-man shows, Lady Patricia exhibited regularly (but apparently reluctantly) throughout her life. She was elected a member of the New English Art Club in 1931, having already exhibited her paintings there from 1928, and she was made an Associate of the Royal Society of Painters in Watercolour in 1940, after several of her works had been included in their exhibitions. She was also an honorary member of the Royal Institute of Painters in Watercolour, and a member of the Royal West of England Academy.

The origin of all this activity must lie in the painting instruction given to both Princess Margaret and Princess Patricia of Connaught around the turn of the century. A series of photographs exist of the two sisters at work in their studio in the Royal Hospital, Dublin, in April 1904, during their father's time as Commander of the Forces in Ireland.[20] The subjects are entirely botanical, in a similar style to some paintings by the

The two daughters of Prince Arthur, Duke of Connaught, in their studio at the Royal Hospital, Dublin, in April 1904, while their father was Commander of the Forces in Ireland. The eldest sister, Margaret, married the future King Gustaf of Sweden in 1905, while the younger, Patricia, married the Hon. Alexander Ramsay in 1919. Both sisters continued to paint throughout their lives. One of the flower studies painted by Princess Patricia at this time is illustrated as Plate 59.

LEFT: Plate 57. *Princess Marie, eldest daughter of Prince Alfred, Duke of Edinburgh, adapted the initial letter of her name to resemble a crown on her marriage to the future King Ferdinand I of Roumania in 1893. This abstract pattern of flowers and wheels was painted on vellum.*

BELOW: Plate 58. *Princess Marie Louise, the second daughter of Princess Helena and Prince Christian, learned the art of enamelling during the early years of this century, partly in emulation of Carl Fabergé. The prelate's morse of the Order of St Michael and St George was both designed and made by the Princess.*

ABOVE: Plate 59. *While Princesses Patricia and Maud were in Dublin in April 1904 they painted a number of different flowers and plants (see p. 178). This study of a day lily shows Princess Patricia's sure handling of watercolour, at the age of eighteen.*

ABOVE: Plate 60. *Princess Patricia only signed those paintings with which she was satisfied, her signature being VP (Victoria Patricia) before her marriage (in 1919), and VPR thereafter. This still-life painting includes the same white vase as that shown in the doll's house watercolour of the early 1920s (see p. 183), and probably also dates from around that time.*

LEFT: Plate 61. *This oil painting of water lilies in the pond at Bagshot Park was painted by Lady Patricia Ramsay in the 1930s. The treatment of the subject-matter, and the almost impressionistic handling of the paint, may be connected with the period from 1919 to 1922 when the Ramsays resided in Paris.*

RIGHT: Plate 62. *The Ramsays visited Ceylon during the mid-1920s and in 1936, when Alexander Ramsay was Commander-in-Chief of the East Indies station. This view of Kandy must have been painted during the first visit as it was included in Lady Patricia's exhibition at the Goupil Gallery, London, in 1928. The effects of her contact with the bright colour of Ceylon (and Bermuda) can be felt throughout her later work.*

BELOW: Plate 63. *When visiting the South of France, Lady Patricia found a similar range of colours to those recorded in Ceylon. In this painting, entitled* Dans le Midi, *the oil colours are applied in short, impressionistic dabs.*

RIGHT: Plate 64. *This rural English scene may have been painted by Lady Patricia Ramsay in the 1940s, after her family moved to Ribsden Holt, Windlesham, Surrey.*

RIGHT: Plate 65. *Queen Alexandra lovingly preserved the early artistic offerings of her children in a leather-bound album. This frieze of totem-like figures was inscribed 'For dear Motherdear From Eddy August 21 1877' by her eldest child, the thirteen-year-old Duke of Clarence.*

ABOVE: Plate 66. *As well as receiving lessons in chalk drawing, the Prince of Wales's daughters were taught the rudiments of watercolour painting. This still-life study was inscribed by the eldest daughter, Princess Louise, in 1881.*

ABOVE LEFT: Plate 67. *The Prince of Wales's second daughter, Princess Victoria, inscribed this sketch 'For darling Motherdear from Victoria 1881'*

LEFT: Plate 68. *Prince George, later King George V, presented this simple view to his mother in 1882.*

LEFT: Plate 69. *Princess Marina inherited her interest in painting from her father, Prince Nicholas of Greece. The year after their marriage (1934) the Kents were left Coppins (in Buckinghamshire) by their cousin, Edward VII's unmarried daughter, Princess Victoria. This painting records an interior in the house.*

BELOW: Plate 70. *This view of the Private Dining Room at Windsor Castle shows the Queen reading a newspaper at the breakfast table, with two paintings by Stubbs on the walls behind. It was painted by the Duke of Edinburgh in the 1960s.*

LEFT: Plate 71. *A group of fishermen's huts with a jetty, painted by the Duke of Edinburgh during a visit to Malaysia in 1975.*

BELOW: Plate 72. *Princess Margaret composed a number of feather pictures during the 1960s creating flower pieces from the feathers of pheasants, partridges and other birds*

ABOVE: Plate 73. *This teapot belongs to a tea service made by Spode to Princess Margaret's designs in 1956. Both the shape and the decoration were devised by the Princess. Around 150 years earlier two of George III's daughters had been involved in porcelain design in a comparable way.*

RIGHT: Plate 74. *The Prince of Wales made this watercolour of Petra during a visit to Jordan in March 1985*

BELOW: Plate 75. *During part of the visit of the Prince and Princess of Wales to Italy in 1985, they were accompanied by the artist John Ward whose influence can be seen in this watercolour of a deck chair on* HMY Britannia

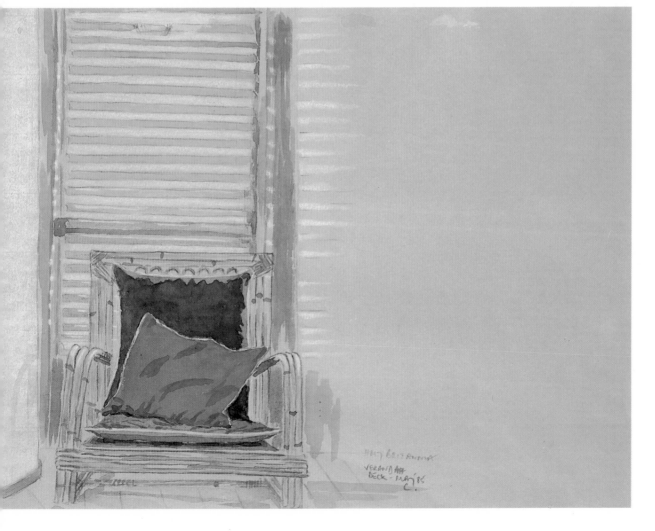

Plates 76 and 77. *These watercolours by the Prince of Wales were painted on board HMY* Britannia *in 1986. The flagpole dominates the view off Skye, while the naval escort HMS* Glamorgan *is seen head-on, but at a distance, off Scrabster.*

Edinburgh daughters at Langenburg (Plate 59). In June 1905, Princess Margaret (1882-1920) left home, following her marriage to Gustaf, Crown Prince (later King) of Sweden: she continued to paint throughout her life, and there have been several posthumous exhibitions of her work in Stockholm.[21] The name of one of Princess Patricia's early teachers is revealed in a letter from her mother to her father the month after Princess Margaret's wedding: 'This morning Patsy painted with Mme Mercier and had quite a serious and *most* instructive time with her.'[22] In an early album of Princess Patricia's work there are also two pencil portraits of Lady Marjorie Manners, inscribed Gosford, October 1904.[23] Following her elder sister's marriage, Princess Patricia accompanied her father on the numerous voyages that resulted from his positions as Inspector-General of the Forces (1904-7) and British High Commissioner in the

A portrait by Princess Patricia of Lady Marjorie Manners, the future Marchioness of Anglesey, drawn at Gosford House in October 1904. Lady Marjorie also portrayed Princess Patricia.

Mediterranean (1907-9). There are watercolour sketches of the sun setting over the Nile at Khartoum and Omdurman in February 1905, very similar in effect to those made by Princess Patricia's aunt, Princess Louise, Duchess of Argyll, on her trip down the Nile in the following year.

From 1911 to 1916 the Connaught family was resident in Ottawa, during the appointment of the Duke as Governor-General and Commander-in-Chief of the Dominion of Canada. The day after their arrival in Ottawa, the Duchess noted in her diary: 'Had fun seeing some of the things P. has brought with her – her sketches too, she has made most wonderful progress whilst painting in London.'[24] Another parallel between the lives and interests of Princess Patricia and her aunt Princess Louise is pointed out in a letter from the Duke of Connaught to his sister in 1912: 'Yesterday I opened the 22nd exhibition of the Royal Canadian Academy, which really owes its inception to you . . . Patsy sent 4 landscape oil pictures which looked quite well, the colouring being distinctly good, 3 were Canadian scenes & 1 Swedish.'[25] Princess Patricia's painting activity at this time is documented, through both photographs and paintings. There is a photograph of her painting in oils on the golf course, Banff (Canada), in the Royal Archives. A number of her photograph albums include snapshots of the artist at work.[26]

Princess Patricia of Connaught (later Lady Patricia Ramsay) was active with her paints during the period 1911-16, when her father was Governor-General of Canada. This photograph shows her sketching at Lake Louise, named after her equally artistic aunt, Princess Louise, Marchioness of Lorne.

One of them contains views of the Princess's sitting room, with her framed landscapes (mostly of Sweden, home of her sister Margaret) around the walls. She labelled one of the views: 'My sitting room, with my sketches around the walls', adding (in 1963) 'now they would be called pictures (oils)!' Only a few paintings can be securely placed during this period. There is a dramatic winter landscape dated 1916, inscribed on the back: 'Ice breaking up in Spring on the Ottawa River, below the Rideau Falls'. Two other oils, both dated 1914, were presented to the National Gallery of Canada in the following year.[27] One of these, a *Still Life with Flowers and Porcelain*, is among the first of a number of flower still lifes by the Princess. The other painting, *A Woodland Glade*, well demonstrates the effectiveness of the Princess's impressionistic use of paint, which remained a hallmark of her style for many years thereafter. During these same years Princess Patricia was also involved in the more serious (and important) work of assisting her father in his official duties. As a Prussian princess, who enjoyed rather poor health, life was far from easy for the Duchess of Connaught during World War I so her daughter's help was important. In the first year of the war a new regiment was formed in Canada to fight with the British army in France. It was named Princess Patricia's Canadian Light Infantry. To mark and encourage the new troop, the Princess designed both their badge[28] and their Regimental Colour, which was also worked by Princess Patricia. It was carried in the many battles fought by the regiment until 11 November 1918.[29]

The Duchess of Connaught died the year after the family's return to England, and two years later Princess Patricia married, thereafter signing her pictures 'VPR' rather than 'VP'. The Ramsays lived a somewhat peripatetic life, moving from Paris (where Alexander Ramsay was Naval Attaché from 1919 to 1922) to Bermuda, Ceylon (where his ship was *c*.1926, and where he returned, as Commander-in-Chief of the East Indies Station 1936-8) and elsewhere. Lady Patricia was herself chiefly resident in England, in the Duke of Connaught's homes at Clarence House and Bagshot Park, until she inherited Ribsden Holt, Windlesham, on the death of her aunt, Princess Louise, the Duchess of Argyll, in 1939. Lady Patricia's master at this time is known to have been A. S. Hartrick (1864-1950), who trained in France in the 1880s and was in touch with Gauguin at Pont Aven. A view of rooftops and chimneypots is inscribed: 'My first pen and ink drawing, done under Mr A. S. Hartrick's tuition – view from Clarence House over roofs at St James's

Following the return of the Connaught family from Canada and Princess Patricia's marriage, she took drawing lessons from A. S. Hartrick. This study is inscribed 'My first pen and ink drawing, done under Mr A. S. Hartrick's tuition – view from Clarence House over roofs of St James's Palace VPR'.

Palace VPR'. A very similar pen drawing of 'My books, in my sitting room at Clarence House', is dated February 1924.

Lady Patricia's work was normally in oils, on a rather large scale, but in the early 1920s she provided a minute watercolour still life entitled 'The White Vase' for Queen Mary's Doll's House. The impressionist handling of the paint has momentarily gone, as it has in another (larger-scale) still life in oils of the same period (Plate 60). The Goupil Gallery exhibition in 1928 included a number of views in Ceylon, and the bright colours which she recorded there and in Bermuda remained an inspiration throughout her life (Plate 62). There is a series of oils of underwater vegetation, also painted in bright tints, through a

glass-bottomed boat or bucket. One of the Princess's commissioned works was an underwater triptych for Mrs Chester
Beatty. A richly coloured view 'Dans le Midi' is in the collection
of HM Queen Elizabeth The Queen Mother at Clarence House
(Plate 63).[30] Other mature works include agricultural scenes, a
self-portrait dated 1945, oxen by a shed in Ceylon (completed
1948), garden views (presumably dating from after the move

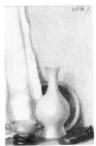

*This tiny watercolour,
reproduced here actual size,
was Lady Patricia Ramsay's
contribution to the art
collection in Queen Mary's
Doll's House in the early
1920s.*

*Lady Patricia was in her late
sixties when she painted
this picture, entitled*
Abstract Sunny Window.

to Ribsden Holt), and *Water Lilies* and *The Tank Garden* at Bagshot Park (Plates 61, 62 and 64). A new style is seen in a painting of 1954 entitled *Abstract Sunny Window*,[31] and in two paintings purchased by the National Gallery of Canada in the 1960s, *Fruit on a Blue Ground* dated 1961 and *The Sea* dated 1965.[32] At the same time Lady Patricia was working on a picture entitled *West Highland Abstract* in which intersecting forms make peaks and slopes with different facets coloured green, white, red, blue and purple. This is indeed a 'very modern' view of Scotland, by someone in her seventies, who also happened to be a granddaughter of Queen Victoria.

Princess Alice, Countess of Athlone (1883–1981), was Lady Patricia's senior by three years. She was the only daughter of Queen Victoria's fourth son, Prince Leopold, Duke of Albany, who died the year after Princess Alice's birth. Both her parents were friends and pupils of John Ruskin, whose lessons to the other Princess Alice were noted above. An album of drawings and prints made up by Queen Mary for the Princess and her husband (Queen Mary's younger brother Alexander of Teck, 1st Earl of Athlone) in 1940 contains both a landscape study drawn by Ruskin for the Duchess of Albany in the 1880s, and a group of watercolours by Princess Alice herself, from around the turn of the century.

Sir Robert Collins was a devoted member of the household of the Duke and Duchess of Albany. He is seen here in a watercolour by the 17-year-old Princess Alice, later Countess of Athlone.

In 1901, Arthur Edward, Prince of Wales, had succeeded his mother as King Edward VII, himself to be succeeded by his only surviving son, 'Georgie' as King George V in 1910. Probably owing to his own very formal and structured upbringing, which had in no way been suited to his temperament, the children of the Prince and Princess of Wales were taught in a much more relaxed way. Indeed, in comparison with most of their cousins they were not well-educated. In addition, from an early age their health was 'most wretched excepting Georgie, who is always merry and rosy', as their grandmother observed.[33] Six children were born of the Prince and Princess of Wales's marriage, of which the youngest, Alexander John, died soon after birth (1871). Following the two boys, Prince Albert Victor, Duke of Clarence (1864-92), and Prince George (1865-1936), came Princesses Louise (1867-1931), Victoria (1868-1935) and Maud (1869-1938: later the Queen of Norway). At Sandringham there is a volume containing drawings by each of the children (excepting John), invariably inscribed 'to Motherdear', and dated between the years 1873 and 1882 (Plates 65-68).[34] When turning the pages of this album one is struck by the similarity between these sketches (even scribbles) and those produced by children in the 1980s. There is a naïve spontaneity about them which is quite distinct from the more polished works of Queen Victoria's children at a similar age. A thorough artistic grounding from teachers such as Messrs Corbould and Leitch was no longer considered necessary from such an early age. Nevertheless, by their teens the girls were evidently receiving some sort of artistic tuition. In the Print Room at Windsor there is a uniform series of head studies, in red chalk on blue paper, by each of the three girls, dated 1881.[35]

In July 1889, at the age of 22, Princess Louise became engaged to be married to the 6th Earl (later 1st Duke) of Fife. As was the case with the marriage of her namesake and aunt, the Duchess of Argyll, Queen Victoria overlooked the fact that the Earl was not of royal birth, and showed a realistic grasp of the necessities of life in her comment to her own eldest daughter about the impending match: 'It is a vy brilliant marriage in a worldly point of view as he is immensely rich.' Princess May of Teck, the future Queen Mary, was one of the bridesmaids at the wedding, and commented: 'The presents were gold bangles with a diamond L & F with her crown & his coronet on top, they were designed by Louise, but honestly I don't think they were very pretty.'[36] The survival of a small group of (mainly undated) drawings by Princess Louise in the

Study by the eleven-year-old
Princess Maud of Wales
(nicknamed 'Harry'), who
was to marry the future King
Haakon VII of Norway.

possession of the Duke of Fife, the son of her daughter Maud, would suggest that she continued to paint and draw after her marriage. There are charming studies of kittens playing, a portrait of a pet guinea pig, and a single pansy painted on a piece of writing paper headed 'Duff House, Banff, N.B.', all indicating the years when Princess Louise's two children, Alexandra (1891-1959; married Prince Arthur of Connaught) and Maud (1893-1945; married 11th Earl of Southesk), were growing up.[37]

Apart from his contributions to the Sandringham album, only one very slim volume of drawings by the girls' brother, Prince George (the future George V), has survived in the Royal Collection. This contains pencil outlines of simple forms such as vases, boxes and an antelope. The volume is inscribed 'Bernstorff, September 1874', and dates from the Prince's eleventh year. Three years earlier the Prince and his elder brother 'Eddy', later the Duke of Clarence and Avondale (1864-92), had been placed under the tutorship of Canon Dalton, who was to supervise their education until 1885. As Prince George had always been destined for a career in the Royal Navy, long periods during his adolescence were spent at sea, in the company of both his elder brother and Dalton, but apparently without

Princess Louise, the eldest daughter of the future King Edward VII, drew this fisher lady knitting in 1884.

any idea of making use of watercolours or a sketch pad. In the context of the serious and active interest taken in the arts by other members of Prince George's family (including his sisters), it comes as a slight surprise (and disappointment) to hear his comment on the Impressionist paintings at the Tate Gallery which he saw, willy-nilly, at the opening of the new extension in 1926: 'Here's something to make you laugh, May!'[38] With some justification, the only portrait of himself that he really liked was Lavery's conversation piece of the King, the Queen and their eldest children, now in the National Portrait Gallery, London.

> When viewing the work in the artist's studio, the King said he would like to have a hand in it, and was allowed to add a touch of blue to the Garter ribbon; the Queen followed suit. It pleased Lavery to recall that Velazquez, when painting Philip IV of Spain, had permitted the King to add the red cross of a Knight of Calatrava to his portrait.[39]

In 1893, four years after his sister Louise's marriage, Prince George had himself married Princess May of Teck (1867-1953), the daughter of the jolly Princess Mary Adelaide (1833-97) who, as the child of George III's son Adolphus, Duke of Cambridge, was a first cousin of Queen Victoria. Princess May and her three younger brothers, Adolphus (1868-1927), Francis (1870-1910) and Alexander (1874-1957), spent their first years in the charming surroundings of White Lodge, Richmond, and Kensington Palace, until their mother's extravagance forced the family into involuntary exile on the Continent from 1883 to 1885. The Teck children were contemporaries of the Wales children, but received a more traditional educational 'grounding'. Their mother ensured that they were all taught to work with their hands, and the children's presents to Queen Victoria bear witness to their varied accomplishments. One such gift was accompanied by a letter from Princess Mary Adelaide: 'The children made the basket for you (all traced, for cutting out with a saw, and therefore not quite so difficult as would appear). They are overjoyed at your kind mention of their work and you cannot think the pleasure they took, in making the basket for you!'[40] Other presents included a box decorated with forget-me-nots 'drawn from nature', a plate painted by Princess May with gold, that had had to be 'fired several times', and a 'novelty for flowers'.[41] At the time of the Queen's birthday in 1877, Princess May, not yet ten years old, informed her that: 'My brothers and I have had great pleasure in working You a pocket-handkerchief case, which we lay most respectfully at Your feet and hope You will kindly use in remembrance of Your dutiful and loving little Niece and Nephews.'[42]

The enforced departure of the Teck family for Italy in 1883 came at an ideal time for Princess May. During their stay in Florence from late 1883 to mid-1885 (except for a lengthy holiday in Switzerland and Germany from July to December 1884), the Princess's love of pictures, museums and galleries was first inspired, just as countless other young English visitors to Florence, both before and since, have left the city profoundly moved by what they have seen there. Later Princess May reminisced about her time in Florence: 'Oh! how happy those days were, I sometimes long to go back there.'[43] At first the Tecks stayed at Paoli's Hotel on the Lungarno, but from April 1884 were able to borrow Miss Bianca Light's fifteenth-century Villa i Cedri, 'which stands in an English garden on the left bank of the Arno, some three or four miles from the Porta San Niccolo, near Bagno a Ripoli . . . There are no buildings between the villa and the banks of the Arno, which here forms a wide translucent weir, its waters momentarily held in check by a low lock at Bagno a Ripoli.'[44] As well as paying frequent visits to all the great churches, palaces and galleries of Florence, Princess May received lessons in singing, painting and Italian. A volume entitled 'Sketches by Queen Mary' contains very competent watercolour views (dated 1884) of the various sights of Florence, including the Arno both in the centre of town and at the bottom of the garden at the Villa i Cedri (Plate 7). These may be associated with Princess May's instruction from an artist called Verwloet, who is known to have taught her at i Cedri in May 1884.[45] Another artist encountered in Florence by the Teck family was the young Irishman Thaddeus Jones, who became attached to their household as a sort of pet. His watercolours of the same Florentine views are also in the Print Room at Windsor. An English family called Purves also befriended the Tecks, and young Daisy Purves taught Princess May 'the intricate art of crustoleum painting in the hotel sitting-room'.[46]

During part of their holiday in 1884 the Tecks stayed at the Hotel Sonnenburg in Seeligsberg, Lake Lucerne. Among the fellow guests at the hotel were the Roman landscape painter Hermann Corrodi and his wife. The Tecks and the Corrodis evidently played bowls together. Maybe the 'Commendatore' Corrodi gave Princess May a few painting lessons, just as he had taught (and continued to teach) the Princess of Wales.[47] However, apart from the Florentine views of 1884, no other works by Princess May have survived in the Royal Collection.

Following their return to England in mid-1885, the Tecks resumed their old (extravagant) pattern of life at White Lodge, Richmond Park, and at Kensington Palace. Meanwhile there was mounting discussion in royal circles about a suitable bride for the wayward elder son of the Prince of Wales, Prince Albert

Victor, Duke of Clarence and Avondale. The Queen summoned the 24-year-old Princess May to Balmoral in November 1891, so that she could get to know her better and judge her suitability for the match. She was well satisfied and reported to the Empress Frederick: 'She has no frivolous tastes, has been very carefully brought up & is well informed & always occupied.'[48] Shortly before the planned wedding, the Prince died during a severe outbreak of influenza. After a suitable pause, his younger brother Prince George proposed to and was accepted by Princess May. Following their marriage in 1893 her ceaseless activity was channelled towards maintaining their various homes, caring for a growing family, attending her husband (by now Duke of York), seeing to the increasing number of charities to which she gave her support, and visiting art galleries. In February 1910, shortly before her husband's accession as King George V, the Duchess of York wrote to inform her French companion Mlle Bricka: 'I have spent all my afternoons lately going to *Museums*, how much one learns & picks up, & how much nicer than going out to tea & gossip.'[49] Another channel for her boundless energy was needlework, which occupied Queen Mary during most evenings throughout the rest of her life. Already in the 1890s she had exhibited some of her work (alongside that of her mother-in-law, Princess Alexandra) at the Home Arts and Industries Association exhibition at the Royal Albert Hall. In 1907 she took part in Lord Grey's scheme for the Mother's Union to provide inspirational banners for presentation to nine Canadian colleges. One of the banners may have been partly worked by the Duchess of York herself.[50]

During the early 1930s Queen Mary began working in gros point, and sewed a number of chair seats, a small screen and a carpet for her room.[51] The Queen made no pretence of the fact that she played little part in actually designing the patterns to be worked. The role of the 'tapissiers' employed by Mary Queen of Scots was now filled by the Royal School of Needlework, but Queen Mary selected the colours, and carried out all the stitching. The most notable piece of needlework to survive from Queen Mary's hand is the carpet, comprising twelve separate stitched panels and a border, now in the National Gallery of Canada.[52] The carpet is remarkable initially as the product of many hours of unstinting work, between 1941 and 1950, by a lady in her seventies and eighties: it contains well over a million stitches. But the circumstances of its arrival in Canada bestow upon it an even greater significance. Queen Mary was anxious to make her own contribution to help Britain

This photograph of the recently-widowed Queen Mary was taken in the summer of 1936, while she was staying with her son and daughter-in-law, the Duke and Duchess of Kent, at Coppins.

out of the 'dollar crisis' into which the country had plunged after the end of World War II, and she gave this carpet, the product of her years at Badminton during the war, to a committee in order to raise funds (in dollars) to be paid into the British Exchequer. It was envisaged that – in addition to the proceeds from the sale of the carpet – entrance fees to the various showings of the exhibition, and income from the sale of leaflets, photographic reproductions and so on, would make some small contribution to Britain's national plight. The plan was extraordinarily successful. Messrs Chubbs supplied a 'special oaken case, lined with metal with an inner lining of silk, four feet square and 15 inches deep', weighing 450 lb, in which the carpet crossed the ocean (on the *Queen Mary*) and then travelled from

The needlework carpet worked by Queen Mary between 1941 and 1950, her contribution to the national effort in the dollar crisis that followed World War II. It was exhibited in numerous locations in North America, and was later presented to the National Gallery of Canada by the organization (the Imperial Order of the Daughters of the Empire) that had purchased it, for Can. $100,000 in June 1950.

exhibition to exhibition. During the first tour, commencing in March 1950, it was seen by 400,000 people in twenty-eight American and six Canadian cities.

It had been specified that the carpet must finally find a home in a public institution of repute, and a number of competing bids for its purchase were considered before, in June 1950, the offer of $100,000 from the Imperial Order of the Daughters of the Empire was accepted. Queen Mary noted in her diary: 'Saw Dow. Ly Reading who told me my carpet had been bought for Canada by the "Im. Daughters of the Empire" for £35,000 to which may be added more money by degrees – This is my gift towards the National Debt --!!'[53] The first stated objective of the Imperial Order was 'To stimulate and give expression to the sentiment of patriotism which binds women and children of the Empire around the throne and person of their Gracious and Beloved Sovereign.' The IODE set up a formidable committee to raise the necessary funds (by a second great exhibition tour), before finally handing over the carpet to the National Gallery of Canada. By July 1951 the Committee was informed that over $2,000 more than was required had been raised, during a tour covering 25,000 miles and 67 exhibition locations, through which over a quarter of a million adults and 100,000 children had seen the carpet. With other miscellaneous revenue, $119,651.86 was eventually handed over to Winston Churchill to be passed on to the British Treasury. The formal presentation of the carpet from the IODE Committee to the National Gallery of Canada was made by Princess Elizabeth during her visit to Canada in October 1951. Queen Mary was naturally delighted by how it had all worked out, declaring it 'Just one of those drops which help to fill the bucket'. The whole affair had an almost touching element to it: so many hundreds of thousands of people being involved in raising funds through Queen Mary's million stitches for the British Exchequer, as if it was some sort of charitable institution.

The few surviving artefacts of Queen Mary's children are likewise more 'craft' than 'art'. In the private family museum organized by Queen Mary at Frogmore House there is a pair of animal heads cast by the eldest sons, Princes Edward and Albert (the future Edward VIII and George VI) at Osborne College in 1907 and 1908 respectively, and a wooden box with 'MAMA' incised on the lid, carefully labelled by the proud mother, 'Made by King George VI when he was at Osborne College'. An even more surprising aspect of the boys' education is raised by a pair of handscreens in the same place, the outlines of the designs (in

Casts of the heads of a fox and a cat made by the future Edward VIII and George VI at Osborne College. Each boy was 13 at the time.

one an orange branch, in the other an apple) stitched with coloured thread, like a child's lacing card. The verso of the handscreen with the orange is inscribed 'worked and painted by Edward of York, 1910' (i.e. at the age of 16), and of the apple 'From George Xmas 1908' (i.e. at the age of 13).[54] Both Princes continued to 'work' into adulthood, following their mother's example. According to Edward VIII: 'At Sandringham my brothers and sisters and I used to sit around her at tea-time. While she talked to us, she was either crocheting or doing some kind of embroidery; and because we were all interested she taught us *gros point*.'[55] Lady Furness, who introduced the Prince of Wales to Mrs Simpson, was also responsible for teaching him petit point. 'His first project was a paper weight for his mother, embroidered with the royal crown and the initials M.R. in gold, his second a backgammon board for Lady Furness, the background beige, the points in the Guards' colours red and blue.'[56] The second brother, the future George VI, also inherited his mother's love of needlework, and worked a set of chair covers with his own hand.[57] Following his marriage to Lady Elizabeth Bowes-Lyon in 1923, Prince George, Duke of York, is said to have personally designed the decorative cipher of two interlaced E's which was embroidered (by the Royal School of Needlework) on the linen ordered for their newly equipped house at Windsor, Royal Lodge.[58] Also at Frogmore is the fully-equipped wooden paintbox given by Edward VII to the short-lived Prince John (1905-19) for his fourth birthday, and a fan painted for Queen Mary with merry men and women 'by Mary of Wales', that is the Princess Royal, later Countess of Harewood (1897-1965).

But if the children of King George V and Queen Mary were

Before her marriage, Princess Alice, Duchess of Gloucester (formerly Lady Alice Montagu-Douglas-Scott), was very active as a watercolour painter and held two exhibitions in London in the 1930s. Her subjects were views around Britain and in East Africa. This watercolour shows a family of wild boar near Lake Elmenteita in Kenya.

not particularly distinguished for their artistic products, in at least two cases they married persons of some artistic accomplishment. In 1935 the third son, Henry, Duke of Gloucester (1900–74), married Lady Alice Montagu-Douglas-Scott (born 1901), the third daughter of the 7th Duke of Buccleuch. She was taught to paint by Mr Gilmour, the art teacher at St James's School, West Malvern, where she was educated. With other members of the family she contributed illustrations to the Buccleuch family magazine, *The Schoolroom Magazine*. In the Duchess's autobiography she describes how her interest in painting developed before her marriage:

> Disapproving of my visits to Kenya, my father warned me that if I was determined to go again it would have to be at my own expense. This confronted me for the first time with the task of earning money, and I decided to hold an exhibition of my sketches. Painting was not something that I had done much before I went to Kenya, but when I got there I found myself taking it up because (this being before the days of colour photography) there was no other way of recording the colouring of the place. My sketching expeditions proved to be one of the most rewarding features of my Kenyan life – peaceful, instructive and full of incident . . .

I succeeded in fixing myself up with an exhibition of these Kenyan watercolours at Walker's Galleries in New Bond Street. I am sure the show met with much more kindly reviews than would be the case today. Even *The Times* gave me several column inches, including the compliment that: 'In Africa the artist seems to have risen to the occasion and, with imagination stimulated by unusual shapes and colours, produced a series of records which are interesting pictorially as well as from the topographical point of view'. I exhibited sixty-four pictures and sold 190 guineas-worth of them at an average of about five guineas a piece.[59]

Thus the money was found for the passage back to Kenya, which took place by flying-boat, not without incident.[60] Following Lady Alice's return from this visit, a second exhibition of her paintings was planned at the Walker Galleries. During the preparations for this exhibition she became engaged to Prince Henry, and the wedding took place quietly at Buckingham Palace on 6 November 1935, soon after the sudden death of her father in October. The Duchess has continued to paint, but latterly has confined her activity to holidays. Her subjects are mainly landscapes in Scotland, Australia, Jamaica and Africa.

The Duchess's second son, Prince Richard, the present Duke of Gloucester (born 1944), read architecture at Cambridge University (1963-9). His mother notes that he chose this course of study because he had always been good at making models, adding that, 'this proved such a success that I am sure that had Richard not succeeded to the title he would, in due course, have become well known in his own right as an architect.'[61] After coming down from university, Prince Richard joined a London firm of architects, where he was responsible for some of the administrative functions involved in a thriving architectural practice. Following the sudden death of his brother Prince William, in a flying accident in 1972, and his father's death two years later, his work at the partnership ceased. However, he is closely involved with the work of a number of organizations connected with architecture or design, and has published three books of photographs of sculpture or architecture.[62]

Prince Henry's younger brother George, Duke of Kent (1902-42), was keenly interested in art, and formed a notable collection of paintings and furniture. When he married Princess Marina of Greece (1906-68) in 1934 he reintroduced into the British Royal Family some of the active continental interest in

Princess Alice has continued to paint, particularly when travelling and while on holiday. This view from Hawley Beach, Port Sorell, Tasmania, was painted in 1946.

art that had been so apparent in the nineteenth century. Princess Marina was the third daughter of Prince Nicholas of Greece (1872-1938), who was himself the third son of Queen Alexandra's brother King George I, King of the Hellenes (1845-1913). Prince Nicholas's family was chiefly resident in Paris while his three daughters were growing up. He was an accomplished painter, his oil sketches of Athens, Switzerland and France conjuring up a curious vision of an exiled Greek Prince with palette and easel at work on the pavements of Paris,

*Cecil Beaton, who
photographed Princess
Marina, Duchess of Kent,
on numerous occasions,
commented that her portrait
of him was 'a hundred times
better than I had expected –
a really excellent likeness'.*

*Viscount Moore (the future
11th Earl of Drogheda) was
portrayed by Princess
Marina in 1937, five years
after her marriage to Prince
George, Duke of Kent.*

occasionally selling his pictures to supplement the meagre family income.[63] Princess Marina studied painting in Paris in the 1920s and befriended several artists.[64] Among these was the Russian-born Savely Sorine (1886-1953), whose style the Princess sometimes imitated. Her own works are in a variety of media and include landscapes and interiors painted in oils with great competence. In the collection of the present Duke there are two charming interiors of the Kent family home at Coppins (Plate 69), which they had been bequeathed by Edward VII's unmarried daughter Princess Victoria at her death in 1935. Princess Marina was also a talented portraitist, using charcoal or sepia wash, her subjects chosen from her family and friends. In the 1930s she portrayed Viscount Moore (now 11th Earl of Drogheda, born 1910). In 1943, the year after her husband's death, she drew Cecil Beaton (1904-80), who described his visit to the 'poor widow, her face strained and furrowed by sorrow and anxiety . . . the picture turned out to be a hundred times better than I had expected – a really excellent likeness'.[65] Sir Cecil wrote fondly of the Princess following her death:

When I think of Princess Marina I remember her deep, serious voice, and her sad smile of compassion. I recall the many photographic sessions in the garden at Coppins with her husband and children, and, at the studio . . . I can see now the expression of intense concentration as, with dust sheet on the sitting-room floor, she worked with crayons and pencils at her easel . . . Beautiful and romantic princesses are a rare phenomenon today, and their mere existence enhances. Even those who saw her only a little were warmed by the knowledge that she was there.[66]

Portraits such as these were exhibited by Princess Marina during her lifetime, at the Society of Women Artists – of which she was a patron[67] – or the Women's International Art Club.[68]

Princess Margaret (born 1930) was among those portrayed by Princess Marina. The early artistic instruction of both The Queen and Princess Margaret was rudimentary, but during the 1960s her innate artistic talents led her to evolve a rather personal art form, of flower pieces made from the feathers of pheasants, partridges and other birds, arranged and pasted on to a board (Plate 72). Around ten years earlier she had designed (with the assistance of Denys Dawnay) the smart blue, white and gold tea service, made by Spode in 1956 and still in regular use in the Princess's apartment at Kensington Palace (Plate 73). Both

CHIN-JAN.XI.LXVI

Princess Marina's dog,
Chin, drawn in January
1966.

Princess Marina used felt tip
and biro to make this study
on board the yacht Daska *in*
August 1961.

of Princess Margaret's children from her marriage to Lord Snowdon are pursuing artistic careers at a professional level. David, Viscount Linley (born 1961), having studied under the furniture designer John Makepeace, set up his own company in 1985 to design and produce high quality furniture. According to his statement at the time of the launching of David Linley Furniture Ltd., 'We design each piece ourselves and oversee each stage of production. Design is of primary importance in making furniture that is a pleasure to live with, but equally important is the choice of materials.' His younger sister, Lady Sarah Armstrong-Jones (born 1964), became a student at the Royal Academy Schools, having done her foundation course at Camberwell School of Art.

On 5 February 1952, Queen Elizabeth and Princess Margaret 'took a trip on the Norfolk Broads which lasted an hour and a half. They went to Ludham to take luncheon with Mr Edward Seago [1910-74], the artist, at his riverside home.'[69] Thereafter they returned to Sandringham and had 'a truly gay dinner, with the King like his old self'.[70] Early the following morning the King died in his sleep. A fortnight later Queen Elizabeth wrote to thank the artist for his letter of condolence, and to inform him of the pleasure the King had derived from the paintings they had brought home on that last evening.

Seago's influence lies behind many of the paintings by both Prince Philip, Duke of Edinburgh (born 1921), and Charles, Prince of Wales (born 1948). Like his first cousin, Princess Marina, Prince Philip has inherited the artistic interests of the many royal families of Europe from which he is descended. His father, Prince Andrew of Greece (1882-1944) – an accomplished watercolour artist – was the fourth son of King George I of the Hellenes, while his mother, Princess Alice of Battenberg (1885-1969), was the granddaughter of Prince Alexander of Hesse and his morganatic wife Countess Julie von Hauke.[71]

According to Prince Philip, it was Denys Dawnay who first suggested during the years immediately after his marriage (in 1947) that the Prince might derive pleasure from painting. Dawnay gave him his first paintbox and easel, which is still in use. Then, in 1956, Prince Philip invited Edward Seago to join part of his world tour on the Royal Yacht *Britannia*, sailing with him from Melbourne to Antarctica. The invitation was made principally in the hope that Seago would enjoy painting the extraordinary landscape and seascape of the South Atlantic. But the Prince was also eager to receive assistance with his own sketches, on which he had already been hard at work before

Seago embarked at Melbourne. On 19 December, while sailing towards the Falkland Islands, Prince Philip painted the artist, and the artist painted Prince Philip: in both cases the sitters are naturally represented at their easels.[72] Later the two collaborated on a lino-cut design for a certificate to be presented to each member of the ship's company in commemoration of their visit inside the Antarctic Circle. Seago wrote in his diary: 'Prince Philip has really done the design for it although the wardroom asked me, but I must admit his idea is better than what I had in mind! I am amazed at his keenness and energy.'[73] But the chief artistic productions of the voyage were paintings in oils by Seago and by Prince Philip. In the bleak surroundings of the South Atlantic, they worked together on paintings of the sea and the sky, with the occasional iceberg or rocky outcrop.

Clouds over Palmerston Island in the mid-Pacific, painted by the Duke of Edinburgh in 1971.

The Prince commented that watching Seago work was like witnessing 'a magician producing a rabbit out of a hat. One could never figure out how he did it':

> Seago wrote down a list of colours he recommended should be put on the palette and Prince Philip always kept the old envelope with the list on the back in his paint-box although he noted that Seago was far more economical in his colours than he was.[74]

Seago continued to act as Prince Philip's painting mentor until his death in 1974. The Prince works exclusively in oils, handling the paint with confidence and flair, and uses boards more often than canvas. At first Seago let him have some of his home-prepared boards, but then the Prince developed his own method of priming hardboard. His paintings are often done at sea, whether on a private voyage (such as that to the Falklands

Watercolour study of the banks of the River Nile made by the Prince of Wales during his honeymoon in 1981.

The Prince and Princess of Wales's Italian visit in 1985 culminated in a journey up the east coast, to Venice. This view from the deck of HMY Britannia shows San Giorgio Maggiore on the left, the Punta della Dogana in the middle, and the entrance to the Grand Canal to right of centre.

in 1954) or an official visit (such as that to South-East Asia in 1975; see Plate 71). The subject matter of his paintings shows that easel and paintbox have frequently accompanied Prince Philip on holiday, whether to Balmoral, Sandringham or Liechtenstein. There is also a charming view of Her Majesty The Queen at her breakfast table in Windsor Castle, painted during the 1960s (Plate 70). Prince Philip is keenly interested in photography, but only a very small proportion of his paintings are based on photographs. The remainder were painted direct from nature, as Seago's portrait of Prince Philip at work on board HMY *Britannia* well indicates. During the 1970s the Prince painted a small number of abstract subjects and still lifes, but has since concentrated on landscape views. The artist's own very honest comment on this activity is: 'I don't claim any exceptional interest or knowledge or ability. It's strictly average.'[75]

Prince Philip imparted his own love of painting to his eldest son, the Prince of Wales, who was introduced to Seago at an early age. Prince Charles recalls:

I'd tried to paint when I was about seven or eight when my father had shown me how to do it with oils. Then, about two years before Ted died, I suddenly had a yearning to try

ABOVE: *Group of houses at Altnaguithasaich, near Balmoral, painted by the Prince of Wales in the summer of 1985.*

LEFT: *The same houses on the Balmoral estate, painted the following year.*

with watercolours – firstly because it was something different and secondly, because I thought it was somehow more expressive than oils and such painting was more alive and had more texture and depth than a photograph. I struggled along and did some dreadful work. I wanted to have a lesson and took my pictures along to the Dutch House [Seago's home at Ludham, Norfolk] and asked Ted to criticize them and tell

In this desert view, sketched during the Prince and Princess of Wales's visit to Oman in 1986, the landscape is described by a very fine ink line enclosing delicate colour washes.

me where I was going wrong. He told me, for a start, I was using the wrong paper and the wrong brushes and where I could get the proper paper and brushes . . . I asked him if he'd give me a lesson. He'd never given lessons in his life; he said he was not a teacher and he didn't like teaching. Then he said, 'Alright, I'll give you a lesson – but only one.'[76]

The lesson consisted of a demonstration by the artist of how a watercolour – in this instance of a pair of Thames barges on a Norfolk broad – develops. In his contribution to Seago's biography, the Prince related that:

Watching the picture grow out of the paper was one of the most impressive demonstrations of sheer creativity that I have ever seen . . . He made it look so easy – but it's not. I went away inspired but it is extraordinarily difficult. I've tried to do it and I still try and I have lessons when I'm at Windsor. I love it because I feel one can express a great deal through it – if it works.[77]

Since this one lesson, in the early 1970s, Prince Charles has received instruction and encouragement from a number of other artists such as Elizabeth Andrewes (the wife of an Eton master), Charles Bone (President of the RIPW), John Ward, Bryan Organ and Martin Yeoman. He has worked hard to improve his technique and has contributed to several exhibitions.[78] Although he realizes that to be a serious painter he should paint 'a sky a day', there are few opportunities to do so except on holiday. His subjects are mainly landscapes or still lifes (Plates 6, 74-77). He has no wish to attempt abstracts, and believes that he is still not sufficiently adept with his brush to tackle portraits. Like the other royal artists whose careers have been charted in these pages, he paints for relaxation, and comments ruefully that when returning to the ordinary world after a sketching session, it is like coming out from behind a curtain to find life going on exactly as it was before. The enjoyment which His Royal Highness derives from his painting is self-evident. The pleasures of artistic creation (or recreation) have probably been appreciated by so many members of the Royal Family over the centuries precisely because of its very personal and private aspect, a fundamental and doubtless very welcome contrast to the relentlessly public nature of the rest of their lives.

BIBLIOGRAPHICAL NOTE

The majority of the works discussed in these pages are in the Royal Collection. In 1979 a new numbering system was commenced, listing all drawings and watercolours by royal artists with a 'K' prefix. Before this Paul Oppé had included some of the eighteenth-century material in his catalogue of the English drawings at Windsor (Oppé). A new catalogue to cover all drawings, watercolours and prints by royal artists is planned. All the nineteenth-century oil paintings in the Royal Collection (including those by royal artists) are to be discussed in a forthcoming catalogue by Oliver Millar.

Previous discussions of British royal art appear to be limited to the catalogues of the two *Royal Performance* exhibitions (1977 and 1980), and Bernard Denvir's article in the 1965 Christmas number of the *ILN*. Royal artists are sometimes included in dictionaries such as Thieme-Becker and Mallallieu. When they have shown their works in public, they are also included in lists of exhibitors, principally those compiled by Algernon Graves.

General discussions of the history of the teaching of drawing and painting often include references to our subject, for instance: F. J. Levy, 'Henry Peacham and the Art of Drawing', *Journal of the Warburg and Courtauld Institutes*, vol. 37, 1974, pp. 174-90; Ian Fleming-Williams, Appendix I and II, in Martin Hardie, *Watercolour Painting in Britain*, vol. III, London, 1968; Kim Sloan, 'Drawing – A "Polite Recreation" in Eighteenth-century England', *Studies in Eighteenth-Century Culture*, vol. 11, 1982, pp. 217-40; David Alexander, *Amateurs and Printmaking in England 1750-1830*, exh. cat., Oxford, 1983.

Individual artists are discussed in general biographical works, and in the following studies: Margaret Swain, *The Needlework of Mary Queen of Scots*, 1973; Warner, AS-E, Corden and Fitzgerald [Queen Victoria; see also H. A. Hammelmann, 'Queen Victoria's Etchings', *Country Life*, 11 April 1968, pp. 878-9, and

'Some Drawings by Queen Victoria and King Edward VII', *Girl's Realm Annual*, 1901]; John Charlton, 'Prince Albert as Artist and Collector', *Country Life*, 9 October 1969, pp.904-6; Alfred St Johnston, 'A Royal Artist' [the Princess Royal], *Magazine of Art*, vol. 9, 1886, pp.300-3; Hilary Hunt-Lewis, Appendix II in David Duff, *The Life Story of H.R.H. Princess Louise*, London, 1940, pp.337-44.

NOTES

ABBREVIATIONS

Alice Letters *Alice Grand Duchess of Hesse. Biographical Sketch and Letters,* ed. Princess Helena, London, 1884
Angelo Henry Angelo, *Reminiscences,* 2 vols, London, 1828
AS-E Aydua Scott-Elliot, 'The Etchings by Queen Victoria and Prince Albert', *Bulletin of the New York Public Library,* vol. 65, no. 3, March 1961, pp.139-53
Aspinall *The Later Correspondence of George III,* ed. A. Aspinall, 5 vols, Cambridge, 1962-70
BL British Library, London, Department of Manuscripts
BM British Museum, London, Department of Prints and Drawings
Callow *William Callow. An Autobiography,* ed. H. M. Cundall, London, 1908
Chambers John Harris, *Sir William Chambers,* London, 1970
Corden Victor Corden, 'The Queen and Painting', *Art Journal,* 1901, pp.99-100
Darby & Smith Elizabeth Darby and Nicola Smith, *The Cult of the Prince Consort,* New Haven and London, 1983
Darling Child *Darling Child. Private Correspondence of Queen Victoria and the German Crown Princess, 1871-1878,* ed. Roger Fulford, London, 1976
Darmstadt Archives Hessisches Staatsarchiv, Darmstadt
Dearest Child *Dearest Child. Private Correspondence of Queen Victoria and the Princess Royal, 1858-1861,* ed. Roger Fulford, London, 1964
Dearest Mama *Dearest Mama. Private Correspondence of Queen Victoria and the Crown Princess of Prussia, 1861-1864,* London, 1968

DNB *Dictionary of National Biography*
Dorment Richard Dorment, *Alfred Gilbert,* New Haven and London, 1985
Elizabeth Letters *Letters of Princess Elizabeth of England . . . Landgravine of Hesse-Homburg,* ed. Philip C. Yorke, London, 1898
Elphinstone Mary Howard McClintock, *The Queen thanks Sir Howard,* London, 1945
Empress Frederick *The Empress Frederick, A Memoir,* London, 1913
Farington Diary *The Diary of Joseph Farington,* ed. Kenneth Garlick and Angus Macintyre, New Haven and London, 16 vols., 1978-84
FitzGerald W. G. FitzGerald, 'Personal relics of the Queen and her children', *The Strand Magazine,* no. 78, June 1897
GPH Grossherzogliche Privatsammlungen. Collection of Princess Margaret of Hesse and the Rhine, Wolfsgarten
Harcourt Papers *Harcourt Papers,* ed. Edward William Harcourt, 14 vols, Oxford, 1887-1905
Hayes John Hayes, *The Drawings of Thomas Gainsborough,* London, 1970
Hedley Olwen Hedley, *Queen Charlotte,* London, 1975
Hubbard R. H. Hubbard, *Rideau Hall, an Illustrated History,* Ottawa, 1967
ILN *Illustrated London News*
KHF Kurhessische Hausstiftung Archiv, Schloss Fasanerie, Fulda
Leitch A. MacGeorge, *Wm. Leighton Leitch, A Memoir,* London, 1884
Marie Louise Princess Marie Louise, *My Memories of Six Reigns,* London, 1956

Master Drawings Jane Roberts, *Master Drawings in the Royal Collection,* exh. cat., The Queen's Gallery, London, 1986
Memoirs of Princess Alice Princess Alice, Duchess of Gloucester, *The Memoirs of Princess Alice, Duchess of Gloucester,* London, 1983
D. Millar Delia Millar, *Queen Victoria's Life in the Scottish Highlands depicted by her watercolour artists,* London, 1985
O. Millar Oliver Millar, *The Later Georgian Pictures in the Collection of Her Majesty the Queen,* 2 vols, London, 1969
NGC National Gallery of Canada, Ottawa
Oppé A. P. Oppé, *English Drawings . . . at Windsor Castle,* London, 1950
Owen Felicity Owen, *Joshua Kirby and Thomas Gainsborough,* exh. cat., Sudbury, Suffolk, 1980.
PAC Public Archives of Canada
Pope-Hennessy James Pope-Hennessy, *Queen Mary,* London, 1959
Potsdam Staatliche Schlösser und Gärten Potsdam-Sanssouci, Abteilung Schlösser, Aquarellsammlung
Pyne W. H. Pyne, *The History of the Royal Residences,* London, 1819
QVJ Queen Victoria's Journal, RA. (The original manuscript survives only for the years 1832-6. There is a reliable typed transcript up to the Queen's marriage in 1840. Thereafter there is the [imperfect] copy made by the Queen's youngest daughter and executrix, Princess Beatrice, who transcribed parts of the Journal before destroying the original.)

RA Royal Archives, Windsor Castle
Royal Performance *Royal Performance*, exh. cat., Hartlebury Castle, Kidderminster, 1980. (An earlier exhibition with the same title was held in the Curfew Tower, Windsor Castle, 1977.)
RPA Royal Photographic Archives, Windsor Castle
Seago J. Goodman, *Edward Seago*, London, 1978
Stuart Dorothy Margaret Stuart, *The Daughters of George III*, London, 1939

Surtees Virginia Surtees, *Charlotte Canning*, London, 1975
Twenty Years *Twenty Years at Court*, ed. Mrs Steuart Erskine, London 1916
V&A Victoria and Albert Museum, London, Department of Prints, Drawings and Photographs
Vertue G. Vertue, *Notebooks*, 6 vols., *W.S.*, XVIII-XXX, 1930-55
Victorian Exhibition *Victorian Exhibition*, New Gallery, London, 1891-2
Walpole, Anecdotes Horace Walpole, *Anecdotes of Painting in*

England, ed. R. N. Warnum, 3 vols., London, 1862
Warner Marina Warner, *Queen Victoria's Sketchbook*, London, 1979
WPR Print Room, Royal Library, Windsor Castle, where the inventory of all drawings and watercolours in the Royal Collection is maintained
WRL Royal Library, Windsor Castle
W.S. *Walpole Society*
Your Dear Letter *Your Dear Letter. Private Correspondence of Queen Victoria and the German Crown Princess, 1865-1871*, ed. Roger Fulford, London, 1971

INTRODUCTION

1 Hilary Hunt-Lewis, Appendix II, in David Duff, *The Life Story of HRH Princess Louise*, London, 1940

2 These include Princess Louise's brother Prince Alfred, Duke of Edinburgh, his sister-in-law Princess (later Queen) Alexandra, and her daughter Princess Victoria. For a discussion of their photographs see F. Dimond and R. Taylor, *Crown and Camera: The Royal Family and Photography 1842-1910*, exh. cat., The Queen's Gallery, London, 1987. More recently the present Duke of Gloucester and Prince Andrew have published selections of their photographs, while a number of other members of the Royal Family are active with their cameras, to form their own private family records

3 RA Add. U32(27 February 1858)

4 QVJ, 27 January 1835

5 Aristotle, *Politics*, Book VIII, Chapter iii

6 Henry Peacham, *The Compleat Gentleman*, London, 1622, Chapter xiii

7 *Your Dear Letter*, pp.203-4

8 *Darling Child*, p.178

9 For this phenomenon see especially Ian Fleming-Williams, Appendix II: 'The Amateur', in Martin Hardie, *English Watercolours*, III, London, 1968

10 Walpole, *Anecdotes*, III, pp.923-4

11 RA M17/2(27 April 1852). E. H. Corbould to Col. the Hon. C. B. Phipps

12 *Master Drawings*, p.14

13 Queen Victoria's drawing of a male nude (WPR, K80; illustrated

p.14) is derived from one of the figures in a study by Raphael now in the British Museum. The Queen noted that her sketch was 'copied from a photograph after Raphael Feb. 6 1860'. A photograph of the drawing (then in the collection of J. Malcolm) was included in the Prince Consort's 'Raphael Collection'

14 Holbein's painting is now in the Staatliche Museum, Gemäldegalerie, West Berlin. For the Crown Princess's copy see Sotheby's, London, sale cat., 29 November 1984, lot 768. For Princess Alice's copy of 'Jonah', see Wolfsgarten, GPH, vol. 1126. Princess Elizabeth's copy is in the Gothic House, Bad Homburg (E 120, Drawer I). The Raphaelesque original (now attributed to G. F. Penni) is WPR, RL 0804 (A. E. Popham and J. Wilde, *The Italian Drawings . . . at Windsor Castle*, London, 1949, No. 811). These works are illustrated on pp.12 and 13.

15 RA Add. 32/1734

16 QVJ, 10 July 1852

17 RA Z24/28(29 January 1870)

18 QVJ, 26 May 1834

19 RA Z20/58(27 November 1867)

20 *The House of Orange*, exh. cat., New York, 1979, no. 104

21 J. Lauts, *Karoline Luise von Baden*, Karlsruhe, 1980, and J. Lauts, 'Jean-Etienne Liotard und seine Schülerin Markgräfin Caroline Luise von Baden', *Jahrbuch der Staatlichen Kunstsammlungen in Baden-Württemberg*, 14, 1977, pp. 43-70. A good cross-section of

artistic German princesses can be found by turning to the entries for those named 'Sophie', for instance, in Thieme-Becker.

22 Information from Dr Lorne Campbell

23 WPR: box of etchings by royal artists. See also Album 3, f.12.

24 Prince Ernest's 'Scene from Woodstock' hangs in Buckingham Palace. 'The Mountain Path' was no. 774 in the old Osborne inventory.

25 Vertue IV, pp.83-4

26 BM, 1927-10-8-143. For Louis XVI's interest in turning, see below, Chapter Two, note 19.

27 F. H. Man, 'Lithography in England (1801-10)', in C. Zigrosser, *Prints*, London, 1963, nos. 48-52. For a drawing by Louis-Philippe himself, see WPR, RL 22336.

28 *Callow*, pp.24-6

29 e.g. QVJ, 9 November and 2 December 1834, 10 March 1835, 2 June and 28 December 1836

30 QVJ, 20 May and 1 June 1850

31 QVJ, 27 October 1851

32 QVJ, 13 January 1853

33 *Callow*, p. 108

34 RA Y52/50(May 1888), in translation

35 *Harcourt Papers*, VI, pp.268-9

36 Quoted in Darby & Smith, p.19

37 RA Y36/26(5 March 1841). Feodora, Princess of Hohenlohe-Langenburg, to Queen Victoria

38 FitzGerald, p.632, repr.

39 Theodore Martin, *Queen Victoria as I knew her*, Edinburgh and London, 1901, p.48

40 Corden, p.96

41 J. W. Fortescue, *Author and Curator*, Edinburgh and London, 1933, p.142

42 RA Add. T275

43 There is also a volume of Princess Charlotte's drawings in KHF, Vol. K339

44 See W. Becker, 'Zum schriftlichen Nachlass der Begründerin der Greizer Kupferstichsammlung' in *50 Jahre Staatliche Bücher und Kupferstichsammlung Greiz*, Greiz, 1970, pp.131-42. The present director of the Staatliche Museum, Greiz, has provided a detailed listing of Princess Elizabeth's collection there (correspondence with the author, May 1987). An album from Princess Elizabeth's collection, including some drawings by the Princess, was recently sold in London (Christie's, London, sale cat., 19 July 1983, lot 1. See also William Drummond, Summer Exhibition, London, 1984, No. 23). The volume had been purchased 'in 1869 at Homburg at the Sale of Pictures, Prints, etc. which had belonged to H.R.H' by Baroness Gremp van Freudenstein. The Princess's Library was catalogued by S. Leigh Sotheby and John Wilkinson, for sale in London, 7-11 April 1863

45 Other papers relating to the family of Prince Alfred, who lived in Coburg from the 1870s (and succeeded his uncle as Duke of Saxe-Coburg and Gotha in 1893), are in the Landesbibliothek, Coburg

46 FitzGerald, pp.632-3, and Corden, p.99

47 The albums belonging to 'Bauerlein' and to Madame Rollande are at GPH and WPR respectively

48 A sketchbook entitled on the cover 'Sketches Vol. II. Sketches from Nature V.R. 1845-1852' was presented by George V to Victoria University, Toronto, on the occasion of the 84th anniversary of the founding of Victoria College and the 80th anniversary of its institution as Victoria University. (Information from Dr Robert Brandeis of Victoria University Library. The volume is *en suite* with volume K25 in WPR.) Another of Queen Victoria's sketchbooks is in the London Museum, to which it was presented by the Hon. Maurice Brett (1882-1934). The cover is inscribed 'Sketches from Nature. V.R. 1857 to 1860'. A third errant sketchbook, containing studies made during the visit to Florence in 1887, was bequeathed to the Library of the University of Rochester, New York, by their one-time librarian, Dr Robert Metzdorf, on his death in 1975.

49 J. Maas, *The Glorious Enterprise,* New York, 1973, p.122

50 *Victorian Exhibition,* nos. 662-4. Lent by the Queen, the Earl of Denbigh and Mrs Manley H. Coulson

51 See Algernon Graves, *A Century of Loan Exhibitions*, London, 1914, IV, p.1580

52 RA Z8/4(10 June 1859)

53 Algernon Graves, *Dictionary of Artists*, London, 1895

54 Theodore Martin, *Life of the Prince Consort*, London, 1879, IV, p.15

I : THEORISTS AND EARLY PRACTITIONERS

1 The reference in H. Mallallieu, *British Watercolour Artists*, Woodridge, 1986, to a watercolour view of Richmond by Edward VI in the Royal Collection seems improbable

2 See Margaret Swain, *The Needlework of Mary Queen of Scots*, Van Nostrand Reinhold, 1973. For the foregoing see also Lanto Synge, *Antique Needlework*, Poole, 1982

3 Henry Peacham, *Graphice*, 1612, dedicatory letter to Sir Edmund Ashfield. See F. J. Levy, 'Henry Peacham and the Art of Drawing', *Journal of the Warburg and Courtauld Institutes*, 37, 1974, pp.174-90

4 For a discussion of this aspect of seventeenth-century miniature painting see John Murdoch's contribution to *The English Miniature*, ed. J. Murdoch, J. Murrell, P. J. Noon, R. Strong, New Haven and London, 1981, ch. 3

5 Roy Strong, *Henry, Prince of Wales*, London, 1986, pp.106-7

6 Bainbrigg Buckeridge, Appendix to de Piles, *Lives*, 1754, p.A3 (Dedication to Robert Child)

7 R. Perrinchief, *Life of Charles I*, appended to the *Icon Basilike*, 1727 edition

8 Vertue I, pp. 46, 47

9 Oliver Millar, 'The Inventories and Valuations of the King's Goods, 1649-51', *W.S.*, XLIII, 1970-2, p.247, nos. 369 and 376

10 Bainbrigg Buckeridge, p.A3. See also the references given in Thieme-Becker

11 *The Diary of John Evelyn*, ed. E. S. de Beer, Oxford, 1955, I, *De Vita Propria*, p.26. The picture letter is now London, British Library, Add. MS. 18738, f. 98. I am indebted to Kate Gibson for this reference.

12 Quoted in E. Godfrey, *A Sister of Prince Rupert*, London, 1909, p.280. Louisa's sister, Sophia, mentioned Louisa's artistic skill in her Memoirs: Louisa 'devoted herself to painting, and so strong was her talent for it that she could take likenesses without seeing the originals' (*Memoirs of Sophia, Electress of Hanover*, translated by H. Forester, London, 1888, p.15).

13 The self-portrait was formerly at Hamstead Marshall (Courtauld Institute Neg. No. B70/708). The portrait of Princess Sophia was Phillips, London, sale cat., 11 December 1984, lot 2. For other works from the Craven collection ascribed to Princess Louisa see ibid., lot 89, and Sotheby, London, sale cat., 27 November 1968, lots 89-93. Princess Louisa is also thought to have painted the group showing Elizabeth of Bohemia

with three of her daughters in attendance, which now hangs in the Gallery at Herrenhausen, Hanover. Her portrait of her cousin, the Duke of Gloucester (1640–60), still hangs in a former Craven residence, Ashdown House (National Trust Inventory, NT/P/(T)23)

14 J. Kerslake, *National Portrait Gallery. Early Georgian Portraits*, London, 1977, p.88

15 A. von Rohr, *Sophie Kurfürstin von Hannover*, exh. cat., Hanover, 1980, p.80

16 Vertue V, p.39

17 Vertue V, p.7

18 P. Morrah, *Prince Rupert of the Rhine*, London, 1976, pp.

393–4. For Prince Rupert's artistic activity see also Orovida C. Pissarro, 'Prince Rupert and the Invention of Mezzotint', *W.S.*, XXXVI, 1956–8, pp.1–9, and Edward Croft-Murray, *British Museum: Catalogue of British Drawings. Volume One XVI and XVII Centuries*, London, 1960, pp.473–5. The etching of Queen Christina and a portrait of King James I, allegedly carved by Prince Rupert, are illustrated in Morrah, *op.cit.*, facing p.178.

19 Walpole, *Anecdotes*, II, p.427

20 Walpole, *Anecdotes*, I, p.338

21 Vertue V, p. 39, and Walpole, *Anecdotes*, II, p.427

22 G. Parthey, *Wenzel Hollar*, Berlin, 1853; expanded by R. Pennington, Cambridge, 1982, nos. 922–5'

23 ibid., no. 1419

24 Vertue II, p.156

25 Vertue I, p.49

26 This was first stated by Bainbrigg Buckeridge during Queen Anne's lifetime, and was repeated by Walpole (*Anecdotes*, II, p.535)

27 *The Illustrated Journeys of Celia Fiennes*, ed. C. Morris, London, 1982, p.241

28 18 September 1875, lot 151. Referred to in Lanto Synge, *Antique Needlework*, Poole, 1982.

29 Oppé 118

2: THE EIGHTEENTH CENTURY

1 Vertue III, p.72

2 Stanway, Collection of Lord Neidpath. The painting by Mercier from which this picture was copied is now untraced, but see John Ingamells and Robert Raines, 'A Catalogue of the Paintings, Drawings and Etchings of Philip Mercier', *W.S.*, XLVI, 1976–8, p.54, no. 229

3 WPR, K459

4 Walpole, *Anecdotes*, III, p.973

5 Princess Mary's drawings are KHF. Her son Frederick (1747–1837) was also an artist, and his paintings are in KHF, WPR and at Schloss Philippsruhe. His daughter, Augusta, married her second cousin, Adolphus Duke of Cambridge, in 1818. The series of etchings by Lens is BM, English Etchings, C.272★, vol.25

6 For the Prince's possible involvement with the composition of George Knapton's portrait of his three younger children see O. Millar, no. 573, and *Frederick, Prince of Wales and his circle*, exh. cat. by Stephen Jones, Gainsborough's House, Sudbury, 1981, p.16

7 Walpole, *Anecdotes*, III, pp.751–2

8 Angelo, I, p.195

9 WPR, K199

10 BM, Bull vol. 1 (189★ b.22), nos. 14–17

11 BL, Add. MS. 37836

12 Pyne, *Frogmore*, p.8. The King's drawings are WPR, K257–K294

13 Oppé 4. The King's devotion both to Kirby and to the profession of architecture led him to finance the stay of Kirby's son, William, in Italy to study architecture in the 1760s. See Oppé, p.70.

14 Royal Academy Archives, CHA/3/17, undated

15 Owen, p.11

16 RA Add. 32/1742. The instrument, invented by Lord Bute, was also described in some detail in Kirby's *Perspective of Architecture*: see Owen, p.8.

17 Angelo, I, p.196

18 Collection of Sir Marcus Worsley, Hovingham Hall. Pen and ink and wash, 253 x 154 mm. Inscribed *Invenit, designavit dedit Georgius III*.

19 *Chambers*, pp.219, 253, with references. Two small gold-mounted ivory boxes, in which the ivory was turned (and carved) by George III, are known. For that in the Royal Collection, see Plate 14. It is inscribed inside the lid: 'The Ivory part of this Box was turned by H.M. KING GEORGE THE THIRD and by him given to my Grandfather JUNE 1774. NB My Grandfather purchased the Lathe in Paris and brought home with him a person to instruct H.M. how to use it.

Henry Duval'. A note inside the box repeats this statement, and adds that the King's teacher 'after two months staying in England, was presented with £100'. The box was given to Queen Mary by Lady Mountstephen at Christmas 1917. The second box (which has the addition of coloured foil beneath the ivory) is in the Herzog Anton Ulrich Museum, Brunswick (Inv. 304. See *Herzoglichen Museum, Führer durch die Sammlungen*, Brunswick, 1887, p.198). It was presented by George III to his sister Augusta, Duchess of Brunswick, in 1772. The identities of the King's aide and instructor are not known, but an invoice dated 22 June 1769 reimbursed John Duval & Sons for the cost of supplying a gold snuff-box and 'a Tourg. Machine a Guilloché' and transporting it from France (£50 plus £288 8s; RA16822). The art of turning was described in the lavishly produced and illustrated *L'Art du Tourneur Mécanicien*, by M. Hulot Père, published in Paris, 1775. (King George III's copy of this work is in the British Library.) In the Introduction Hulot writes: 'Tout le monde sait . . . que bien des Amateurs attirés par les agréments qui en résultent, ne dédaignent point de se livrer à ce travail; & qu'on voit même les plus grands Princes se délasser de leurs occupations importantes, en se livrant aux travaux du Tour' (pp. vii-viii). For Louis XIV's activity as a turner see Svend Eriksen, *Early Neo-Classicism in France*, London, 1974, pp. 180-1

20 George III's picture-hanging plans are to be the subject of an article by Francis Russell in the *Burlington Magazine*, August 1987.

21 *Court and Private Life in the time of Queen Charlotte*, ed. Mrs V. D. Broughton, London, 1887, I, p. 42. For the King's designs for Kew Palace, made during his first illness in December 1788, see Robert Fulke Greville, *Diaries*, ed. F. Bladon, London, 1930, p. 117.

22 *Farington Diary*, IV, p. 1354. For an illustration of Bradley's house, built to the King's design, see Lord Thorneycroft, *The Amateur*, London, 1985, p. 127.

23 Oppé 2

24 *Diaries of a Duchess*, ed. James Greig, London, 1926, p. 35. The King's drawing of Syon is K237: see illustration p. 64.

25 The second series is discussed as Oppé 1. *Kew Ferry* was Society of Artists, 1767, no. 86. Kirby's surviving oil painting of an archway in a classical landscape (Owen, no. 5) is related to George III's drawing, WPR K212 (Oppé 1).

26 Quoted in W. T. Whitley, *Thomas Gainsborough*, London, 1915, p. 51. The catalogue of the 1767 exhibition in the National Art Library at the V&A has a manuscript addition beside no. 86, Kirby's view of Kew Ferry: 'said to be painted by the King' (200.8.403A). The notes are stated to have been 'copied from those of Horace Walpole'.

27 Owen, p. 11

28 Quoted in Wilfrid Blunt, *The Art of Botanical Illustration*, London, 1950, p. 55

29 Hedley, p. 139

30 Information from Mrs N. Round, British Museum, Natural History. According to the list of subscribers to Miller's *Illustrations*, Queen Charlotte ordered two copies of the work.

The Princess Royal's drawings K1149 and K1155 copy Miller, vol. I, Class XII, Order 1 and Class I, Order 1, respectively. The *Crinum pendulum* is K1162.

31 Robert Thornton, *New Illustration of the Sexual System of Linnaeus*, London, 1799-1807

32 Hedley, p. 179

33 Christie's, London, sale cat., 16 August 1819, lot 25

34 Quoted in Stuart, p. 150

35 RA Queen Charlotte's Diary

36 Pyne, *Frogmore*, p. 11

37 H. Clifford Smith, *Buckingham Palace*, London, [1931], p. 91. The frame was supplied by the cabinet-maker Charles Elliott (1752-1832). The following reference in J. Sisson's invoice to King George III dated 26 February 1771 suggests that the Queen shared her husband's interest in perspective drawing: '2 December 1770 – For a Geometrical Square for drawing in Perspective of brass divided to 1/16 of an inch & 16 Screws with Studds for the Queens use – £1:0:0; 19 February 1771 – For dividing & Stamping 2 tangents on an Ivory scale for her Majesty – 0:5:0' (RA 16826).

38 WPR, K437 and K438

39 Oppé 6

40 *Harcourt Papers*, VI, p. 52

41 *Farington Diary*, XII, p. 4330: 11 April 1813

42 Pyne, *Frogmore*, p. 9

43 Christie's, London, sale cat., 26 August 1819, lots 139-146

44 O. Millar, no. 1142

45 *Mary Hamilton at Court*, ed. E. and F. Anson, London, 1925, pp. 55-6

46 *Harcourt Papers*, VI, p. 16

47 *Horace Walpole's Correspondence*, ed. W. S. Lewis, Oxford, 1944, vol. 12, p. 198

48 Ruth Hayden, *Mrs Delany*, London, 1980, pp. 164-5. See also *Farington Diary*, III, p. 919 (7-9 November 1797): 'The Princesses are so eager in pursuit of their studies they often rise in the summer at 4 o'clock in the morning.'

49 H. Clifford Smith, *op. cit.*, p. 91

50 Oppé 16, K371

51 Oppé 16

52 See Becker (*op. cit.* in Introduction, n. 44), p. 134. Some of Princess Elizabeth's

drawings in the Gothic House, Bad Homburg, appear to be copies (even tracings) of works by Sandby (e.g. E83). The Princess's collection at Greiz includes works by Sandby (see Introduction, n. 44).

53 RA 36842-948, *passim*

54 Pyne, *Frogmore*, p. 12

55 RA PP George IV Box 6

56 *Court and City Registers*, 1782-8

57 A copy of an Italian landscape composition by Marco Ricci in the Royal Collection, formerly in Queen Charlotte's portfolio of drawings by the princes and princesses, was attributed to Alexander Cozens by Paul Oppé (Oppé 157; see also A. P. Oppé, *Alexander and John Robert Cozens*, London, 1952, pp. 39-41). On the basis of its similarity in style and technique to drawings by Princess Elizabeth at Homburg, it must however be by the Princess.

58 *Mary Hamilton, op. cit.*, p. 95

59 WPR, Engraved Topography. Another example, printed in brown ink, is in the BM, Bull vol. I, no. 27.

60 William T. Whitley, *Thomas Gainsborough*, London, 1915, p. 115

61 Angelo, I, p. 194

62 See Oppé, p. 11

63 Quoted in Hayes, p. 70

64 Hayes, p. 70

65 cf. Hayes, no. 865, plate 325

66 O. Millar, no. 791

67 BM, English Etchings, C.3★

68 Ashmolean Museum, Oxford: Hayes, no. 266, plate 86

69 BM L.B.1. Two etchings, one in soft ground and the other in line, of the same subject are known: the line etching of 'The Wood Girl' in the Bull volumes at the BM (Bull vol. II, no. 15) is dated 1805. For related drawings by Gainsborough see Hayes, nos. 840-53 and plates 203 and 233.

70 Examples at the Gothic House and in the BM, 1887-9-22-135

71 O. Millar, no. 668. A landscape by the Duchess of Gloucester is included in the Duchess of Kent's album of drawings by Princesses Victoria and Feodora (WPR, K14, f.27)

72 Pyne, *Frogmore*, p. 12

73 BM, 1847-7-13-82. Other lithographs are at the Gothic

House, Bad Homburg (e.g. E18, E19, E40).

74 Angelo, I, p.196. For a mezzotint by Princess Elizabeth see Gothic House, Bad Homburg, E21.

75 Helmut von Erffa and Allen Staley, *The Paintings of Benjamin West*, New Haven and London, 1986, p.431, n.1. A bound series of these etchings, together with the single plate of a flowering bulb plus bee and butterfly, has a draft (pencil) title-page (V&A, E.489-499-1950).

76 Angelo, I, p.200
77 Pyne, *Frogmore*, p.13
78 Angelo, I, p.194
79 Stuart, pp.224-5
80 *Farington Diary*, V, p.1804
81 RA 36940. Queen Charlotte's diary is RA.
82 Stuart, p.185
83 *Farington Diary*, I, pp.158-9
84 The etching is WPR. The Princess's preparatory study is WPR, K1166. Giulio Clovio's original is A. E. Popham and J. Wilde, *The Italian Drawings . . . at Windsor Castle*, London, 1949, no. 243, RL 0453.
85 WPR, K513, dated 1786
86 G. Parthey, *Wenzel Hollar*, Berlin, 1853; expanded by R. Pennington, Cambridge, 1982, no. 345. Cf. WPR, K379.
87 For instance, WPR, K389, K410 and K429 are based on engravings by Jan de Visscher after Berchem; K392 is based on a print by C. Visscher, and K391 on one by Danckerts, also after Berchem
88 *Farington Diary*, III, p.919: 9 November 1797
89 Pyne, *Frogmore*, p.16
90 BM 1857-5-20-80. The inscription is on an etching other than the one illustrated.
91 The drawing is WPR, K514. The etching exists in WPR and BM.
92 WPR, K315, K316 and K515. See also Oppé 13 and 14. The posthumous inventory of the effects of her younger sister Elizabeth lists a volume of that Princess's copies, also after Piazzetta (Darmstadt Archives, Abt. D11 Nr. 142/9 (ii)).
93 O. Millar, no. 666. For an early drawing by Princess Augusta see the oval landscape dated October 1778, WPR, K313.
94 Gothic House, Bad Homburg.

For the copy of Jonah, attributed to Raphael, see illustration p.12.
95 Stuart, p.47
96 Stuart, pp.24-5. Benjamin West's portrait of the young Princess Royal with her mother had already suggested this interest in embroidery (O. Millar, no. 1142).
97 Aspinall, IV, p.306
98 Aspinall, IV, p.341
99 For this activity see Bevis Hillier, *Pottery and Porcelain 1700-1914*, London, 1968
100 *Diary and Letters of Madame d'Arblay*, ed. Charlotte Barrett, with Preface and Notes by Austin Dobson, London, 1905, V, p.282
101 or 1798. BM, Banks Collection C.1-5346. The collection was made by Miss Sarah Sophia Banks (1744-1818), only sister of Sir Joseph Banks. A slight pencil study of Cupid rowing a sailing boat was presented by the Princess to an unknown recipient in February 1812 (V&A E.457-1948).
102 *Elizabeth Letters*, p.320
103 Gothic House, Bad Homburg. Several of her prints are also WPR, BM and V&A.
104 Angelo, I, p.195
105 T. Fisher, 'The Process of Polyautography Printing', *Gentleman's Magazine*, vol. 78, pt. 1, 1808, p.195
106 Mounted into a small album in the Royal Library. Formerly in the collection of Sarah Sophia Banks (see note 101 above), to whom the individual silhouettes were presented between 1807 and 1817. Other silhouettes by Princess Elizabeth are incorporated into the album made up by Princess Augusta, Duchess of Cambridge (WPR, Album 5, ff. 1, 17 and 76. Folio 17 is illustrated on p.81).
107 Darmstadt Archives, Abt. D11, Nr. 142/10. See also Introduction, n.44.
108 Register No. W31-1984, purchased, with the aid of a gift from Mr J. A. Fothergill and his family (descendants of the original recipient). For Princess Elizabeth's rolled paper work see G. Bernard Hughes, 'English Filigree Paper-work', *Country*

Life, 21 September 1951.
109 The tea service is in the Royal Collection, Windsor: presented by Miss Montgomery Campbell in 1907. The accompanying note states that the service was 'designed by Princess Elizabeth . . . & painted by H.R.H. & her sister the Queen of Würtemberg on Royal Prussian porcelain'. Two of the fans are in the Royal Collection: one at Windsor (240 WC 13) and another at Kew (Kew 1). See also London Museum, Fans 48.109/1, presented to Miss Goff in 1789
110 Pyne, *Frogmore*, p.18. For Princess Elizabeth's decorative painting, see Edward Croft-Murray, *Decorative Painting in England*, II, London, 1970, p.204.
111 *Farington Diary*, III, p.919: 9 November 1797
112 Hedley, p.230
113 Hedley, p.186. The celebrations for the King's Jubilee in 1809 included a fête at Frogmore, to which over a thousand guests were invited. For the occasion a doric temple was built on the island in the lake: 'the designs were furnished by the Princess Elizabeth, and executed under the direction of Mr Wyatt,' (*Annual Register*, 1809, p.338).
114 The improvements evidently included the introduction of 'very necessary conveniences'. When Queen Victoria wrote to the Princess Royal about the alterations that could be made to her new home in Berlin, she advised: 'Now I told you last year that my Aunt the Landgravine, sent for a person from here to make a number of these really necessary affairs in the Palace at Homburg.' (*Dearest Child*, pp.170-1, 2 April 1859).
115 Royal Collection, Windsor
116 *Elizabeth Letters*, p.137
117 ibid., p.220
118 ibid., pp.358-60
119 For Möller see M. Frölich and H.-G. Sperlich, *Georg Möller*, Darmstadt, 1959.
120 coll. The Hon. Christopher Lennox-Boyd. The British Museum drawing is BM 1962-7-14-34.
121 BM 1857-5-20-87
122 Apparently on the

recommendation of Sir Thomas Lawrence: *DNB*. See also Rupert Gunnis, *Dictionary of British Sculptors*, London, 1968, p.402 and Terry Friedman, 'Turnerelli's Bust of Queen Charlotte', *Leeds Art Gallery Calendar*, no. 75, 1974, pp.12–18. Two landscape studies by Princess Caroline, both dated 20 July 1810, representing Richmond (near Brunswick), and Moel Stabod, Wales, were with William Drummond in 1979. In view of the date on each and the distance between the relevant localities, they may both have been copies.

123 NPG 244. Richard Walker, *National Portrait Gallery. Regency Portraits*, London, 1985, I, p.98

124 BM. The head of Hannibal is ultimately derived from Plate 63 of Fulvio Orsini, *Illustrium imagines Fulvium Ursinum*, Antwerp, 1606.

125 For the view of Windsor Castle by Ernest Augustus, Duke of Cumberland (1771–1851; WPR, K368, Oppé 16) see Plate 15. There are two paintings in

bodycolour by Augustus Frederick, Duke of Sussex (1773–1843) in WPR: K369 of 1780 (Oppé 16; see our Plate 15) and K509. A further two items are attributed to Adolphus Frederick, Duke of Cambridge (1774–1850): K370 of 1780 (Oppé 16) and K460 of 1828. There are also two drawings by Prince George of Cambridge (1819–1904): K461, and K462 of 1832.

126 PAC. There are drawings by Lord Falkland in WPR. A paintbox used by Queen Adelaide has survived in the Brighton Museum, but no works by her have been located.

127 WPR, K308-K312. See Oppé 8–10.

128 The Prince's Lodge and Music Pavilion are illustrated in lithographs by T. Moore, Boston, in William Eagar, *Nova Scotia* (n.d.). An item in the posthumous sale of the Duke's property could well have come from this music pavilion: Lot 29. A most complete music stand, designed by His late Royal Highness, adapted for a

band of forty performers, made of mahogany, in the most substantial manner . . . (James Denew, sale cat., Castle Hill, Nr. Ealing, Middlesex, 16 October 1820).

129 e.g. WPR, K377 (Plate 25), K464-K466, K516, K517

130 Mainfränkisches Museum, Würzburg, Nr. 60468

131 According to the anonymous description of the Rosenau in *Coburgisches Taschenbuch für 1821* (Coburg, 1820, p.227-8), the paintings in this room were the responsibility of one of the court painters of the Prince of Leiningen, and although the Princess oversaw the project, the only part that she actually painted was the waterfall to the left of the entrance. The correspondence of Duchess Louise, Duke Ernest I and the Princess of Leiningen allows a dating of 1815-17 for this work. The Leiningen court painter Eckardt was almost certainly involved in the project. (Information from Mr Herbert Appeltshauser, Coburg.)

3 : QUEEN VICTORIA AND PRINCE ALBERT

1 QVJ, 6 December 1836

2 WPR, K22 (f.329). Two volumes of drawings made as teaching aids by Richard Westall are WPR (see *Master Drawings*, no. 126).

3 WPR, K14. *Master Drawings*, nos. 126 and 127

4 *Victorian Exhibition*, no. 662

5 Warner, ch. 1, 2. The majority of Princess (later Queen) Victoria's portrait drawings are contained in two volumes of 'Original Portraits' in WPR: K6 and K7.

6 WPR, K14. See, for instance, Warner, p.19.

7 *Letters of Feodora*, London, 1874, p.16

8 RA Z123 'Massaroni', and Z124 'Lady Maria'. The Princess's list of her wooden dolls is Z118.

9 Museum of London (46·16/8) and *Elphinstone*, p.95

10 *Victorian Exhibition*, no. 664, lent by Mrs Manley H. Coulson. For other Hayter copies see K22, the Duke of Kent's album.

11 Retzsch's illustrations to Schiller's *Pegasus im Joche* were given on New Year's Day 1834, those to Schiller's *Das Lied von der Glocke* were given on 7 December 1834. Shakespeare's *King Lear* illustrated by Retzsch is noted on 24 May 1838, and *The Tempest* on 29 December 1840. The last was a gift to the royal couple from Prince Ernest of Saxe-Coburg and Gotha. The Princess's copies from the *Glocke* are dated August-December 1833 and December 1834, from *Faust* December 1833-November 1834, and from *Hamlet* and *Macbeth* December 1834. All these are in album K22. See also K113 and K114.

12 QVJ, 21 May 1836. For portraits by Queen Victoria of Prince Albert see Warner, pp.89-91.

13 QVJ, 24 June 1837

14 QVJ, 7 December 1837

15 Queen Victoria's studies of the

Coronation were gathered together by her in an album entitled 'Recollections of the Coronation' (WPR, K21).

16 See RA M5: Education of Princess Victoria, for a self-portrait made at Ramsgate, October-November 1835 (illustrated p.91). Two other presumed self-portraits are illustrated in Warner, pp.24 and 44. Another self-portrait, dated 19 August 1838, was illustrated in *Country Life*, 5 October 1961, as in the collection of G. A. Parrett, County Wicklow, Eire.

17 QVJ, 15 October 1839

18 WPR, K24. Many of these are illustrated in Warner, ch. 4. A watercolour sketch of Princess Louise (aged 6 or 7) by Queen Victoria belongs to Prince Michael of Kent. The Queen's study of Princess Beatrice is at Potsdam, Aquarellslg. Nr. 3441.

19 Warner, p.21

20 QVJ, 14 January 1836

21 e.g. QVJ, 20 March 1836
22 For a full discussion of this activity see AS-E. Earlier treatments of the subject are Christian Brinton, 'Queen Victoria as an Etcher', *The Critic*, vol. XXXVI, No. 6, June 1900, pp.501–9; Algernon Graves, 'Queen Victoria as an Engraver', *The Printseller*, vol. 1, no. 12, 1903, pp.505–11; H. A. Hammelmann, 'Queen Victoria's Etchings', *Country Life*, 11 April 1968, pp.878–9
23 See, for instance, Warner, pp.97, 98
24 Christie's, London, sale cat., 13 May 1986, lot 50
25 RA Add. U171/141
26 For this lawsuit see Daniel F. Tritter, 'A Strange Case of Royalty: The singular "copyright" case of *Prince Albert v. Strange*', *Journal of Media Law and Practice*, September 1983, vol. 4, no. 2, pp.111–29
27 QVJ, 2 July 1842
28 Royal Collection
29 QVJ, 14 February 1846. For Prince Albert's lithograph see AS-E 93.
30 WPR, K15 (f.79 b)
31 There are copies by Queen Victoria after the works of both artists in the Royal Collection.
32 Surtees, p.101
33 ibid., p.137
34 ibid., p.138
35 WPR, K25 (f.24). Lady Canning's view of the Glen also survives at Windsor (RL 19516).
36 WPR, K25 (f.22)
37 QVJ. For the sketch see WPR, K54 (f.3). See also Warner, p.129.
38 *Leitch*, p.61
39 A number of sheets bearing sketches and notes by Leitch, which are self-evidently of a didactic nature, have survived in the Print Room (e.g. Plate 3). In 1864 the artist had offered the Queen the two Books of studies that he had made, for her and for Princess Alice (RA PP 17988/1864). Other teaching sheets were purchased by the Queen five years later, among 35 studies by Leitch (PP VR PEA). Lot 538 in Leitch's studio sale (Christie's, 13 March 1884) was 'Lochnagar, a lesson with the Queen'.

40 *Leitch*, p.62
41 Surtees, p.172
42 D. Millar, Plate 21. The Queen's sketches from this visit are mainly WPR, vol. K26. See, for instance, Warner, pp.174–5.
43 D. Millar, p.42
44 e.g. WPR, K26 (f.41), a view from Craig Gowan towards Abergeldie, inscribed as having been painted by the Queen at Windsor in October 1848, after the original sketch made in Scotland on 21 September 1848.
45 QVJ, 6 July 1849
46 WPR, RL 19851. Queen Victoria's copy of Leitch's view, also in watercolour, was presented to the Duchesse de Nemours.
47 QVJ, 3 August 1851
48 *Twenty Years*, pp.133–4, 10 October 1846
49 ibid., p.273, 27 September 1854
50 QVJ, 15 March 1849. Most of these copies were in watercolour, e.g. WPR, K504 (reproduced in D. Millar, p.62) and K505. However in 1851 the Queen presented her mother with a copy in oils, by herself and Prince Albert, of a 'Tyrolese Woman and Child' by Foltz. This painting is now in the Forbes Magazine Collection, New York, P 71076.
51 e.g. WPR, K22 (ff.55–58), K42 (f.13v), K143, K144, K503, K506
52 D. Millar, p.85
53 QVJ, 8 and 12 July 1854, etc.
54 QVJ, 29 July 1854
55 WPR, K143. Another hallmark of Haag's style, the scraping out of highlights, is seen in Queen Victoria's copy of Haag's watercolour of mountains, dated 1853: WPR, K42 (f.13v). For a full discussion of Haag's technique see D. Millar, Appendix, pp.143–4.
56 RA PP2/55/2646
57 Warner, p.169. The Queen's painting activity in the mid-1870s is referred to in the background of Charles Burton Barber's portrait of her dog, 'Noble' (Royal Collection). This shows a bound sketchbook (stamped VR on the cover), brushes and water containers.
58 Thirty days at four guineas a day: D. Millar, p.105.
59 *Leitch*, p.64. See also QVJ,

30 September 1863.
60 *Leitch*, pp.65–6. See also QVJ, 5 and 6 October 1863.
61 Detailed statements of Leitch's lessons in 1864 and 1865 survive in the Privy Purse papers at Windsor. The account dated 10 October 1864 is described as: Note of the lessons in water colour painting that Mr Leitch had the honour of giving to Her Majesty the Queen, & also to HRH the Princess Louis of Hesse & to their R.H.ss the Princesses Helena and Louisa & the Prince Leopold in August last. August 6, 8, 9, 10, 12, 13, 15, 16, 17, 18, 19, 20, 22. 13 days at 4gs. Queen Victoria inscribed the docket as follows: The Account to be divided between the Queen's own & the Royal Children's Education (RA PP2/87/7756). Leitch's account for lessons in 1865 is 'Note of lessons &c in Water colour which Mr Leitch has had the honor of giving to Her Majesty The Queen in April last', i.e. 11 April (2 gns.), 13 April (1½ gns.), 15 April (1½ gns.) (RA PP2/95/8986).
62 BM 1951-11-10-41. For the circumstances of this commission see FitzGerald, p.633, and Darby & Smith, p.17, plate 16. The BM drawing may be identifiable with no. 623 in the 'Royal Room' exhibition at Earl's Court, 1897: 'The Prince Consort, 1864, lent by E. H. Corbould'.
63 Theodore Martin, *Queen Victoria as I knew her*, Edinburgh and London, 1901, p.49
64 But see WPR, K500–K508, which are all copies by Queen Victoria after original works by other artists, and which still hang at Balmoral.
65 For illustrations of Queen Victoria sketching during her last years, see *ILN*, 6 May 1893, and D. Millar, fig.118 (in 1901). The Queen's travelling satchel, box of watercolour paints (from R. Ackerman), small tin watercolour box, travelling case of watercolour brushes, silver ruler and wooden watercolour box, were presented to the Royal Academy of Arts by Edward VII in 1906. Another paintbox belongs to the Royal

Pavilion, Art Gallery and
Museums, Brighton (supplied
by T. J. Morris of Birmingham,
colourman to the Duke of Sussex,
the Queen's uncle).
66 *Twenty Years*, p.133
67 QVJ, 26 January 1851
68 QVJ, 20 December 1850 and
17 January 1851. The drawing
is WPR, K141: see *Master
Drawings*, no.128
69 WPR, K507
70 QVJ, 6 and 18 September 1851,
etc.
71 Now RPA
72 QVJ, 1 October 1873
73 *Dearest Child*, p.178
74 QVJ, 14 April 1834. Queen
Victoria's box of oil paints was
presented to the Royal Academy
of Arts, London, by her daughter,
Princess Louise.
75 QVJ, 8 May 1840
76 C. Grey, *Early Years of the Prince
Consort*, London, 1868, pp.321-2
77 QVJ, 11 May 1840
78 Oliver Millar, *The Queen's
Pictures*, London, 1977, p.171
79 Corden, p.99
80 QVJ, 23 June and 27 June 1851
81 QVJ, 1 July 1852
82 QVJ, 4 November 1851
83 QVJ, 8 July 1851
84 QVJ, 3, 13 and 15 August 1851.
The paintings are both at
Osborne House.
85 QVJ, 19-22 August 1851. See
also QVJ, 6 April 1852. The
painting is likewise at Osborne
House.
86 All these works of 1852 are at

Osborne House
87 QVJ, 5 January 1848
88 QVJ, 26 August 1850
89 D. Millar, p.100
90 The lessons were to be twice
weekly, between 1 and 2 on
Wednesday and Saturday
afternoons. See C. Grey,
op. cit., p.107
91 AS-E 11
92 WPR, K98
93 QVJ, 21 May 1840
94 QVJ, 12 April 1844
95 QVJ, 13 August 1845
96 QVJ, 15 July 1840
97 WPR, K19 (f. 25)
98 WPR, K54 (ff.17, 18, 22 and 26).
See also QVJ, 22 October 1850,
indicating a renewed interest in
drawing at this date, of which
no examples appear to have
survived.
99 QVJ, 30 April and 27 May 1854
100 Corden, p.100
101 The painting can no longer be
traced in the Royal Collection
but was formerly Redgrave,
Windsor no. 223.
102 QVJ, 21 May 1851
103 Dorment, p.17
104 QVJ, 1 March 1844
105 QVJ, 3 March 1844
106 QVJ, 31 July 1844
107 AS-E 87
108 QVJ, 8 October 1844
109 QVJ, 1 November 1844
110 QVJ, 30 September 1845
111 Elfrida Manning, *Marble and
Bronze*, London, 1982, p.34
112 RA Y190/29 (13 April 1859)
113 WPR, K542 and RL 21425:

presented to Her Majesty by the
sculptor's granddaughters in
1959. The resulting bust,
dated November 1861, is at
Buckingham Palace (Courtauld
neg. no. B69/427). A plaster
version is at Osborne House
(neg. nos. 958/16/7 and 8).
114 Royal Collection. In the
scrapbook of G. Whitford of
Garrard Jewellers 1857-91 (RA
Add. T233) there are a number
of other royal designs for jewels.
Queen Victoria's designs for a
cross, dated 16 July 1878, and for
a bracelet, are on ff.5v and 6 (now
WPR, K529 and K530). Her
drawing of a sprig of orange
blossom from this album is
WPR, K532. There are three
designs by Princess Alice relating
to jewellery to be worn at the
Prince of Wales's wedding
(ff.13-15), and a design for a
bracelet by Prince Arthur, dated
December 1880 (f.8, now K531).
115 Both pieces are still in the Royal
Collection. The 1861 Cowes
Regatta Cup, now in the Festung
at Coburg, is also apparently
dependent on the Prince's design.
116 QVJ, 27 September 1860. See
also RA M42/76 (16 July 1853),
Prince Albert to Marie, Duchess
of Saxe-Coburg and Gotha:
'Eberhardt has designed the plans
and we have tested them here.'
117 RA Y204/110
118 BM 1972-12-9-1
119 D. Millar, p.59

4: THE NEXT GENERATION

1 Darby & Smith, p.6
2 The Princess's timetable for
January 1848 does not mention
drawing, but dancing,
geography, history or 'work'
occupied the period between
5 and 6 on weekday afternoons
(RA M12/66).
3 WPR, K1028. For a watercolour
portrait by Winterhalter of Prince
Arthur in the same costume, worn
by him on 11 January
1853, see Sotheby's, London,
sale cat., 13 March 1986, lot 19.
4 QVJ, 10 February 1853
5 QVJ, 24 May 1853
6 KHF, K5. It is signed and dated

6 July 1853, Buckingham Palace.
7 KHF, K9. This drawing was
made at the start of Corbould's
professional career, in September
1836, and is very reminiscent of
the work of Retzsch, whose
outline illustrations the royal
couple had also copied as
children. Through Corbould
the influence of his dramatic
linear style was also introduced
to the princes and princesses.
8 *ILN*, 7 April 1855. A copy of the
catalogue of the *Exhibition of
Water-Colour Drawings and
Pictures by Amateur Artists . . .
in Aid of the Fund for the Relief of*

*the Widows and Orphans of British
Officers Engaged in the War with
Russia*, London, 1855, is in the
Royal Library. This lists the
contributions of members of
the Royal Family as follows:
H.R.H. The Prince of Wales – The
Knight; H.R.H. The Princess
Royal – The Field of Battle;
H.R.H. Prince Alfred – The
Prince of Wales, afterwards
Henry V; H.R.H. The Princess
Alice – Prayer; H.R.H. The
Princess Helena – Girl Asleep. In
addition the Duchess of
Gloucester contributed sixteen
pictures.

9 FitzGerald, p.636
10 *ILN*, 7 April 1855, p.336
11 ibid., 31 March 1855
12 *Dearest Mama*, p.29 (26 December 1861)
13 RA Z5/26 (23 February 1858)
14 An undated timetable of the Princess Royal's lessons at this period (c.1855-6) includes instruction from 'The Prince' every afternoon at 4.00 and a single lesson with Corbould on Tuesday at 12.30. At the same time Princess Alice was receiving twice-weekly instruction from Corbould, on Wednesdays at 3 p.m. and Fridays at 12.30 (RA M17/55).
15 Fans Inventory, 240 WC 28
16 WPR, K1101. Leitch's watercolour of the same view is also in the Royal Collection, RL 17635. It was acquired at his studio sale (Christie's, London, 13 March 1884, lot 159) as 'A View from the Garden at Osborne – the last lesson to H.I.H. the Princess Royal before her marriage'.
17 BM 1951-11-10-43. Another of the Princess's drawings, in the Forbes Magazine Collection, was evidently given to the Scottish artist, Sir Joseph Noel Paton, in 1863. It is inscribed 'This study of The Princess Helena was made in my room at Windsor Castle by the Crown Princess of Prussia, and presented to me by H.R.H. on the eve of her departure from England, Nov.ʳ 1863. J.N.P' (P 82078-D).
18 *Dearest Child*, p.74 (5 March 1858)
19 RA Z5/16 (12 February 1858)
20 RA Z5/35 (enclosed with letter of 11 March 1858)
21 RA Z5/48 (April 1858)
22 Manchester City Art Gallery (1977.165)
23 RA Z12/47 (12 December 1861)
24 RA Z14/29 (10 January 1863)
25 RA Z7/114 (19 April 1859). Two of the Princess Royal's watercolours from the early years of her marriage are illustrated in Walburga, Lady Paget's *Embassies of Other Days* (London, 1923, vol.I, between pp.74 and 75, and 140 and 141). They represent the Princess's ladies-in-waiting Marie Lynar and Walburga Hohenthal (the author of the reminiscences).

26 In addition, Corbould was in Berlin for short visits in 1858 and 1859: see the Princess Royal's correspondence, RA Z7/11 (22 September 1858) and Z8/47 (10 September 1859).
27 QVJ, 30 May 1859
28 Royal Collection, WCI 2838
29 WPR, K1261. Signed and dated 25 July 1859.
30 RA Z7/107 (4 April 1859)
31 Royal Collection, WCI 2839
32 Forbes Magazine Collection, P 79273-D
33 RA Z9/15 (10 December 1859). The Album was returned to England in January 1860, see RA Z9/19.
34 WPR, RL 21321-21372
35 KHF, K17
36 Curiously, the equivalent scenes from *Richard II* in the Queen's album (RL 21342-21347) are by Lundgren rather than the Princess's teacher, Corbould.
37 *Callow*, pp.124-31
38 ibid., illustration facing p.128. Now in the collection of Dr Francis Callow Place.
39 ibid., p.139
40 The view of Sans-Souci was among a group of pictures sent by the Crown Princess to the London printseller, Algernon Graves, with the following explanation: 'I want to help one of the charities here but I don't want to give a sum of money direct. I want to feel that whatever I give I have earned' (FitzGerald, p.638). Graves presented the picture to Queen Mary in 1918, and it has now passed into the Royal Collection. A watercolour by Callow of the Neue Kammern, Potsdam (misidentified as Sans-Souci by the artist), is inscribed 'Sketched with the Princess of Prussia September 23 1874' (illustrated in J. Reynolds, *William Callow*, fig. 89, as formerly with Agnew).
41 *Your Dear Letter*, p.128
42 Royal Collection
43 Quoted in *Empress Frederick*, pp.191-2
44 RA Z16/50 and 60 (May and 6 July 1864). A set of these prints, entitled *Erinnerung an den 18ten April 1864* (Berlin, 1864), survives among the engravings

of European History at Windsor. A preparatory watercolour study for the fourth subject is in one of the Crown Princess's albums in the Fulda Archives (KHF, K5).
45 *ILN*, 1 October 1870, p.359, and 19 June 1880, p.602. Princess Louise also contributed to this exhibition: see p.150.
46 RA Z26/61 (29 March 1872). The paintings are WPR, K174-176.
47 William II, *My early life*, London, 1926, p.57
48 RA Z27/28 (August 1873)
49 *Darling Child*, p.123 (2 January 1874)
50 Sotheby, London, sale cat., 29 November 1984, lot 768. See Introduction, note 14.
51 RA Z31/28 (28 May 1877)
52 *Darling Child*, p.252
53 *Empress Frederick*, p.268
54 *ILN*, 19 June 1880, p.602. An illustration of the drawing was included as an extra supplement to the *ILN*.
55 RA Z35/40 (5 September 1881)
56 RA Z31/27 (24 May 1877). The Crown Princess feared that the painting might frighten the cows at Balmoral.
57 RA Z30/3 (14 May 1877)
58 RA Z31/28 (28 May 1877). The passage referred to in note 51 above follows on immediately after this one.
59 *Elphinstone*, p.194
60 ibid., illustration facing p.194
61 ibid., pp.199-200. The painting, a still life, is in the Royal Collection. The Crown Princess's portrait of Princess Louise Margaret, painted in the year of her marriage (1879), belongs to a descendant.
62 ibid., pp.200-1
63 *Darling Child*, p.252
64 RA Z30/7 (7 December 1881). The paintings are still in the Royal Collection.
65 A. von Werner, 'Eine fürstliche Malerin', *Gartenlaube*, Leipzig, XXXIII, no. 46, 1885, pp.761-2. This provided the basis for an article in an English magazine the following year: A. St Johnston, 'A Royal Artist', *Magazine of Art*, 9, 1886, pp.300-3, in which the same illustrations were used.
66 H. J. Thaddeus, *Recollections of a Court Painter*, London, 1912, p.248
67 QVJ, 17 October 1898

68   E. C. Clayton, *English Female Artists*, London, 1876, II, pp.429-30

69   RA Z1/37 (11 September 1858) and Z2/15 (9 April 1859)

70   RA Z3/51 (22 December 1860), Postscript

71   RA Z10/58 (19 February 1861)

72   RA Z4/22 (14 June 1861)

73   RA Z10/23 (11 December 1860)

74   *Leitch*, pp.71-2

75   In addition to the following, the correspondence mentions a pair of angels in oils, and a series of watercolours for a cupboard in the Blue Room at Windsor. The latter are WPR, K182 and K188.

76   *Dearest Mama*, p.29 (26 December 1861)

77   *Dearest Mama*, p.32 (29 December 1861)

78   *Dearest Mama*, p.36 (8 January 1862)

79   RA Z13/28 (21 June 1862)

80   Darby & Smith, p.15

81   *Dearest Mama*, p.185 (24 March 1863)

82   Neither original, nor casts, nor even photographs of this bust appear to have survived

83   Darby & Smith, pp.30-7

84   Corbould's drawing is KHF, Album K6, while Princess Alice's copy is WPR, K1108. A volume of miscellaneous writings concerning Princess Alice, published soon after her death, contains a transcript of her letter to Corbould of 24 May 1861, following the death of his daughter, less than two months after the Princess had herself suffered the loss of her grandmother, the Duchess of Kent: 'If the sympathy of one who feels, and that most warmly, for your grief, can bring you the slightest consolation, I do sympathise with all my heart' (C. Bullock, *Doubly Royal. Memorials of the Princess Alice*, London, [1878/9,] p.16).

85   QVJ, 19 April 1858

86   *Leitch*, ill. p.67

87   WPR, K1177

88   Wolfsgarten, GPH, vol. 1127 (Frl. Bauer's Album)

89   WPR, K912 and K916

90   WPR, K933 and K940, and Wolfsgarten, GPH, vol. 1125

91   WPR, K962

92   Wolfsgarten, GPH, vol. 1125

93   Wolfsgarten, GPH, red 1865 vol.

The following description, sent to the future Queen Victoria by her half-sister Princess Feodora of Hohenlohe-Langenburg, of the drawing she had made following the death of her sister-in-law Agnes in September 1835, may provide a precedent for these memorial pieces:
I have made a drawing for my poor mother-in-law and sent it to her, and I think it will please her. It represents Agnes lying dead on her bed; at her head bends an angel over her kissing life away, and at the same time showing upwards where her sister Eliza and brother Harry open their arms to receive her, to welcome her in Heaven: in the foreground a kneeling angel over a faded and torn wreath, the angel of life lamenting her death (*Letters of Feodora*, London 1874, p.43).

94   Darby & Smith, p.7. In Theed's letter accompanying his invoice for recent work he wrote: 'The next item, £250, is for the Octagon pedestal executed after the design of H.R.H. the Princess of Hesse' (RA PP2/80/6668).

95   As, in turn, were this child's eldest daughter Alice (Prince Philip's mother), and her second son Louis, later created Earl Mountbatten of Burma

96   Wolfsgarten, GPH, vol. 1125

97   RPA, Stags Album III (f.16)

98   Wolfsgarten, GPH, vol. 1126

99   *Alice Letters*, p.111. The painting is at Osborne.

100   ibid., p.124

101   Wolfsgarten, GPH, vol. 1126

102   WPR, K989

103   Darmstadt Archives, Gross-herzogliches Familien-archiv, Abt. D. 24, Nr. 20

104   Wolfsgarten, GPH, red 1865 vol.

105   For this relationship see J. S. Dearden, *Facets of Ruskin*, London and Edinburgh, 1970, chapter x: 'John Ruskin and Prince Leopold'.

106   E. T. Cook, *The Life of John Ruskin*, London, 1911, II, p.200. See also RA Add. A30/119. I have not been able to find the occasion on which Ruskin's 'advice was rather ill-advisedly sought . . . about the art education of the young princes and princesses' (Bernard Denvir,

'Royal Artists', *ILN*, Christmas 1965, pp.16-17). The Curator of the Ruskin Galleries, Bembridge School, has informed me of a watercolour of a fern growing on a rock presented to the Galleries by Princess Alice, Countess of Athlone. It had apparently been given to Princess Alice's mother, the Duchess of Albany, as part of a drawing lesson from Ruskin. Another drawing of this type, made in the garden at Claremont in 1883, is in an album compiled by Queen Mary for the Earl and Countess of Athlone (property of Lady May Abel-Smith). It was inscribed by Princess Helen, Duchess of Albany: 'Sketch done by Ruskin when giving me a painting-lesson Autumn 1883 at my sitting-room window'.

107   *Diaries of John Ruskin, III: 1874-89*, ed. J. Evans and J. H. Whitehouse, Oxford, 1959, p.847

108   RA Add. A30/124. Quoted in *Letters of Ruskin* (Library edn), II, p.174.

109   RA Add. A30/125. See *Letters of Ruskin*, pp.178-9

110   RA Z207/17 (18 December 1875)

111   For instance, the Queen's birthday in 1868. See *Alice Letters*, p.200. A waistcoat embroidered by Princess Louise for her father is in the Museum of London (58.121/1).

112   G. Noel, *Princess Alice*, London, 1974, p.231

113   Marie Louise, p.17

114   WPR, K953, K963-6, K971. See also the undated pen sketch of a lady on a balcony in the Museum of London (37.79/29).

115   WPR, K973. A volume of sketches by W. L. Leitch in the Print Room (RL 20116-20144), was formerly in Princess Helena's collection. Her daughter, Princess Marie Louise, gave it to Queen Mary, by whom it was presented to the Royal Library. It is possible that the volume only came to the Princess after Leitch's death, rather than dating back to the time of her lessons with him. Queen Victoria's purchases at Leitch's posthumous sale were intended as gifts for her children (RA L20/9 (12 March 1884)).

116   The watercolour is WPR, K523

117 e.g. WPR, K899, K900, K907, K908, K913, K918, and Wolfsgarten, GPH, vol. 1127. At an early age the Princess also received lessons from Miss Mills of the Female School of Art (RA PP Vic. A250 (28 January 1860)).

118 WPR, K976

119 QVJ, 16 February 1864. The memorial pictures are WPR, K978 (illustrated p.147), K980, K983 and K984. For Prince Albert Victor's christening gift see Darby & Smith, p.17 and Plates 14-15.

120 Duchy of Cornwall; acquired as part of a lot of drawings from Corbould's estate, Christie's, London, c.1980; see also Darby & Smith, p.17 and p.108, n.77

121 WPR, K1003

122 WPR, K808 and *Royal Fans*, exh. cat., Harewood House, 1986, no. 94. Other early drawings by the Princess are referred to in invoices submitted to the Privy Purse by picture framers, e.g. 'A light fancy gilt frame for a water colour portrait by the Princess Louise Sight of Picture 10½ x 7.7/8"' in July 1864. A group of her sketches were framed up in January 1869. See PP2/87/7723 and PP2/140/15638. In April 1867 an invoice was submitted 'To Reeded Gold Oxford Frame Inrich^d with Ivy Leaves from a Drawing by H.R.H. Princess Louisa' (PP2/119/12628).

123 e.g. WPR, K988, dated 1862

124 RA Add. A15/228 (12 January 1863)

125 *Leitch*, p.65

126 RPA, Stags Album III, K614 and K616

127 RA Add. A17/1785/130

128 WPR, K95, dated 19 July 1865

129 WPR, K37 (f.60)

130 QVJ, 24 December 1867. The picture is at Osborne House.

131 e.g. WPR, K705, cf. K42 (f. 26)

132 Royal Collection, Balmoral

133 RA Add. A17: Folder I

134 RA Add. A36/170 (19 November 1870)

135 *ILN*, 1 October 1870, p.359

136 RA Add. A17/1788 (4 September 1871)

137 See Jehanne Wake, forthcoming biography of Princess Louise

138 WPR, K830

139 RA Add. A17/1777 (23 January 1877)

140 Used for a letter from Lorne to Queen Victoria, RA Add. A17/1794 (24 March 1876). A pencil drawing of 'A Kentish Farm Labourer' by Princess Louise, dated December 1876, was presented by the Duke of Kent to the Maidstone Museums and Art Gallery in 1940.

141 J. L. Roget, *A History of the Old Water-Colour Society*, London, 1891, p.122. Princess Louise's contributions to the RSPW exhibitions include the following:

1880-1 23. Lieut.-Col. F. de Winton; 183. Sir John McNeil, v.c.

1882-3 252. Canoeing on the Cascapedia River, Canada

1883-4 105. Sketch of the Canadian Falls, Niagara; 278. Sketch of Greenhithe

1884 174. Study of a head; 224. The Mission, Santa Barbara, California; 263. A Freshet on the Cascapedia, Canada

1884-5 97. Schloss Heidelberg; 122. A Peep of a Tyrolese Village; 142. Pencil Sketch – Princess Victoria of Hesse

1886 18. Dorothy Heseltine Child's Head

1888

1890 194. Study of a head

1899 192. Dorothy; 227. Provençal Garden

1899-1900 259. Dawn, Mediterranean

1907 259. Near Luxor; 254. Philae in February; 250. Outskirts of a village by the Nile

1908 54. A Portrait

1911 1. A seascape; Cottage in a Wood; A Portrait

142 *Good Words*, London, 1882, XXIII, pp.217-52

143 In *Round the Globe*, ed. W. C. Procter, 1887

144 Illustrated Hubbard, p.56

145 RA A17/1797 (23 February 1880)

146 NGC, Acc. No. 144

147 NGC, Acc. No. 14637

148 e.g. 1882: no. 73 – Portrait of Henrietta Montalba (illustrated p.153 above); 1889: no. 117 – Col. The Hon. Charles Lindsay as a knight in antique armour. For Myra Fontenoy see *DNB*.

149 Colonial and Indian Exhibition, London, 1886, no. 1984

150 e.g. September 1907 – January 1908: nos. 879, 886 and 920 were by Princess Louise, and had each been shown at the RSPW summer exhibition for 1907. The 1920 Liverpool exhibition included two works by the Princess: nos. 632 and 633

151 1888, no. 228 (Cascapedia Valley, Canada), and no. 242 (Coxwain of HMS *Comus*); 1903 (A study: oil painting on easel)

152 1893, no. 36 (A study); 1910, no. 34 (Portrait of a Lady); 1912, no. 157 (A Maltese Girl)

153 RA Add. A17/803 (undated)

154 RA Add. A17: Folder I (10 July 1905)

155 Princess Louise's drawing is K422. For the print see F. O'Donoghue, *Catalogue of Engraved British Portraits in the . . . British Museum*, IV, 1914, p.358, no. 184

156 BM 1976-9-25-8, gift of Sir John Pope-Hennessy. Inscribed by him on the back of the mount: 'given to my mother who was her [Princess Louise's] Lady-in-Waiting in Venice in 1888'.

157 Sandringham House, S 69

158 WPR, K439

159 WPR, K668-K683. Three finished watercolours resulting from this voyage were exhibited at the RSPW in summer 1907 (see above, note 141).

160 RA Add. A17/80 (30 August 1863)

161 RA Add. A17/88 (10 November 1863)

162 RA PP2/88/7924. The same invoice, dated 8 December 1864, mentions two casts of the bust made in May, and two casts made in December, at three guineas per cast. A further cast was included in the 17 May 1867 invoice (PP2/118/12350).

163 RA PP2/118/12350 and PP2/130/14071

164 No. 931

165 RA PP2/127/13738 of January 1868; PP2/132/14451 of 17 July 1868

166 *Your Dear Letter*, pp.178-9 (18 March 1868)

167 RA PP2/132/14451 and PP2/142/15870, dated April 1869. The bust was displayed at the summer exhibition of the

RSPW in 1868, and the following year at the Royal Academy, to which it was presented by the Queen. Other pieces of sculpture from this early period include a female figure entitled 'Resignation', presented to the Queen at Christmas 1865 (formerly at Osborne), and a medallion portrait of Lady Churchill, the Queen's Lady-in-Waiting, mentioned in a letter from Prince Arthur to Princess Louise, 16 January 1866 (RA Add. A17/135).

168 RA Add. T104, Sahl to Queen Victoria, 10 February 1869. Quoted in Mark Stocker's forthcoming biography of Boehm, ch. 3, n.6

169 The first in marble (Windsor Castle), the second in plaster (Osborne). Stearine casts of both these were sent to the German charity exhibition at the New British Institution Galleries, London, in 1870. See *ILN*, 1 October 1870, p.359.

170 RA Add. A36/170 (3 May 1870)

171 No. 1536

172 Royal Academy *Annual Report*, 1877, p.7

173 RA Add. A17/1772 (22 April 1878), Boehm to Princess Louise

174 Dorment, plate 4

175 RA Add. A17/1773 (8 December 1890)

176 Dorment, pp.105–8

177 RA Add. A17: Folder 1

178 Dorment, p.107

179 Dorment, p.144

180 Another figure of the Queen by Princess Louise was destined for the west front of Lichfield Cathedral. See A. St Johnston, 'A Royal Artist', *Magazine of Art*, vol. 9, 1886, pp.300–3

181 Dorment, p.332

182 RA Add. A17/905 (30 December 1897), Princess Louis of Battenberg to Princess Louise

183 RA Add. A17/927 (25 October 1898)

184 Information from Dr Mark Stocker, who has also informed me of the Princess's relief portrait of Sybil, Duchess of St Albans, at Emmanuel Church, Bestwood, near Nottingham. A statuette group by Princess Louise of John Brown with the Queen's pony 'Flora' and her collie 'Sharp' was

lent by Osbert Sitwell to the exhibition of Queen Victoria's etchings at the Brook Street Art Gallery, London, in 1925. The group still belongs to the Sitwell family, at Renishaw, Derbyshire. It is presumably identical with the bronze statuette group signed and dated by Boehm in 1869 which exists in three versions in the Royal Collection. (See RA Add. T174/September 1883 for a payment to Boehm for three bronze copies of the group.)

185 For the St Paul's memorial see Frank Atkinson, *St Paul's and the City*, London, 1985, p.29. A replica of the Colonial Monument was exhibited at the Summer exhibition at Tooth's Galleries, London, in 1907. Jehanne Wake has informed me of the following additional memorial projects in which Princess Louise was involved: Mrs Erskine Wemyss (1895–7; the Chapel, Wemyss Castle); Mrs Thurston (Kensal Green Cemetery); War Memorial for Heritage Craft Schools (Chailey, Sussex); plaster relief 'In Memory of our Nurse' (exhibited Fine Arts Society, 1902, no.32).

186 Two of her busts are in the National Portrait Gallery: Sir Henry Streatfield, and the Princess's self-portrait (illustrated p.2). Other miscellaneous works include the bronze of Richard Coeur de Lion on horseback (Inveraray), and the bronze statuette of Nelson dated 1906.

There are obvious parallels between Princess Louise's sculptural activity and that of members of the Gleichen family, descendants of Queen Victoria's half-sister Feodora of Hohenlohe-Langenburg. Victor (1833–91) the third son (and fourth child) of Feodora's marriage to Prince Ernest of Hohenlohe-Langenburg, and his daughter Countess Feodore Gleichen (1861–1922), were both talented and prolific sculptors and are represented in the Royal Collection. Prince Victor adopted the surname Gleichen following his morganatic marriage in 1861

to Miss Laura Seymour. He studied under Theed and had the use of a studio at St James's Palace. His elder sister Eliza (1830–51) was considered a talented painter (*Letters of Feodora*, London, 1874, pp.62, 152 and 201), while his other daughter Helena was also a trained artist. (See Thieme-Becker.)

187 D. Millar, pp.138–9

188 *Royal Children*, Brighton Museum, exh. cat., 1977, no. B112

189 Sandringham House, S290

190 M. E. Sara, *The Life and Times of H.R.H. Princess Beatrice*, London, 1945, p.41. Princess Beatrice exhibited at the Institute of Painters in Watercolour between 1883 and 1885. Her works were illustrated in the catalogues. In 1881 she had designed *A Birthday Book*, privately printed in 1881 by Smith, Elder & Co., London (with illustrations, printed by colour lithography in Leipzig). Queen Victoria gave away copies of this book to members of her family, for the addition of autographs under the appropriate dates.

191 RA M14/39 (26 April 1849)

192 WPR, K424 and K1023

193 WPR, K1047. The two volumes of teaching drawings are now K477 and K478

194 WPR, Brown volume

195 F. Dimond and R. Taylor, *Crown and Camera*, London, 1987, p.108, no. 26.

196 WPR, K1222 and K1223, dated March 1861. The seaport is K902.

197 *Dearest Child*, pp.350–1 (26 September 1861)

198 *Dearest Child*, p.127 (8 November 1862)

199 *Leitch*, p.64

200 WPR, K157, August 1863

201 WPR, K130–K139

202 WPR, K163. See also K158–K160. A number of other Scottish watercolours by Princess Alexandra are in the possession of the Duke of Fife.

203 *Leitch*, p.71. Lessons with Leitch are recorded in RA, Princess Alexandra's engagement books, February, May and June 1873 and August 1876.

204 Sandringham House, P269

205 RA, Princess Alexandra's

engagement books (incomplete
series), 7, 15, 20 March 1877,
16, 17, 18, 19 November 1880,
29 March to April 1882, 3, 8, 10,
12, 17, 22, 24, 26 July and 31
October 1884, 15, 16 February
and 26, 27 April 1887, 7, 9, 10,
14 October 1888. See also 6 June
1873 when Princess Alexandra
saw some of Harper's work.

206 ibid., 18 May 1883, September
1886, 11 July 1888, 27-29 July 1892
207 ibid., 22, 23, 25 October 1886
208 ibid., 27 July 1887, March and
April 1889
209 ibid., 13 February 1876 and
17 March 1890
210 '9 small Oil Paintings' by Queen
Alexandra were listed among
the contents of her Painting
Room at Marlborough House in
the Picture Inventory taken by
H. S. Middleton following her
death in November 1925 (RA,
p.205).
211 WPR, K135 and K136; S005,
S504, S505, S551 and S724
212 RPA, Album: Norwegian
Cruise, 1893, p.27
213 Sandringham House, S496
214 WPR, Green Alexandra vol.
215 WPR, K432 (f.4v)
216 WPR, K432 (f.1)
217 WPR, K458, after RL 21675
218 WPR, K156
219 WPR, K147 (dated 1895) and
K150. See also two
watercolours in the possession
of the Duke of Fife.
220 e.g. Fans Inventory, F24. It is
perhaps relevant to mention here

the Queen's Carving School
and the Queen's School of
Needlework, set up at
Sandringham c.1920. The objects
of these institutions were,
respectively, to train the boys
from the estate to become
cabinet-makers and the girls to
become needlewomen.
Although it is unlikely that
Queen Alexandra had a hand in
the design of any of the
products of these schools, she
(and later George V and Queen
Mary) took a close personal
interest in their activities. The
School of Needlework appears to
have been short-lived, but the
School of Carving – which
specialized in the production of
high quality inlaid pieces – was
only closed in 1957. Information
from Sir Edmund Grove. 'An
Exhibition of Hand-made
Furniture from H.M. The
Queen's Carving School,
Sandringham', comprising 170
items, priced between £7 and £1,
was held at Walker's Galleries,
London, in April 1933.
221 WPR, RL 23188
222 D. Millar, p.121
223 Royal Collection, Balmoral
224 WPR, K1131
225 WPR, K894. Among Prince
Alfred's lesson books in the Royal
Archives is an uninscribed
watercolour study of a peony,
which presumably dates from
the early 1850s.

226 WRL, I IB 5A
227 RA PP2/30/9191 (payment for
twenty lessons between 29 March
and 9 June 1858, and for drawing
and painting materials), PP2/31/
9395 (two lessons in July 1858),
and PP2/48/1589 (unspecified
lessons at Osborne during 1860)
228 A doll's house used by the young
Edinburgh children, and partly
decorated by their parents, is
now at Wallington,
Northumberland (National
Trust. See *Royal Children*,
Brighton Museum, exh. cat.,
1977, No.B155)
229 KHF, Album K9: drawing of
boats, 1859. Presumably a gift to
the Princess Royal.
230 WPR, K914 and K915
231 *Elphinstone, passim*
232 *Leitch*, p.63. See also RA Add.
A15/208, 225 and 228
233 RA Add. A17/135 (16 January
1866)
234 WPR, K90-K92
235 RA Add. A17/279
236 At Christmas 1867 Queen
Victoria received a watercolour of
Windsor Castle in the floods,
from her frail youngest son,
Prince Leopold, Duke of Albany
(1853-84). It was a copy of a view
by William Evans, and is
recorded in the Royal Collection
at Osborne until 1902, when it
was presented to the Duchess of
Albany by King Edward VII.
Present whereabouts unknown
(Osborne cat., p.413).

5: QUEEN VICTORIA'S GRANDCHILDREN AND THE TWENTIETH CENTURY

1 Kenneth Rose, *King George V*,
London, 1983, p.318
2 The letter continues: 'It is just the
same with music, & Charlotte
with needlework. – I suppose the
prussian family comes out in them
in these respects' (RA Z25/78
(20 May 1871)). Two years later
the Crown Princess sent the
Queen drawings by both
William and Victoria, but none
appear to have survived in the
Royal Collection (RA Z27/35).
3 RA Z26/85 (25 July 1872)
4 Potsdam, env. 3663c. The

Crown Princess's watercolour
of the same sitter, inscribed
'Elena Hajens and Mina
Jacobson. Niblum 18 August
1865', is KHF, K5.
5 Potsdam, 3659 and env. 3663c.
The troop carrier was sketched on
the back of an envelope
containing 'Der Deutsche
Sportsman', addressed to 'Ihr.
Hoheit Dem Prinzen Wilhelm von
Preussen' at Potsdam. A study of
a German warship at her
moorings, dated December
1893, is in the Forbes Magazine

Collection (P74001-D).
6 Potsdam, 3660
7 Potsdam, 3663c
8 William II, *My Early Life*,
London, 1926. The original sketch
is dated 27 March 1861. For an
interview with the Kaiser's
great-granddaughter, the artist
Victoria Achache, see *Observer*,
colour supplement, 8 March
1987, pp.76-7.
9 Osborne House, K527
10 In the possession of the Duke of
Fife, RL Neg.6089
11 WPR, K468, undated.

12 Marie of Roumania, *The Story of My Life*, New York, 1934, pp.378-80

13 Pope-Hennessy, p.253. See, however, Hannah Pakula, *The Last Romantic*, London, 1984.

14 Georgina Battiscombe, *Queen Alexandra*, London, 1969, p.193, quoting Francis Knollys, Private Secretary to the Prince of Wales

15 Osborne, K524. The painting incorporated the following poem:

    Prayer is the burden of a sigh
    The falling of a tear –
    The upward glancing of an eye,
    When none but God are near.

16 Marie Louise, p.117

17 ibid., pp.118-19. The Royal Academy has been unable to find any record of this event.

18 ibid., p.155

19 R. H. Wilenski, 'The Art of Lady Patricia Ramsay', *Apollo*, May 1928, pp.222-4. Her other two one-man exhibitions were held at the Lefevre Galleries in May 1946, and in the Adams Gallery in May – June 1959.

20 RPA. In the Royal Collection there is a small abstract in oils, and a French poem alongside an orchid outlined in gold, very much in the style employed by the Edinburgh daughters (WPR, K167). Two pen and ink drawings by Princess Patricia are in the Swedish Royal Collection.

21 1949; 1979 (at Prince Eugen's Waldemarsudde); 1982/3 (at the Royal Palace, Stockholm). Over 250 paintings, watercolours and drawings by Princess Margaret survive in the Swedish Royal Collection. Other works belong to members of the Danish and Swedish royal families (information from Göran Alm, Curator of the Swedish Royal Collections). The uncle of Princess Margaret's husband, Prince Eugen of Sweden (1865-1947), was also a distinguished artist.

22 RA Add. A15/8017 (18 July 1905)

23 These are close in style to drawings by Violet, Duchess of Rutland (1856-1937), by whom there are a number of works at Windsor.

24 RA Add. A15/8445 (10 December 1911)

25 RA Add. A17/1122 (29 November 1912)

26 See e.g. illustration p.180 and Hubbard, pp.129, 139

27 NGC, Acc. nos. 1047 and 1048. Another painting of this time is 'View from Government House, Ottawa', sold Sotheby's, Toronto, 26 November 1984, lot 50.

28 The badge consisted of a marguerite – a pun on Margaret, her sister's name – encircled by the regiment's name and surmounted by a crown. See Hubbard, p.137

29 For the regiment, of which Princess Patricia was Colonel-in-Chief from 1919 until her death in 1979, see Jeffry Williams, *Princess Patricia's Canadian Light Infantry*, London, 1972

30 Exhibited *New English Art Club Centenary Exhibition*, Christie's, London, 1986, no. 227

31 *Royal Performance*, no. 69

32 NGC, Acc. no. 9927 (bought in 1962 for $400) and Acc. no. 14824 (bought in 1965 for £500).

33 *Your Dear Letter*, p.222

34 See Plates 65-8

35 WPR, K1008-10

36 Pope-Hennessy, pp.180-1

37 The three small drawings by Princess Louise in the Royal Collection were acquired in 1965, having formerly belonged to the Princess's masseuse (WPR, K541a-c).

38 Kenneth Rose, *King George V*, London, 1983, p.317. In Queen Mary's diary for the relevant date (26 June 1926), she noted: 'At 12 we went to National Gallery – Milbank where G. opened the Modern foreign & Sargent Galleries given by Sir Joseph Duveen. We then went round the galleries – Most interesting' (RA). The King merely noted the visit, without comment, in his own diary (RA).

39 K. Rose, *op. cit.*, p.318

40 Pope-Hennessy, p.50. The original letter is dated 13 June 1878

41 ibid.

42 ibid., pp.50-1

43 ibid., p.158

44 ibid., pp.130-1

45 ibid., p.133. Probably Victor Verwloet, born 1829.

46 ibid., p.121

47 ibid., p.143

48 ibid., p.208

49 ibid., p.113

50 Beryl Platts, 'Symbols of Trust', *Country Life*, 3 June 1982, p.1695, fig. 4

51 A floral carpet worked in six sections from April to October 1950, was lent by HM Queen Elizabeth The Queen Mother to the posthumous exhibition of Queen Mary's Treasures in 1954. Two pieces of Queen Mary's needlework were lent by Princess Alice, Countess of Athlone, to *Royal Performance*, nos. 65 and 67; see also no. 66.

52 NGC, Acc. no. 6081. The following details of the history of the carpet are based on papers in PAC from the Office of the Governor General, RG 7, G 26, vol. 99, file 3185A: 'Her Majesty Queen Mary: documents relating to Queen Mary's carpet'.

53 Pope-Hennessy, p.616. The IODE, founded in 1900, is still in existence with its headquarters in Toronto, Ontario.

54 Fans Inventory, F14 and F13

55 Frances Donaldson, *Edward VIII*, London, 1976, p.140

56 ibid., p.140

57 *Royal Performance*, no. 72

58 *Aberdeen Press and Journal*, 7 April 1933

59 *Memoirs of Princess Alice*, pp.90-1. The catalogue of *An Exhibition of Water-Colour Sketches of Kenya Colony and Elsewhere* by Lady Alice Scott, July 1933, lists 64 items, views in Africa, Scotland, Northamptonshire and Sussex. The prices range from one to ten guineas. The exhibition two years later was confined to Kenyan subjects. There were 43 exhibits, and the prices were between two and seven guineas.

60 *Memoirs of Princess Alice*, pp.92-3

61 ibid., p.187

62 *On Public View* (1970), illustrating London statues, *The Face of London* (1973), and *Oxford and Cambridge* (1980)

63 Prince Nicholas of Greece, *My Fifty Years*, London [1926], pp.19, 153, 282, with illustrations. Two of his

paintings hang at Windsor Castle. A number of others are in the collections of the Duke of Kent and of Prince Michael of Kent. A silhouetted figure of Napoleon, signed and dated 'Nicky '99', is in the Print Room at Windsor: RL 22626A, in Album 6, f.38.

64   Drawings and sketches from this time are in the collection of Prince Michael of Kent.

65   Hugo Vickers, *Cecil Beaton*, London, 1985, pp.268-9

66   *Self Portrait with Friends. The Selected Diaries of Cecil Beaton 1926-1974*, ed. R. Buckle, London, 1979, pp.395-6

67   1936 – 647. The Duke of Kent 1937 – 532 and 541. Two (unidentified) charcoal studies

68   1950 – 22. Portrait of a Man. For illustrations of these and other works by Princess Marina, see Stella King, *Princess Marina*,

London, 1969, between pp.204 and 205.

69   *The Times*, quoted in *Seago*, p.212

70   *Seago*, p.213

71   Prince Philip's sister, Princess Margarita of Greece, also painted, but most of her works were burnt in the fire at her married home, Schloss Langenburg

72   Illustrated in *Seago*, opp. p.217

73   ibid., p.219

74   ibid., p.220

75   Quoted in D. Judd, *Prince Philip*, London, 1980, p.209. Apart from loans to the two *Royal Performance* exhibitions, Prince Philip's paintings were included in a small display in the hall of the Royal Academy of Arts, summer 1976, and in the exhibition at Sotheby's, London, on the occasion of a charity sale in aid of the Duke of Edinburgh's

Award Scheme.

76   *Seago*, p.235

77   ibid., pp.11-12 and 235-6

78   The Prince of Wales has exhibited annually at the RIPWC since before his marriage, and his work was included in the loan exhibition to the Federation of Canadian Artists in Vancouver, 1986. In 1987 he also contributed to the RSPW exhibition in London. Item 860 in the 1987 Summer Exhibition at the Royal Academy of Arts ('Farm Buildings in Norfolk', signed with the initial 'C'), was submitted by the Prince of Wales under the alias of Arthur G. Carrick: one of the Prince's courtesy titles is Earl of Carrick. Two works by his cousin, Lady Sarah Armstrong-Jones, were nos. 488 and 573 in the same exhibition.

LIST OF ILLUSTRATIONS

COLOUR PLATES

BLACK AND WHITE

INDEX

NOTE

Monarchs and their children are referred to under their Christian names. The grandchildren of monarchs are generally listed under the family name of their birth (e.g. Connaught, Edinburgh). Illustrations are referred to in *italics*.